Indian Swans
Literary Methodology

Indian Swans

Literary Methodology

Charu Sheel Singh

ADHYAYAN

ADHYAYAN PUBLISHERS & DISTRIBUTORS

New Delhi-110002

Published by
ADHYAYAN PUBLISHERS & DISTRIBUTORS
4378/4B, 105, J.M.D. House, Murari Lal Street
Ansari Road, Darya Ganj, New Delhi - 110002
Ph.: 011-23263018, 011-23277156, Fax: 23280028
Email: adhyayanpublishers@yahoo.com

Indian Swans : Literary Methodology

Edition 2010
ISBN 978-81-8435-118-7

Printed in India

Published by Harish Chandra Yadav for Adhyayan Publishers & Distributors, Delhi. Laser Typesetting at V. M. Graphics and Printed at Tarun Offset Printers, Delhi

For

Professor P.S. Sastri

with Reverential Gratitude

and

Methodical Piety

Editorial

The considerable body of Indian literature in English has created enormous problems of its evaluation. This is largely because the ethos in which this literature grew and is flourishing is an ethos which evokes traditions going back to thousands of years. Application of Western critical models and paradigms for a literature having its roots in a different native tradition is neither judicious nor desirable; it will have to be confessed that it only be speaks of the poverty of our mental apparatus and the sheer lack of technical acumen and methodological skill. The time is more than ripe now for the institutionalization of literary studies in India with a view to giving an Indian orientation or idiom both to literature written in English (or in any Indian language) and the critical models evolved to study such literature. Where are, for example, the critical models in the light of which we could study Aurobindo's *Savitri,* Tagore's *Gitanjali,* or Raja Rao's *The Serpent and the Rope?*

Critical models in the present century have come to acquire great cognitive value—in fact have their base in different epistemologies. In the Indian tradition a whole range of possibilities is waiting to be exploited— possibilities which could be malleated into durable critical models—in the form of the *Vedas,* the *Upanishads,* and of course Buddhism. It is here that the universal principles of form—of the utmost limits of human consciousness—lie latent. The configurations of the particular, however, are not neglected. *Tantric* symbolism, typologies, and archetypes, with which such literature is immanent, could well form the base of any reasonable theory of literature, theory of reading, or model of evaluation.

The need is to look within, understand the native tradition, and devise flexible rules and methods that could go a long way both in furthering the growth of such literature and in accounting for such a growth. It has been demonstrated beyond doubt that India does have authors who have given an Indian idiom to English, often supposed to be a foreign language: languages are tools of expression and one cannot limit the scope and dimension of their use. Since the use of English as a medium of expression by Indian writers is no more a controversial matter now (in fact, English is the only language which gives us a unitive sense of *Indian literature* in a multilingual society as in India), there must, however, be issued a note of caution.

We have a great tradition of "sacred texts;" however, 'commentary' in our tradition never lagged behind, and came in the form of *Bhasyas* and *Puranas.* This is where the beginnings of the concept of a university could be traced. *Primary texts* required continuous preservation and interpretative skill for their endless survival. We have a consistent line of philosophical, philological and textual criticism in our literary-philosophical tradition best exhibited by our Sanskrit theoreticians. However, an over-reliance upon the familiar modes of Sanskrit literary criticism has often led us to dead-ends of inappropriateness as this habit simply blocks our imagination to the numerous possibilities open within the fabric of the text.

Due to historical circumstances, Indian literature, particularly the one written originally in English, is still shying away from its own legacy. The need of the hour is that Indian creative writers in English, as well as critics who study such literature, try to relate themselves to the interpretative, philological, philosophical and literary legacies of their own tradition. It will indeed be a landmark in the history of Indian literature in English if it could consider itself as a *secondary text* in relation to the *primary text* of the *Vedas* and the *Upanishads*, Buddhism, among others. The sense of continuity with the tradition which is broken by historical circumstances is yet to be established by Indian writers in English to a reliable extent.

It will not be out of place here to suggest that ideas, from whatever source, always float around a wakened consciousness. As the West has perhaps energised itself, if not benefitted, from the influx of ideas from Indian subcontinent, so should the East come forward and make use of the ideas available, especially literary-critical and philosophical, in order to devise critical models which suit the demands of a text set in a particular local colour and a reality that is locally contemporaneous with itself. Major contemporary literary-critical movements, like Structuralism and Deconstruction, show a positiveaffirmation of such cross-cultural tendencies. In fact, the time has come when the major texts of Western literary-critical-philosophical-philological movements should be translated into Indian languages in order that Indian literary-critical scene refurbishes itself and escapes stereotypes of dread and dreariness in favour of freshness of insight and novelty in approach.

Heidegger evolved the method of taking the object as given and considered all modes of enquiry as relating to the secondary discourse which tries to apprehend the primary text. The method of course came from Kant. The distinction between the *primary* and the *secondary* text has largely manifested itself in the European tradition in the form of Formalist Criticism, Phenomenological Criticism, New Criticism, Structuralism, Deconstruction (the entire controversy of the supremacy of the voice over the written character) and other branches of semiotics. Where are such theoretical movements with reference to the study of either the literature in English or literature in any other Indian language? How long shall we make Sanskrit Poetics a shield to cover the sheer poverty of our imagination and technical skill?

The need for the Indian critic is not only to evolve native methodologies to study a native tradition, but also to study the nature of relationship of such methodologies to their own necessity. This is, in a way, going beyond methodology and posing the question: "why do we need methodological tools at all to make a text accountable to our sensibility?" The question of the necessity of methodology of course raises the issue of the strategies of reading, into the development of which Indian critics should venture now.

We have had the model of the apparent and the hidden (inside/outside). This could be seen as the basic principle of construction in most of our *primary* and *secondary* texts. In fact this phenomenon has occurred in cultures where there has been a long oral tradition. Krishna Himself will serve as the best example of the inside-outside model. This is true of literature on Yoga as well. The other model is the expressionist, where nothing is hidden or revealed; everything is *expressed.* Buddhism offers the dialectical model. A deep study of Buddhist epistemology and dialectic could help in solving the phenomenon of meaning in many otherwise mysterious texts. The *Puranas* offer the allegorical model where the multiple layers of meaning configure to create a literary text as for example, most of the novels of Raja Rao. Such methods notwithstanding, all great works of literature or art have their own layered configurations of meaning and metaphor, and an ingenious critic loses no time in perceiving totalities or divergences that unravel the fabric of images and symbols. It is in this context that an Indian critic is wanted who could formulate critical models for a literature and sensibility that is essentially bi-polar, bi-focal, and cross-cultural in its roots. This is where the new aesthetic should point to and dwell upon.

The articles in this anthology critically examine the nature of available contemporary Indian literary criticism, especially with regard to Indian literature in English, as well as provide critical models for the evaluation of such literature. By Indian literature is to be understood the literature written originally in English as well as literature written in any other Indian language but translated (though not as a rule) into English. Since the intention is to let the articles by distinguished contributors speak for themselves, I would briefly mention that the articles by John Oliver Perry, Norman Simms, and G. N. Devy deliberate upon the nature of climate in which Indian literary criticism (of Indian literature in English) has so far flourished, and the kind of possibilities it could grow into, given the exploitation of such a climate. My own article and those by R. S. Sharma, Kapil Kapoor and Ranga Kapoor, and Javier Ugaz Ortiz provide critical models for the analysis of literary texts. Whereas I base my critical model on the Buddhist *mandala* concept, R.S. Sharma provides a linguistic model, Kapil Kapoor and Ranga Kapoor give a model of the Indian theory of discourse based largely on Panini the grammarian, while the article by Javier Ugaz Ortiz makes a significant contribution towards decoding a 'religious' text providing a hermeneutical model based chiefly on certain of Abhinava Gupta's Kasmir Saivism concepts. Professor P. S. Sastri's brief article is a masterly examination of the central concepts of Sanskrit literary theory; his emphasis falls upon the ethos of the creative work that should be related to the critical endeavour that wishes to understand it. This critical anthology is humbly dedicated to Professor P. S. Sastri for his yeoman services in the field of comparative study of literature and literary theory—British, American, Indian, among others. G. S. Balarama Gupta's article briefly reflects upon the contemporaneous in contemporary Indian English literature, and emphasizes upon what he calls its 'Indianisation'. The article on three middle English romances and medieval literary theory by Professor Norman Simms is mainly included to serve the purpose of a model article, surely the one which could stimulate other critics to study other literary texts with the same degree of critical incisiveness and taxonomical acumen. Ragini Ramachandra's article examines the *Indianness* of a major Indian English novel. R. S. Pathak's article follows a diachronic approach in deeply and critically examining the issues involved in formulating a viable aesthetic theory for the study of Indian literature in English.

I take this opportunity to sincerely thank all the distinguished contributors—both from India and abroad — who responded within time to my brief write-up for this anthology, much of which forms part of the Editorial now. The editor hopes that the articles presented here are a step in the right direction. The purpose of presenting these articles will be more than served if further studies on method could grow—both by way of divergence in opinion and by way of affirmation of what is said here. This book appeared under a different title in an earlier edition.

Charu Sheel Singh

List of Contributors

Charu Sheel Singh, Professor, Department of English and Modern European. Languages, Kashi Vidyapith (University), Varanasi, India.

G. N. Devy, Professor of English, M.S. University, Baroda, India.

G. S. Balarama Gupta, Former Professor and Chairman of the Department of English Studies, Gulbarga University, Gulbarga, India.

Javier Ugaz Ortiz, Post-Doctoral Fellow, Department of Indian Philosophy, Banaras Hindu University, Varanasi, India.

John Oliver Perry, Professor of English (Emeritus), Tufts University, USA.

Kapil Kapoor, Former Professor and Chairman, Department of English, Jawaharlal Nehru University, New Delhi, India.

Norman Simms, Professor of English, Waikato University, Hamilton, New Zealand.

P. S. Sastri, former Professor and Chairman of the Department of English, University of Nagpur, Nagpur, India.

R. S. Pathak, Former Professor and Chairman, Department of English, Sagar University, Sagar, India.

R. S. Sharma, Former Professor and Chairman of the Department of English, Banaras Hindu University, Varanasi, India.

Ragini Ramachandra, Professor, Department of English, Bangalore University, Bangalore, India.

Ranga Kapoor, Professor in English, I. P. College, University of Delhi, India.

Contents

Editorial vii

List of Contributors xiii

1. Literary Criticism in India: Its Multi-Cultural Scope and Opportunities, Especially Relevant to Indian English Poetry *John Oliver Perry* 1
2. Crisis? No Crisis?—Indian English Criticism *G. N. Devy* 14
3. Critique of Indian Criticism *Norman Simms* 26
4. Notes on Literary Methodology *P. S. Sastri* 45
5. Indianization of English Studies: Some Tentative Reflections *G. S. Balarama Gupta* 52
6. Study of Poetry: A Linguistic Model *R.S. Sharma* 58
7. *Mahāvākya:* The Indian Theory of Literary Discourse *Kapil Kapoor and Ranga Kapoor* 85
8. Towards the Development of A Hermeneutical Model for Understanding Traditional Religious Literature *Javier Ugaz Ortiz* 100
9. Readerly Text, Ideas in Motion, and Kinaesthetic Form: An Indian Approach *Charu Sheel Singh* 137

10. The Trauma of Birth, Abandonment, and Homelessness in Three Middle English Romances: New Approaches to Medieval Literary Criticism *Norman Simms* 157

11. Raja Rao's *The Serpent and the Rope:* An Indian Novel *Ragini Ramachandra* 188

12. Towards A Viable Aesthetics for Indian Literature in English *R.S. Pathak* 200

Index 222

1

Literary Criticism in India: Its Multi-Cultural Scope and Opportunities, Especially Relevant to Indian English Poetry

John Oliver Perry

If literary criticism in India today is to be described, with or without overt recommendations, a good deal of preliminary definitions and attendant arguments will have to be repeated. First of all, it should be readily agreed that at least since India's political independence from the United Kingdom, the situation of criticism in India has been regularly deplored by poets, novelists, journalists, critics and academics both from within India and from abroad. Up to the present time this body of criticism has not been comprehensively reviewed and formally analysed so as to produce a serious meta-criticism or theory, of criticism relevant to post-independence India. Although I, for one, have attempted to become widely and deeply informed about the large, perhaps predominant, amount of this material that is written or translated into English, recently some significant cultural events— new publications and institutions and changes in old ones—as well as the generally scattered and multifarious nature of

Indian literary culture have made a sufficiently thorough understanding of the entire scene practically impossible. Even if research is limited to Indian English poetry (my particular focus) critical reviews of Bruce King's ground-breaking *Modern Indian English Poetry* show that one cannot do a truly credible job by depending mainly on knowledge of what has occurred in one or two metropolises and three or four presses.[1]

As the present decade has passed, it has become clear that a historical crisis in Indian literary culture (as part of the wider culture) has been occurring— namely, a struggle for cultural independence from both the United Kingdom and the United States as well as, to a lesser extent, the so-called English-speaking or Commonwealth nations. It is now evident that the crisis is being resolved in the distinct favour of what can be called an indigenous Indian multiculturality. Thus, for Indian English poetry the pre-eminent leadership (and control) has now effectively passed from such pioneer stalwarts as P. Lal, R. Parthasarathy and Nissim Ezekiel, each supporting through the 1960-1980 period his own, basically anti-Aurobindian model, respectively (and over-simply), a free-flowing modernistic, somewhat American tolerance; a tight-fisted "Indian but alienated" stance; and, the most powerful and useful for post-independence India, a well-disciplined, somewhat British and moralistic model. Within Bombay, Calcutta and Delhi, but even more so outside those centres, independent groups have formed, some being urban or regional in scope (*e.g.*, Bombay's and Delhi's poetry societies, various Orissans it inspired by Jayanta Mahapatra; Calcutta's comparative literature association, growing interactions among intellectual workers in Hyderabad—at CIEFL, ASRC, Osmania and Hyderabad Central Universities), some being more nationwide (*e.g.*, various women developing an Indian feminist criticism from Trivandrum to Delhi, Bombay to Hyderabad and places in between). This resolution of the cultural crisis is resulting in an even greater variety of literary production, with increased fragmentation and some laxity in upholding common critical standards but, at the same time, an openness to new critical ideas and artistic talents in a vital, de-centralized cultural organism. The decentralization has occurred both in institutions and in issues together with characteristic responses that now concern literary critics. New avenues of intellectual communication—in carefully edited new journals like *The Indian Literary Review, The Bombay Literary Review, Kāvya Bhāratī, The Commonwealth Review,* in new or revised institutions like the Bhopal Arts Centre, Dhvnyaloka, even at the Sahitya Akademi, in a maturing indigenous women's movement, in new relationships between men and women, between the literati and the academics, among writers around India and between those abroad and those at home—these and other specific changes in the conditions and context of Indian intellectual work have been swiftly developing a good deal of common critical understanding and optimistic good will. Thus, the old despairing complaints about criticism in India, while they still hold for all too much of what is produced academically, journalistically, artistically, and ignorantly, can no longer be repeated. It is necessary not simply to make a few more very important qualifications but more generally to take cognizance of major cultural developments in a highly dynamic, indeed characteristically explosive, contemporary Indian literary scene.

The present, highly promising cultural movement recognizes that while the populace of the world's second most populous nation is predominantly Hindu and imbued with traditional agricultural village mores, the growing literate population in the towns and cities—and indeed in villages touched by modern technology and communications—can no longer be even roughly described in monolithic cultural terms. The current resistance to cultural stereotyping has been especially important for recent growth in both the production and the critical understanding of Indian English writing. Most of all, Indian English poetry early on had suffered from widespread denigration as largely foreign in medium, form, motive and attitude, at best merely metropolitan in content and expression. Whatever the political implications and threats to certain models of national unity, it is now generally admitted that the "Indianness" of Indian society cannot be reasonably defined, that to attempt to do so results in marginalizing the multitude of minority cultures and undemocratically privileging the Hindu majority. Instead India is best describrd as radically multicultural, divided as a whole and increasingly divided — or better, multi-stranded — in every part. Not only is there an enoromous variety of cultures within the predominant Hindu tradition, there is perhaps even more variety outside it, some quite resistant to absorption, others more adaptable. Furthermore, in anyone educated person (meaning to some extent English-medium educated), the mix of cultures — including traditional and modern, rural and urban, local and national and international— is bound to be significant. Yet "alienation" from one's indigenous mix of cultures (native and acquired) is not an inevitable consequence of one's inevitable mutli-culturality. A tenuous, sometimes perilous, yet often enough reliable, irreversibly modern self-consciouness among Indian intellectuals balances different degrees and applications and meanings of the various strands which compose their thought and their everyday living.

One of the most difficult realizations for an outsider to come to that for many, perhaps most, well-functioning Indian writers this multi-cultural condition is not essentially, though it may be quantitatively, different from that of other highly educated persons in Western Europe or the Americas. Except for a few Social isolates, anyone living in the late twentieth century inevitably deals with a number of cultural contradictions in his or her thought and life. Some of these logical disparities may by consciously recognized and dealt with by intellectuals, though, many logical or psychological problems concerning other equally contradictory ideas and attitudes will characteristically be ignored or suppressed. Another frequent human pattern in such situations (and perhaps a conscious strategy for dealing with them) is to see-saw between different, opposed cultural positions as required by or appropriate to different social and cultural contexts. When apparent confusions or carelessness or crass ignorance in critical thinking arise in a particular Indian writers, readers without sufficient appreciation of Indian multi-culturality may be tempted to ascribe the supposed fault to a general cultural condition, to what has been called, by ethnocentrists of both the East and the West, a 'bad mix' of the two cultures. This judgement must be resisted, not only from outsiders liable to unconscious imperialist prejudices or from Indians bent on narrow nativist or orientalist ideologies. They should be resisted by any thoughtful critic aware of how the multi-cultural Indian society operates in its diverse and rapidly changing situation, that is, by varying the mixtures of cultures in different contexts. The result on any one critical occasion is not, in fact, a mixture to be judged good or bad according to some single (and necessarily ignorant/reality-ignoring) notion of national or cultural purity or of what constitutes a so-called civilized society. Rather each cultural event subject to criticism needs to be seen as functioning within a partly homogenized, largely heterogeneous, yet cohesive and coherent multi-cultural organism. Such flexible and complex operations we can readily observe in politically strong social institutions throughout India and in myriads of culturally active, psychologically strong and complex and resourceful individuals. Some of the letters are proper subjects for critical analysis and judgement only if they are considered in terms relevant to their actual cultural functioning.

Another dimension of contemporary criticism in India that bears repeated affirmation is its enormous range, both theoretical and actual. Users of contemporary Indian English may need occasionally to be reminded of the immense critical resources that lie relatively untapped in the often ancient literatures of the many regional languages. Because the numbers of languages are so many and the interconnections so various, Professor C.D. Narasimhaiah, with many other scholars[2] has sought present -day critical and aesthetic norms by adapting those found in the supposedly unifying languages of Sanskrit (or, less so, Hindi) rather than relying solely on the less indigenous, though more current, English norms. However, among other scholars, Professor G.N.Devy[3] is calling our attention to the more scattered, less widely known 'desi' traditions as providing a different, often a more popular, literary culture than the so-called 'marga', or 'greater', more centralized traditions—the Sanskritic and the Hindustani/ Urdu/Persian as well as, lately, the Amero-British/ Commonwealth/European "international". Another source of India's multicultural energy comes from its connections with other commonwealth nations, some predominantly English-speaking like Australia and Canada and Jamaica, others perhaps a bit more like itself in Africa, where English is the elite language of government, higher technology and education but not of the people. No other society, however, is so large and complex in its range of multiculturality as India, whatever the varying degrees of centralization, homogenization, and majoritarian domination in other nations.

Furthermore, the range of Indian criticism is great because, at least in practical terms, it includes a great deal of reviewing in newspapers, weeklies, and of course, literary and scholarly journals. Reviewing is more than usually crucial to criticism in India partly because India's post-independence literary history is relatively brief and extremely dynamic, even explosive, and it is important to have current understanding of what is happening year by year, if not day by day. Partly also reviewing offers some relief from the pressures of an exceptionally conservative academic establishment where the doctrines of Eliot and Leavis and, more rarely, older Marxists are all that, until recently, have enlivened an otherwise ponderously pedestrian reiteration of old saws, established examination themes, and textual paraphrases passing as commentaries. Finally, with respect to the relatively high importance of reviewing, it should be noted that quite properly not a great deal of India's scarce economic resources have gone into scholarly production and publication, especially considering the vast numbers of persons, indeed the inordinately and unusably high proportion (perhaps 25%) of the literate population (only 30% of the whole), that pursue higher education—*i.e.*, college level and above. On the positive side, these numbers of persons constitute in theory, and in concrete potential, a large academic base for creating and marketing a wide range of serious criticism in the future. As several commentators have remarked, once major university syllabuses required or allowed study of Indian English writing (*e.g.*, Delhi University in the 1970s, Bombay University in the 1980s) and the practice spread throughout India, then more effort (and responsible editing) has gone into books about Indian English writing (often intensifying the academic dimension, being based on Ph.D. dissertations now allowed in this area).

Foreign, particularly American and British, cultural institutions, including academic study abroad, have tended to import the latest critical fashions; such as Structuralism or Deconstruction, into the Indian literary scene. The success of such foreign adventures has been minimal in view of the innate conservatism of the Indian cultural establishment, paradoxically strongly controlled by vested interests despite and in reaction to explosive changes on its margins. It also has soon become clear that such imports offer no easy solutions to the perceived critical crisis, for these supposedly 'higher' theories and methodologies are inappropriate technologies for the Indian literary culture, which is and must be, on the whole, much more socially responsible and responsive than Western literary work. Another paradox is evident here in-so-far as Indian aesthetics classically has been, by Western standards, not merely conservative of ancient traditions, including the social hierarchies of caste as well as literary modes and genres, but consequently also more aesthetically isolated, its forms more dissociated in most ways from dealing with problems in everyday living, especially, of course, the modern urban situation.

As Adil Jussawalla's testimony has revealed,[4] the increased degree of social responsibility felt by contemporary Indian writers potentially broadens rather than narrows the range, of Indian cultural criticism. Inevitably the social pull and tug of feelings about national and community and regional issues help to make both writer and critic aware of the enormous complexity of living which is going on, however perilously and contradictorily, in India today. Despite the long-standing tendency of all but a few folk or folk-oriented poets to create their art as if 'for the ages' and thus 'above local frays', there is a growing body of work based in common experience, not idealizing or moralizing about 'village life' nor surrealistically expressing a dream or nightmare sense of an 'Indian' or a cosmopolitan world-view, but instead responding directly and honestly to the mixture of values and social forces interacting in one or another concrete human situation that is experienced somewhere or other in India. Also contributing to the exceptionally broad actual and potential range of Indian English criticism, the impact of intensified social awareness can further help to make somewhat less marginal than in Western democracies the liberalizing efforts of feminists, anti-imperialists, regionalists, Marxists, populists and similar untraditional critics in their dealings with main-stream academics and crude cultural nationalists. Thus, to some extent, the margins of indigenous criticism have, in fact, been both extended and strengthened by infusions from outside and pressures from inside India. The result is that, at least potentially and it seems not too optimistic to predict soon, the effective range of critical thinking in India can be described as exceptionally broad in comparison with even American criticism, which is supposedly so multifarious with its myriad adaptations of often imported critical fashions. As distinguished from the American standardization processes, the tendency towards homogeneity in Indian criticism arises not so much from a rigidly structured academic hierarchy nor especially from powerful technologies of communication and networking that dominate America's highly academicized criticism; rather the main force for sameness in Indian criticism is the cultural lag between the initial appearance of new ideas and approaches and the dissemination and testing of them. Such a so-called 'lag' may be appreciated, however, as helping to keep foreign fashions from sweeping across the continent, as they have done in the past few decades in the USA and even, the more conservative U.K. The slower movement in criticism may also be attributed to well-known Indian hierarchical and traditional resistances, but it is surely as well the product of continuing economic scarcities, including not merely in various forms of communication but also in employment opportunities. Thus, as elsewhere, support for artistic and critical innovation is hindered by the need to conserve present status rather than risk drastically felt losses in hopes of gains not clearly foreseable.

Nevertheless, indisputably an explosion of social and cultural changes is now going on in India, including the nearly completed revolution in common attitudes toward and effective functions of Indian English literary work. This situation makes all the more evident what enormous human resources are readily available in a society that operates in a truly multicultural way. For what has been required is an unusual resilence and responsiveness amidst very threatening circumstances. Those virtues are certainly central to any sensitive critical endeavour in a changing world. They have surfaced sufficiently strongly and widely to permit whatever progress is perceived in Indian criticism however it is measured and, most strikingly, to avoid any number of catastrophic collapses of value systems, whether merely literary or cultural or, most broadly, human. It is in the context of these observations, none of them especially new or profound, that one should begin to develop a criticism of Indian literary criticism. Aware of the hazards in both the enormous range of possibilities and the actual historical pressures—social, economic, institutional and psychological—one cannot realistically or appropriately propose that Indian literary criticism works towards cultural unification or even a common standard, particularly not one based on any single prior tradition, no matter how complex or flexible Indian literary criticism is, will be, and surely should be, as multicultural as the society at large. There will be those who draw heavily on European or American, so-called 'International' traditions and those who work from traditions closer to home, drawing on ancient Indian classics (including, as Professor Narayana Rao has suggested, ideals the poets themselves mention)[5] or on often equally old, but perhaps more viable, regional or folk traditions. There will be those who emphasize comparisons across cultures, both with those inside' India (probably the most relevant, least reductive to overly broad generalities) and those outside, whether in the Third World, the Commonwealth, other Asian or South Asian nations. And there will be those who do the necessary work of close reading, hermeneutically aware of contemporary controversies surrounding concepts like 'context' and 'content', 'text' and 'subtext', 'objective interpretation' and a fat dictionary of other fashionable critical terms, but not over-whelmed by the exaggerated philosophical scepticism of so much current literary theory. With continued expansion of the whole field and consequent optimistic expectations of intellectual and, indeed, institutional gains, there will soon be more critics in India contributing their individual efforts towards developing distinctly and appropriately Indian species of feminist criticism,[6] of area and ethnic studies (with probably less concern for social psychology, more for social and cultural history), of neo-Marxist criticism (again more historically oriented, thus concerned more with current forms of imperialism, including those of Indians, rather than with dogmatics) and so on. As throughout the world, literary criticism will draw inspiration, specific ideas and techniques of analytical understanding from a variety of other disciplines, both in the arts and humanities and in the sciences, social and physical, computational and psychological.

To attempt here a comprehensive list of the present alternatives would suggest limitations (including gaps in this writer's knowledge of the entire literary scene) rather than the virtually unlimited series of options that surely offer themselves. With confidence in the resourcefulness of the broad-ranging, multicultural Indian literary intelligentsia it should not be necessary either to counsel caution about fragmentariness and dissolution of standards or incite to socially responsible enterprise in response to foot-dragging reactionaries and entrenched elites. Plenty of criticism is being produced today in India, and as institutions and technologies expand communication among the multiple varieties and mixtures of multicultures, these will interact in unpredictable and uncontrollable ways. That consequence should not be occasion for renewing the old chorus of disapproval and despair about the state of criticism in India today, but for rejoicing in the appropriateness of its multicultural processes. More specifically, as a personal contribution to the study of contemporary Indian English poetry, I can conclude with a list of my own practical concerns in that area. Given an open and flexible anti-imperialist approach appropriate to and responsible towards Indian liteary culture, several persistent issues seem to me to arise in considering the actual production of this poetry by a variety of writers in India and some few abroad. These issues suggest organizing principles for going beyond or behind theory to practical criticism of currently published work. In effect, they provide chapter headings for a book of critical argument and demonstration yet to be written, and, as such, they cannot here be more fully explicated. Many, perhaps all, of these topics have been raised by critics in India, often in theoretical contexts, but they have not yet received extensive treatment with respect to a range of poems by different poets scattered throughout India and abroad. By giving them such treatment, a book of practical criticism would show the diversity of usually defensible responses to these issues, consciously or unconsciously chosen at different times in different poems. I list them not in order of importance, but in what seems a progression from older critical cruxes concerning medium, authenticity, etc., towards newer concerns with particularities of poetic achievement and the broadening poetic canvas:

(1) problems of Indian English language limitations and opportunities;
(2) differing poetic strategies of indigenization;
(3) differing strategies for dealing with alienation used by the deracinated and the diasporized poets;
(4) problems of philosophical, political and social commitment and their consequences in social-ethical overdetermination;

(5) simple (and overly simple) rhetorical stances in populist and folk protest;
(6) common problems of primivitism, anti-feminism, anti-formalism, etc., in Indian English poetry struggling to be new;
(7) the cultural politics of revision, rejection, rebellion with regard especially to differing aesthetic authorities of form, vitality, etc.;
(8) conservative traditionalism, classical imitation and acceptable derivativeness in the context of differing indigenous and indigenized ideals of authenticity, individuality, selfhood; and
(9) opportunities and hazards in the current opening up of literary and critical canons for discovery, development and democratic pluralism.

Perhaps the final, most appropriate, gesture would be to invite disagreement, discussion, and contributions of ideas from other disciplines, other approaches, other concerned individuals. For though contemporary Indian criticism, like literary criticism in most other nations, has the deserved reputation for being often cantankerous, personally vindictive or dogmatically biased, the energy in such confrontations may have positive effects indistinguishable from efforts towards achieving a new commonality in criticism. What we can all value is critical work that provokes productive interaction among various strands in the multiculturality which so strongly characterizes Indian society, its educated citizenry and its literary achievements.

Notes and References

1. Bruce King, *Modern Indian English Poetry,* Oxford-India U.P., 1987. Besides complaining about how narrowly King defined his topic, Indian critics pointed to limitations in his understanding of this field in the broader cultural context. See, *e.g.*, Meenakshi Mukherjee's review, "Over-enthusiastic Chronicle", *Sunday Observer,* August 30, 1987, p. 22.
2. C.D. Narasimhaiah, Introductions and commentaries on several

Dhvanyaloka seminars on the subject of a common Indian literary tradition, proceedings of which he published in *The Liteny Criterion, e.g.*, one on the Indian critical climate (XVII:2; 1983) and *A Common Poetic for Indian Literatures* (1984). See also V. Rangan, "Towards a New Indian Poetic for Our Times", *Literary Criterion,* XXIII:4 (1988), 97-102 (a review of Krishna Rayan, *Text and Sub-text,* New Delhi, 1987; and *The Burning Bush,* New Delhi, 1988) and comments from a different perspective in various reviews of M.K. Naik's anthologies of criticism, his own and others', as well as his *A History of Indian English Literature* (Sahitya Akademi, 1982), all of which seem to be somewhat condescending about the 'Indianness' of contemporary Indian English poetry.

3. See G.N. Devy's forthcoming book, *After Amnesia: Tradition and Change in Indian Literary Criticism* and his essay in this volume. Professor Balachandra Nemade has been a major spokesperson for a more 'nativist' approach, *e.g.*, in a *New Quest* devoted to the topic, *NO* #45, May-June, 1984.

4. Adil Jussawalla, "Being There: Aspects of an Indian Crisis", also the relevant comments—*e.g.*, "how many of us are consciously or unconsciously against poetry with a political content. . . . We don't have poetry that takes a definite political stance" (p. 77)—in his 'Interview' with Eunice DeSouza, *Bombay [Literary] Review,* 1:1 (1989) 20-27 and 75-79.

5. Guest Lecture in A.K. Ramanujan's course, Harvard Divinity School, December 1987.

6. See K. Radha (ed.), *Feminism and Literature,* Institute of English, University of Kerala, Trivandrum, 1986; and the forthcoming work of such leaders in the field as Susie Tharu, Svati Joshi, and Meenakshi Mukherjee.

2

Crisis? No Crisis?—Indian English Criticism

G. N. Devy

Any consideration of critical approaches and methodology employed for the study of a specific literature immediately turns both the criticism considered and the literature concerned into problems to be investigated. There is no critical approach or method of literary study that is inherently valid for a universal application. Some methods of literary study are useful for understanding, interpreting, or analysing certain kind of literature written in specific periods of history. Some schools of critical thought grow out of specific changes in the social and cultural contexts; some others are inferred from the grammar of literature existing in specific languages. Literary criticism may have claims to many virtues; but it certainly cannot claim to be an autonomous discipline. Therefore, it cannot approach literature, if it has to be a fruitful intellectual exercise, with predetermined notions of literary beauty, style, forms and the functions of literature. Literary criticism essentially is a systematic articulation of linguistic and cultural conventions formed by long literary practice. A consideration of critical approaches to be used in the case of a specific literature, therefore, presupposes the question, 'which literature?', verging on an inquiry into the ontological status of that literature. In fact, the two issues are so intricately associated that a sensible description of the ontological aspect can in itself be a reasonable clue to the epistemological tangle. The primary function, of criticism is, in other words, to state with great clarity the nature of literature which it seeks to interpret, analyse, elucidate. It ends well if it begins well.

I will not raise the question, "why an Indian should write in an alien language?", for it is a completely unuseful question. Many Indians have been writing in English, and some of them have written well. Hence, there is no wishing away of this body of writing on ideological grounds. But it is necessary to answer another question, "is Indian 'writing' in English a 'literature'?" in order to gain a clear critical perspective. The term 'literature' combines two meanings, among many others, *(a)* that which exists in language, and *(b)* that which exists in a community or a culture. It is a language-text as well as a culture-text. It conditions, and is conditioned by, language as well as culture. The minimum conditions of literature are that it must have the support of a language code and a culture code. It must have a language code in order to be able to circulate meaning in and through that code. It must have a culture code in order to circulate itself in and through that code. A literary work in one language will cease to be meaningful if it were introduced to the audience using another language unless that work is amended, adapted or translated. In order to be literature, literature needs to be linguistically foregrounded or distinguished in some ways, but it also needs to be communicated to an audience, published in printed form or read out or spoken to it, who articulates its life experience within a shared linguistic system. Here comes the issue of the status of the English language in India. Is it just a language that can be used by anyone who wants to use it? Is it a foreign language in India? Is it an Indianised language? Or is it a language that is international, and hence in that degree Indian? It is possible, also very entertaining, to argue in favour of each of these positions. It is also possible, also very entertaining, to argue in favour of each of these positions. It is also possible, even profitable, to argue in favour of all the above positions simultaneously. The uncertain status of the language code and the ambivalence of culture code of Indian "writing" in English are closely interdependent.

Language is a highly dynamic system of signs. Every language keeps changing continually. This change occurs irrespective of whether it is the mainstream language or a marginalised language. Language varieties on the margin keep replacing the central norms of language. These new norms, then, are replaced by newly emerging violations of the norm. In the case of Indian literature in English, the socio-linguistic situation involves a certain kind of strange anachronism: Being a "new" literature—a bilingual practice carried out mainly through the "other" language—it should pose a threat and a challenge to the established cannon of monolingual literary practice in the native languages of India, and should move gradually towards the centre of literary transactions in India. However, this possibility is exhausted even before it begins to exist. Thanks to the colonial cultural regime in India, a vast body of literature in English or translated into English already occupies the central place in the literary sensibility of Indian writers and critics in Indian languages. Simultaneously with the growth of Indian literature in English there is evident among literatures in Indian languages a tendency to decolonise literature, a tendency to move away consciously from this colonially sanctioned awareness of world-literature. Also, the place given to the English language in various activities related to the operative political structures in India—the Constitution, administration, the media, social debates, etc.—has made it quite unnecessary for the Indian writer in English to create a variety of English which will move from its hypothetical marginal place to its destined centrality in the imaginative and social life of India. The colonisation of social thought and the imagination in India, which preceded the emergence of Indian English literature, has rendered this new body of literature superfluous and redundant. Even before it can start speaking of its past with any pride it has been robbed of its future, or at least of a very meaningful dimension of its future.

Language and culture dynamics also works in an opposite direction. There is a continuous effort on the part of the border-line sectors of language and culture groups to appropriate and manipulate the hegemonic centres of language and culture. As examples one could mention the history of Christianity or Hinduism. The central church, scripture/s, nature of faith and symbolic rituals have been over the centuries, constantly amended and revised by smaller groups within the larger Christian or Hindu societies. Similarly historical linguistics shows that when a language-empire grows outsize, it breaks into varied splinter groups. Thus broke Latin into several modern European languages, thus broke the Middle-Indo-Aryan into a variety of Modern-Indo-Aryan languages. Such breaks become visible often through development of a consciously marginalised literature, or more appropriately, sub-literature. The growth of Commonwealth Literature – literature that are in fact many but written in one language – is in the nature of this kind of language-culture dynamics. One is tempted to look at the viability and cheerfulness of Indian Literature in English from this angle, as if this new literature was nothing but an act of defiance of the empire of the English language. This angle is indeed very fruitful in understanding Australian or Canadian (Anglophile) literature. There, English is the only choice of language available to the writers. In India, however, the decolonising of the mind and sensibility is more easily possible through the use of Indian languages. English is not the only choice of language to Indian writers in English, excepting the cases of writers who are mentally too lazy to learn any Indian language well enough to write in. Whether one likes to accept it or not, it is a fact that Indian English Literature seems greatly Indianised when looked at from outside India, but appears highly Anglicised when looked at from the Indian languages perspective. It has a dual personality, it is conscious of being so, and tries to play up both at once.

The more one thinks about it, the less one is sure of the exact ontological status of Indian literature in English. It starts appearing increasingly singular, with no parallel that would offer useful critical hints for its correct diagnosis. Yet, that may not be the case. It is not completely true to believe that Indian English literature is without a precedence of its kind. In India itself, there is a long history and tradition of writing in alien languages. Sanskrit literature is one great example of literature in alien language. Persian literature produced in India is another such example. Both Sanskrit and Persian—one may add Arabic too—were languages well developed before they reached India. Both were languages of the rulers that had come to India from outside. They were imposed on Indian people from above, and they became powerful mediums for the expression of Indian imagination and genius. But there the comparison should end. The differences between the role played by Sanskrit-Persian-Arabic in Indian life and the role being played by English today are many. Sanskrit ceased to be, having arrived in India, a non-Indian language. Its literary development took place entirely within India. In due course, it became the central language of Indian metaphysics. Persian and Arabic continued, after their arrival in India; to flourish in their native lands; but they produced a graft language in the form of Urdu in India, and also quickened the growth of Hindi, becoming subsequently the language of political culture and power structures. Sanskrit offered India a language of dialogue with the soul and god, Persian and Arabic shaped the dominant speech of political transactions. When English arrived in India these two had been so deep-rooted in Indian sensibility that English could not, and could not have possibly done so, replace the already established dialects of thought to any great extent.

The English language did, of course, function as a powerful medium of the modern Indian understanding of materials as manifest in the discourse of science, industry, commerce and communications. Thus, to employ a very crude mode of classification, Sanskrit remains the language of the "self", the culture shaped by Persian and Arabic the language of the "other", and English as the language of the inanimate. Today, the birds and trees in India still bear their traditional, native-language names; but the things in markets, the shops, streets, vehicles, machines admit, in a natural way, names of English origin. This is not to deny that there has been some transition and "translation" of Indian sensibility from Sanskrit-Persian-Arabic to English, and *vice versa.* But the act of pervasion of the entire life by the English language in India has been limited in comparison to that by its alien predecessors. It is necessary here to remind ourselves that in "comparison to them English had a far greater power to dehistoricise and to abstract language from its actual speech act, a power endowed on it by availability of the printing technology. A large part of the English language as it operates today in India is this "abstracted", printed language – Shakespreare and the *Bible,* English literature and other European literature in English translation, libraries, newspapers, periodicals, and so on – only a very small part of it is "living", spoken and developing. The English language ranks 87th in the order of the numerical strength of speakers who claim it as their mother tongue. It does, albeit, rank very high in the order of strength of speakers who claim it as their "other tongue". English literature produced in India is therefore literature produced in the "other tongue" context. But, while much of this otherness brought to India by the English language has been assimilated by most Indian languages, the English language in India still remains largely an abstraction without a living body.

With so many problems of ontological nature, with so many uncertainties about its exact status and social role, and with so much of socio-linguistic complexity within which it is enveloped, Indian English literature should be a theoretician's paradise. Literary theory always receives a new impetus from unprecedented literary situations. But in reality this body of literature has generally experienced a lack of adequate critical response. The normal range of criticism includes some condescending praise, some indiscriminate comparison of Indian writers with writers from other countries, and some mindless condemnation. The available criticism of Indian English literature is full of review-level introductory essays, and only occasionally cogently argued book-length studies. But, at no time in its not very long history has Indian literature in English given rise to a relevant theoretical statement.

Some years back, I and Prof. S.K. Desai tried to put together statements of theoretical nature produced by Indian critics in English language. The anthology we produced (*Critical Thought,* 1987) included essays by Sri Aurobindo, Ananda Coomaraswamy, M. Hiriyanna, B.S. Mardhekar, R.B. Patankar, Nissim Ezekiel, V.K. Gokak, Krishna Rayan, Ashok Kelkar and some others. We thought that this anthology would provide a groundwork to discuss the modem Indian tradition of literary theory in English. While collecting the essays for inclusion in it, we felt more disturbed than before by the total absence of any awareness of this modern tradition on the part of the critics considered for inclusion. Most of them go straight to the critical tradition of Aristotle-Kant-Croce, or that of Jonson-Coleridge-Arnold. The others derive their substance from Bharata-Anandavardhana-Abhinavagupta. In either case, there is a heavy reliance on critical traditions originating in distant culture-space or distant culture-time.

Ananda Coomaraswamy was dedicated to his avocation of art-criticism and literary criticism. He had an impressive mastery over arts, literature and philosophy of the West and the East. His explication of the *rasa* theory, though he saw it mainly through Visvanatha's commentary on it, is lucid and perceptive. But, the contemporary literature of India left Coomaraswamy cold. He does not explain whether, and how, the *rasa* theory can be pressed into service for analysing modern Indian writings. For him literary theory is more a branch of metaphysics and philosophy than a branch of linguistics and sociology. Sri Aurobindo had, unlike Coomaraswamy, a profound love for mediaeval and some modern Indian poets. He was aware of the more recent developments in European literature. His *The Future Poetry* shows unmistakably a sophisticated literary sensibility and a sharp critical intelligence. And yet, when it came to theorising about poetry, Sri Aurobindo chose to turn to the spirit of poetry, projected a universal romantic view of it, and ultimately entered into an area where the limits of language merge into silence, that is, mysticism. Though his fascinating theory of poetry as the *mantra* of the real lacks nowhere in its conviction, it nevertheless adds little to one's understanding of modern poetry. B.S. Mardhekar, who was an *avant garde* poet in Marathi, using all devices of modernist poetry in his work, his theory of literature takes up an ambitious course of collaboration with Aristotle, Croce and Collingwood. In the process, Mardhekar leaves all his understanding of Marathi poetry from Tukaram to himself out of his theory. His theoretical structure, like Sri Aurobindo's, is interesting in itself. And there its utility ends. On the other hand, the critics like Krishna Chaitanya and M. Hiriyanna have tried to revive the *rasa-dhvani* theories. Ashok Kelkar, a linguist, and Patankar, an aesthetician, speak a proper modern idiom. But even they have little to offer to a practising critic by way of guidelines in analysing literature. The professors of English in India who institutionalised Indian literature in English sometime in the 1970s have often spent their energy advocating the case of this or that writer for inclusion in the newly established canon of Indian English literature. In short, no critic has so far tried to describe Indian English literature on its own terms in order to offer at least a tentative framework of theoretical issues within which this body of literature can be investigated. Thus, while a whole new body of creative works has become available, and has started posing interesting theoretical issues before us, no significant critical apparatus has emerged to meet the challenge during the last quarter of a century.

It may not be an exaggeration to say that the situation of literary criticism and literary theory is not better in Indian languages literature too. In a study of literary criticism in

Marathi and Gujarati, which I undertook some years back,[1] I noticed that though these two languages have a flourishing literary tradition of more than seven hundred years they have not given rise to any significant and original literary theory. In fact, after the decline of Sanskrit poetics in the post-classical period—particularly after the great work by Abhinavagupta—and even after the emergence of new literary traditions in modern Indian languages, rarely was an attempt made to formulate a new literary theory. This conspicuous absence was certainly not a result of ignorance in the field, but it was more a conscious collective decision to do without a theory. Mediaeval India produced novel poetics, forms of poetry and communication, but never once a theory of literature.

The need to have a theory of literature was felt in modern India only after the arrival of the British colonials with their education system. The context of that education deserves to be noted here. English literature teaching was first introduced in England as a tool to "civilise" the lower classes of people such as factory workers and mechanics, for they had no access to higher education couched in the Greek and Latin traditions. The same "civilising" zeal was the guiding passion of the British colonials when they introduced English literature teaching in India. A vast new market thus became available to English critical texts. When this side industry prospered in England owing to the colonial need, a metaphysics of criticism shaped in the thinking of Matthew Arnold and F.R. Leavis. Ideas which equated active literary criticism and dynamism of culture came in good circulation in England, and subsequently in Anglo-American academic circles. These ideas percolated down to the Indian literary sensibility too. The genesis of the sense of crisis in criticism, the urgency with which Indian critics started wandering in search of adequate literary theory, is in the colonial situation. The easy leap that Indian theoreticians included in the anthology referred above to distant cultures or times in order to grab foundations for their own literary/critical sensibility is, in fact, a symptom of their lapse of cultural memory, memory that for nearly six centuries Indian writers of modern languages had managed without literary theory. We tend to forget, thanks to our colonial intellectual make-up, that there is no direct link between creative literature and literary theory as such. At best literary theory can introduce some rigour in our analysis of literature, but it never can enhance the literary sensibility. I am not advocating the case of abolition of literary theory. It has its own justification for existence. It is certainly an achievement for any culture to have produced an Aristotle, a Kant, an Abhinavagupta. They are the linguists and philosophers of literature. But at the same time I do maintain that the absence of literary theory does in no way indicate decline of a culture. That decline is indicated by the absence of literature itself.

It is because we tend to overlook such ideas that we get bogged down in purposeless debates about "which theory?" One of the most favourite pastimes in modern Indian social and cultural thought has been to debate about the possibilities of synthesising the East with the West, to post a non-existent polarity between "the ancient Indian" and "the modern European" – the *sanatana* and the *nutana*. The so-called "Indian Renaissance", a long period of social churning which has the same intellectual concerns at its conclusion as at its beginning, is an eloquent testimony to the futility of thinking in terms of this dichotomy. While sociologists have firmly established that India has within its culture an invisible apparatus that can smoothly assimilate modernity with the tradition, literary critics have constantly wondered whether they should go back to Bharata-Anandavardhana or they should internalise Derrida, Barthes, Lacan, Freud, Marx, Kant, etc. As if Indian literature is at the crossroads. As if a conscious choice is indeed possible or even necessary. Theories of literature take birth under social and cultural pressures, and in the context of well-established literary conventions. The idea of lifting them up from one culture or period and bring them over to another substantially different literary culture or social period is credulous and misguided. It received currency during the colonial phase which advocated all Eurocentric ideas as being universal in import.

The other credulous and misguided notion about Indian English literature is that it is comparable to other literatures in the Commonwealth. The reason forwarded in justification of this idea is that all Commonwealth literatures share the colonial experience as part of a common history. They also share the English language inherited from the "mother" culture. In the initial years of the academic institutionalisation of Indian English literature these views dominated its criticism. However, these views need to be looked at critically. The fact is that though the British colonial rule prevailed in all colonies that have started producing literature in English, the patterns of colonialism in each of these countries show major emergences. In the white Commonwealth the pattern was developed by and through a settlers economy. In the black Commonwealth it was dominated by a more romantic missionary exploitativeness. In India the situation was much more complex: India is the only country where the British followed a strict policy of religious non-interference, of sexual segregation between the colonisers and the colonised and also of a minimum government. Had the British found India without its linguistic diversity and cultural heritage, without its sophisticated system of administration, without its polytheism and multiculturalism, the British rule in India would have become more closely comparable with that in the other British colonies. Since these vast differences do exist between India and the other colonies, since India happens to be the only country among the colonies included in the Commonwealth literature group that already had a rich and long literary tradition, it is necessary now to view Commonwealth literature more as a "period" in its literary history rather than thinking of Indian English literature as a perpetual little sister in a monolithic church of literature.

I have argued so far that the first condition for evolving a sensible critical approach to Indian English literature is a sensible definition of that body of literature, an exact description of its ontological status. The second condition for that activity is the need to overcome the amnesia introduced in Indian sensibility by the British colonial rule, the need to realise that literary criticism is not a sacrosanct activity. I have further argued that the bipolar choice between the Western critical theories and the ancient Indian critical theories is a superfluous choice. I have also maintained that the established fashion of hitching the mare of Indian English literature within the compound of Commonwealth literature is not consistent with the facts of the colonial history. I will add here that a theory appropriate for understanding Indian English -literature will emerge when the intellectual discourse in India develops in a full native form, when an Indian branch of linguistics, psychology and sociology attains maturity. Such a discourse will offer the initial theoretical premises which, then, can lead to the formulation of a theory. But till such a time that this discourse is not well developed there is no need whatever to feel uneasy about the absence of native theory of literature. The history of literature in Indian languages shows that literary theory is in no way the pivot of literary growth. Till then a confident use of simple common sense and the inborn literary sensibility should be our Critical prescriptions. There is a plenty of useful work awaiting research and attention, work like preparation of good editions, translations, bibliographies, literary biographies and so on. Hence, the literary scholar in Indian English stands no risk of being without his profession. In some distant future he may have a theory or two, too!

Note and Reference

1. *After Amnesi : Tradition and Change in Indian Literary Criticism* (to be published).

3

Critique of Indian Criticism

Norman Simms

Readers of the *Journal of Indian Writing in English* will be familiar with a series of book reviews I have been called upon to contribute to this periodical during the past several years, reviews in which I have often felt compelled to indicate not so much the fault of individual contributors or to the deficiencies of editors compiling these volumes of critical essays as the lack of a pervasive, essential critical perspective at all. In terms of individual writers dealing with particular authors of Indian writing in English, whether poets, novelists or essayists, the task has often been handled deftly, with an eloquent style accompanying careful close-reading of specific texts or balanced overviews of an oeuvre or a genre or an historical period; and in terms of editorial direction, while perhaps less balanced and more riddled with theoretical problems (for reasons I shall have to discuss below), the compilers have generally achieved what they set out to do. Nevertheless, for all the eloquence and all the surveying involved, the result is most unsatisfactory, and this dissatisfaction rests in the lack of a clear engagement—a critical engagement—with particular texts and authors, with oeuvres, genres, periods, and literature itself. Before I begin, then, to examine specifics in greater detail than I have been allowed to within the brief compass of the book reviews undertaken for *JIWE*, it will be necessary to define what I mean by some of the key terms used in the opening paragraph. Without that, it will not be possible to question the premises of the particular volumes of critical essays that seem to represent, at the moment, the heart of Indian critical writing in English. For these premises, often—if not always—unstated, because essentially unperceived or misperceived, also determine the brief given by the publishers to the editors, a brief which I can only suppose arises from the publishers' sense of what actually will sell because what is actually being taught (and therefore, dare we say, thought?) about literature in Indian colleges and universities.

Two words above all demand elucidation: criticism and literature, and then, having grasped some of these theoretical points, we can move on to a discussion of two further words which encompass problems (and problematics) in methodology, essay and perspective. I put the question of criticism first because that is precisely what we are called upon here to describe and evaluate, and which is the ostensible directive in the compilation of the essays constituting our subject. There is a general sense in which criticism merely means any "reading" of a literary text, and then it is a fairly neutral and vague term, the "reading" being the "writing out" of any and all responses to a text by a (not necessarily professional) reader. A similarly general, but somewhat less approved of, sense takes criticism as a negative reading, a way of criticizing associated with journalistic book-reviewers who act as both intermediaries between the book-purchasing public and the publisher, guarding, as it were, that public's rights (and purses) from fraud and deception, by exposing faulty writing and sloppy thinking, and as entertainers, often pillorying authors to the delight of the readers who will never purchase, let alone seek to read, the titles involved. Even at a somewhat higher level of intellectual integrity, such criticism at best offers an ephemeral—daily or weekly—monitoring of the publishing industry, with rare attempts (or rarer knowledge in the reviewer or presumed in the readership) to keep adjusting the received canons of taste and the contours of the accepted (able) literary canon to emerging works by old and new authors. The very nature of this kind of criticism disallows the performance of critical reading.

Critical reading implies an incisive and reflexive dialectic between text and reader, the reader here meaning not only the professional writer of such essays but the cumulative experience of the community he or she comes from and writes towards. Critical in this sense means questioning of more than the superficialities of subject matter, stylistic address or generic decorum. At the core, it means a probing, eversceptical questioning of the literary act itself, an act encompassing writing, publishing and reading. It is incisive because it defies superficial, gratuitously assumed truisms, and reflexive because it considers that at precisely that point when the reader thinks he or she has "understood" the text the questioning process has reached its limits and a new mode of address must be initiated. Evaluation of the text, then, rests on how far the critical reading takes the reader away from superficial truisms, even from faddish *apercus*, towards new insight. Not that, and perhaps mostly when the text is least overtly *avant garde,* grotesquely original, will it begin to tease apart what is already presumed to be known, begin to disclose what is suddenly recognized in a new light as already known, and then lead hesitatingly forward into what is always unknowable. In other words, the critical reading I am concerned with is not and cannot be one that simply spreads a grid of given questions over the book to be read and then reads out those answers which show through. To do merely that, as much of what passes for critical writing in the books I have had to review, is to engage in undergraduate exercises in the outmoded close-reading of the so-called New Criticism.

Literature will then be seen as something distinct from other forms of controlled language, such as philosophy, clinical reportage or journalism, and criticism itself as a department of literature rather than an alien presence juxtaposed to it.

While literary texts may work within the forms and appearances of other rhetorical modalities, such as the probitive, the heuristic and the polemical, they are above all distinguished by their textuality, their critical densities, their polyvalence and polysemiousness. This kind of view of literature as a form of language—whether oral or written is not determinative—that not only engages but already always is critical of its own textuality at once extends and loosens the received lines separating the literary from the non-literary, and indeed may be said to problematize the definitions inherited from Romantic and post-Romantic theories, at the same time as it removes from the field a range of superficial, self-serving, positivistic forms of speaking and writing. Virtually nothing remains as given or assured in this literature, and the reading of texts becomes a constant critical engagement between active participatory reading and a textuality always dialogically alive, influenced by and influencing prior, current and subsequent readings. The text is no longer "fixed" as a verbal icon, a well-wrought urn or even self-consuming artifact; it is a seething, squirming field of activity between its own shifting relationships to readings which have and continue to constitute it and the reader, always a congeries of innocent and guilt-ridden experience.

Neither the New Criticism nor its equally non-humanistic relative, Structuralism, address the deeper complexities of that controlled language we are calling literature. These complexities reside both within the densities of articulation, where texts weave themselves into textualities, and in the psychological, social and ideological contours of the creating matrix. For to be humanistic, literary criticism must be concerned with values, with the content of texts as more than neutral verbiage or a-historical thematics. The processes of the text exist before and after, as well as through the footy of the printed book, and share as well in the indeterminacies and inferential qualities of the ostensible presentation. Critical reading, while it teases apart the strands of the text, also becomes radically involved with it, and needs to address its reflexive presence as a creative and interpretive con-comitant of that text.

No one can imagine the text of a piece of Indian writing in English that is, not thus entangled in these problematic dialectics of social, historical, religious, cultural and linguistic densities, riddled with dysfunctions, incongruities, misprisions, non-sequiturs and a hundred other slippages and seepages. Again and again Indian writing in literature comes into being at the very nexus of these problematics. No one could thus imagine a criticism that does not equally address the tangled web of densities, but yet, alas, it seems the writers of the so-called critical essays we are dealing with do all the time, or at best merely caption the simplified pictures they present and then limn them in with bold colours, never daring to go outside the prescribed lines. And not merely simplistic, but often times dull: for the over-seriousness by which these critics come to worship at the verbal icons does not allow them to treat the playfulness of textuality with the equally playful repartee of true criticism. This means that the fun has gone out of literature, especially where farcical, comic, and satiric stratagems are involved. The critics picture book is very pretty indeed, but dull and often infantile.

So much for the critical reading of Indian literature, which, when we approach it in itself, in all its complexity, diversity and spectacle, reveals the very qualities of reflexivity, with and perspicacity characteristic of the culture but woefully missing in the criticism.

Often I have to backtrack on my own critical terminology when trying to explain to undergraduate students in the university what is meant by an essay in literary criticism, since we use the word "essay" in so broad a categorization that we neglect to distinguish between formal themes and arguments, on the one hand, and the informal, self-reflective essay on the other. We have further to distinguish such essays from the non-essayistic reports required of clinical writing, experimental records and other positivist writings with their pretence at objectivity, at keeping the writer's own sensibility and sensitivity out of the text, and with the presumption (or is it arrogance?) that the positivist perspective is a non-judgemental one. We often ask our students to do exercises in close reading, to write what are in effect descriptive or interpretive commentaries on given passages of prose or short extracts of verse, and these, symbiotically—if not parasitically—attached to the structures of the literary text follow the argument of narrative or the development of emotion through events, images and psychological maturation or breakdown. The writing that emerges, then, has no inner direction of its own and no structure other than that of the text to which it is attached. Interpretation turns out to be little more than, at best, paraphrase of the author's own—or one of his or her own character's—argument, and the words of the commentary are predetermined as "your own", meaning a reduction of literary complexity to adolescent simplicity, or a transcoding to some psychological, political or sociological jargon.

I am, of course, not saying that all criticism that appears in Indian academia is of this sort, but too much actually is; and much essay writing that does move beyond simplistics and immaturity is not critical. It is not critical because it is neither reflexive nor dialectical, because it entails no critical engagement with the densities of the text, the complexities of the reading processes, or the relationship between all facets of the problem. Necessary historical backgrounds and genre-classifications are undertaken in many of the collections of so-called "perspectives", although, even here, it is sometimes questionable as to how often the positivist labours need to be re-done. I have suggested that editors ought to consider collecting already prepared general assessments of this type, rather than calling for new surveys, since the advances on previous work, in the few pages allowed to each scholar, are minimal and marginal.

While it is useful for novices in the literary profession to demonstrate a capacity for the exercise in close-readings which prove the mainstay of the collections of articles we are concerned with mostly, the truly critical essay begins to move into the reflexivity and critical temper of the literary enterprise only when it can do more than describe what is given in a specific text. While we cannot ask under-graduates with their immature minds—immature due to age and hence lack of what are called life-experiences and immature because naive in their familiarity with the literary traditions which feed into our own—to write yet in a relaxed meditative way but must require a degree of formality that derives from thematic structures we built into the projects we assign, the assignment of a theme essay entails at least an incipient critical attitude: to move out of the passive into the critical mode, to begin to question the coming-into-being of the text and the place of the reader in that process. When the Indian essays we have read raise these questions, and they do, even if only rarely, they tend in almost all cases to perceive the coming-into-being as a unilateral, univocal procedure. Either a *Zeitgeist* directs the course of literary history or some quirk in the author's personality determines his or her choice of subject matter or genre, or the two zigzag their way through an otherwise empty, neutral or backgrounded space towards the completed works of the author. But time-spirits, zigzags and simplified reality hardly constitute a critical view of literary history.

My own preference is for what I call the mentalities (or *histoire de mentalités)* approach to literature. This is a procedure involving three stages, each of increasing complexity and engagement, and cumulative in their "englobement" of the literary act. In the initial stage, the text is addressed so as to try to describe all that it actually is, both in its content—as a rhetorical presentation conducive to the scrutinies of the close-reader—and also, significantly, as a performative and productive enterprise. The text needs to be identified and defined as a work of a particular time and place, arising from specific personal and social motives, though it should not be limited to them, since as text it is neither a mirror nor a window of reality. The second stage begins to engage the complexities of its densities by seeking to determine not only what it is—what it actually says, sees and thinks, as it were—but also what it; could have been in other words, by determining what choices were available to the author, the critic begins to assess the nature of those choices, the strategies of the conscious and unconscious motivation, and the range of implications and ironies enfolded by the text. Here the text exists not only in what it actually is but in what it suggests as inferential alternatives, as denied possibilities, and as silent and invisible pressures weighing in upon it from near and far.

In the last stage of this mentalities approach, never separate from and always dialectically involved in the reflexive reassessment of the first two stages, the critic begins to ask what qualities of textualization were not available to the writer, could not be seen, spoken, or thought in the situation out of which he or she creates.

This is, to a great extent, a deconstructionist stage—not a destructive, nihilist methodology, as some would have it; but rather, as we hope we have indicated, an intensified version of close-reading based on the careful expansion ("englobement", to use Lucien Goldmann's term) to the contexts, subtexts, intertexts of the original "text"; so that we begin to discover qualities I am calling un-texts, anti-texts and non-texts, these neologisms referring to "readings" which are partly inside and partly outside the specific verbal configuration itself but all within the dimension of critical perspective. Briefly, by an un-text I mean some presumed discourse of the fictional situation which pretends either not to be present at all, such as an historical romances illusion of being written or spoken in some language other than that it actually appears in, or only partly and fragmentarily so, as when an inarticulate character becomes the focal point out of which the narration arises. The anti-text is even more radical since it implies the existence of a counter-text which would deny, invalidate or destroy that which the reader seems to have in hand. It is not just that one text (the one we actually read) pretends to be another, but that as we weave together allusions and suppressed references the very stability of the primary text is threatened, and this may or may not be the intention, or within the control, of the author.

The non-text is of a somewhat different nature, insofar as it can be either a conscious or unconscious aura around the primary text, a discourse which defies articulation because it is constituted by what, at least for the author or the focal (articulative) fictional character, is unspeakable, unimaginable and unthinkable. The non-text often becomes apparent only at the intersection of mentalities or in a time of crucial shifts in sensibility.

To begin to engage the densities of the real India, in this way, is already to textualize a mentality constituted by these very breakages in mentality and sensibility, both in the time frame of its history over the past hundred years—the dissolution of political and social structures—and in the geography of its religions and ethnic and linguistic diversity, as well as its juxtapositions of psychological modes and awarenesses. In this mentality where Indian literature comes into being an essay in critical reading not only has to be dialectical and reflexive in itself, forever questioning its own premises and its non-innocent presence in relation to the text, but it cannot assume a single clear perspective. What I have had to read for critical review is, however, not an attempt to clarify complexity, but often no more than the self-limitation of pre-determined themes or superficial images to be discussed in regard to some author's work or a particular novel or poem. It may mean, also, a decision to list all the books that were written on a particular subject over a given number of years, arranging them by chronology, by ostensible purpose,. and perhaps by some other positivist category (length, number of sales or editions, etc.). What is not attempted, for the most part, is a critical examination of what is perspective itself, and especially in a series of volumes entitled "Perspectives" anything at all like a range of differing, mutually hostile or reinforcing critical views.

Granted the large number of Western schools of critical thought that have flourished in our century and the range of indigenous Indian philosophies, religions and ethnic creeds actually present, the insistence on a narrow, perhaps univocal, approach is remarkable. Merely varying the number of books within each critic's brief—this one will write on a single title, that one will look at a cluster of novels or poems, this one will survey the development of the genre, that one will divide into subject categories the titles produced in such and such a period—does not at all constitute a coordination of perspectives.

Each language, Elias Canetti has written, has its own silences. Each mentality, too. The paradox I have tried to draw out here, before moving into specific remarks extrapolated from some of the reviews I have written of English-language essays on anglophone literature, is this: that while India can produce a mature, self-critical literature in her novelists, dramatists and poets, in her critics there seems to be, on the whole, a reluctance or a constitutive inequality, to engage those texts with the same intellectual honesty in which they were written. If this silence, though, arises merely from academic structures or institutionalized journalistic modesty, then: bold critics can swerve from the established ways and write essays that open new insights. If not, then the best criticism of Indian literature must remain more Indian literature, poems, novels, stories and plays which engage each other in dialogue and debate.

As I look back over the reviews I have written, at once the name of Prof. M.K. Naik stands out because of his important work in editing the series of volumes in these apparently influential collections of "perspectives" on Indian prose, poetry and so on; yet I do not want to be seen to be making him the butt of my critical comments about what is characteristic of most of the contributors to his anthologies and of other essayists such as B.K. Das, R.K. Srivastava, A. Rahman and A.N. Dwivedi. With rare exceptions, which it would be invidious to bring forward at this time, all these Indian writers are not at fault as individuals, and there is no suggestion that their academic credentials are in any way compromised, nor even that they lack insight, tact or whatever else it is that makes a good reader of literature. But there is, as I have suggested above, a radical dysfunction in the anglophone Indian critical enterprise itself, made most evident in the failure of such writing to fit with—or match up too-the high achievement of Indian creatiye writing in English.

Some of the difficulties I have noticed in the books and articles that have come into my purview are, what are best termed external ones, problems that arise from the brief given to the compilers of the anthologies as well as to the delegated assignments passed on to individual essayists. One of these difficulties would be an unclear focus; we are never sure whether the collections of essays requested are to serve immature undergraduate audiences or to provide a guide to professional (or academic) critics coming to the field of Indian writing in English for the first time. (I think the audience is always imagined as Indian and not overseas, though perhaps, as indicated below, the realization that there are foreigners interested and eager for aid in reading might be a key towards a better critical posture altogether.) Once that question is asked others flow on: because there are very different kinds of intellectual expectations to be met depending on the kind of readership involved. Why is it necessary, for instance, to compile a collection of essays on Indian essayists in English from the mid-nineteenth century to the present? Would it not, perhaps, as I have already suggested elsewhere, be better to gather together the best of what has already been written, leavening that selection of articles from diverse periods with a concern for representation from a diverse range of critical schools of thought? That might be one rationale for a series of "perspectives". If a collection is made with students in mind, then pedagogical methodology dictates a graduated approach, leading the inexperienced reader from simple to more complex thoughts, indicating clearly the kinds of intellectual procedures involved, and not merely piling up repeated lists of names and titles, on the one hand, and undirected running commentaries, oil the other, as is too often the case with the books current in Indian criticism. If directed towards a more specialized audience, however, then much of the simplistic close-reading would have to go, and certainly the random surveys have no place: more substantial annotations would have to appear and vague, impressionistic generalizations should give way to full-scale argumentation.

It also seems that the editors of the anthologies have not thought through their projects sufficiently, or not assumed (or been allowed by their publishers to assume) sufficient editorial control over incoming materials. I know from my own experience as an editor that it is very difficult to engage the sustained attention of busy scholars in such programmes and to ensure that those registered in the project understand clearly—and thoroughly—the parameters of their specific contributions. Nevertheless, putting aside the obviousness of the lack of proper funding or the inefficiencies of postal and telephonic services, internal academic politics and the sheer bureaucratic finesse required to communicate effectively with farflung correspondents to the side, the task of the editor should be precisely to monitor each contributor, direct rewritings to particular categories of amplification or deletion or even correction that emerge as the essays themselves come to hand. Since the compiler does not work with already prepared and published articles in these collections we are discussing, he or she must either have the ability to direct each potential contributor towards a balanced production or, perhaps more realistically if at the same time also more difficult to achieve, to keep reshaping and reshuffling the project itself to the actual materials coming to hand. But probably the most serious and most politically sensitive task of the editor is the outright rejection of work that does not fit within the requirements of the anthology as a whole, or which may simply be poorly written and poorly thought through. Because this does not seem to have occurred, the resulting anthologies are uneven not only in their scholarly rigour but their aesthetic focus, even as they tend towards a bland sameness of approach—even to a repetitiousness of content—in the constitutive essays.

Another form of external problem lies in the length of essays. Trying to cover something so amorphous within a volume of sometimes only one or two hundred pages as (all of) the poetry or the prose of Indian writing in English means that each of the twenty or so contributors finds him or herself with about ten pages, and ten pages is not enough to say anything meaningful about all the novels of one writer, all the poetry of a century, or the implications of some stylistic strategy in a major work. In ten pages an undergraduate can rattle off a list of slogans about this or that genre, can make obvious statements about an ahistorical close-reading of a poem or story, or—as under-graduates do!—pretend to draw simpleminded analogies between social or political contexts and aesthetic decisions within a creative piece of literature. Even when the subject is more limited, as in a compilation of essays on a particular author or even a small selection of his or her works, the tendency has been to reach out towards encyclopedic descriptions or judgements, rather than to focus it on incisive discussions. R.K. Srivastava's anthology of essays on Anita Desai particularly fails on this count, despite a few rather good pieces, which do make the collection a valuable contribution to scholarship. What happens is that most of the essayists overlap in their generalities, and find themselves with a page or two to say something distinct from those around them. What is distinct is tantalizing and ultimately unconvincing to the reader because there is no space to analyse, discuss and extrapolate implications.

Related to this, we must say, is the annoying habit of some (though hardly all) essayists to try to bolster their remarks by citations of "authorities". It is an old ploy, of course, to set up straw men in order to structure an argument around readily available false evaluations and misreadings. But what there tends to happen is the citation of other critics merely for the sake of giving the appearance of scholarly endeavour. Since there are often no substantial critical examinations and apparently no sustained surveys of the materials covered by the recent books of criticism, the writers go to newspaper review, radio interviews, "personality" pieces in the popular magazines, and other essays on the same level with themselves—that is, busy lecturers trapped into the situation of writing hasty pieces for anthologies supposedly necessary to feed the opinion-hungry masses in the universities! When the writers do this, the result is all too predictable. Casual remarks reinforce one another; simple variations in reader response (of an emotional or impressionistic variety) are overblown into theoretical contentions; and nothing new gets said—just glib repetitions of the same old descriptive models. This does not, naturally, mean that there is no merit in combing the press or sieving the airwaves for insights; but that material, like everything else, must be approached critically, within and with a sceptical, questioning dialectic.

Yet it is not only external problems, matters which time and effort could overcome, as the above remarks indicate. The internal difficulties require a shift not just in attitudes but in the whole way in which the critical enterprise is conceived. This enterprise, of course, does not begin or end in the anthologist's brief. It extends into the way in which literature is taught at Indian universities and, from there, to the way in which publishers in Delhi, Calcutta and elsewhere envisage their role in supplying books for students, individual scholars and libraries. There is certainly no question of addressing a general, lay audience, although some of the essays in the adoption—or perhaps continuance of the journalistic posture of book-reviewer do make this presupposition. Since popularity is not a factor, the publishers and editors must decide clearly who they are writing for, provide the adequate means to carry this through—the authority if not the funding—and then insist on consistently high standards. There must also be no attempt to keep repeating with variations what already has been done, but to evaluate real areas of need, real perspectives that have not been touched. It would be foolish of me, the outsider, to venture a paradigm for future work; that must come from within India, or at least from those intimately involved in the whole cultural complex. All I can do, because I am asked to provide some disengaged perspective; is crystallize opinions already taking shape within India as vague feelings of discomfort or muted cries of pain.

What are the majority of Indian critics doing when they

write about literature? I have already suggested that they are engaged in a basically positivist exercise rather than a dialectical or dialogical, critical engagement with a whole process of creativity. When they attempt to survey the origins of a genre, they unroll a list of names, times, and taxonomic details; they are, in this way, vulgar Darwinists--or perhaps better, pre-Darwinists, in their sense that authors respond simply and directly to external pressures, that literature produces literature with no mediation of other arts or cultural factors involved. Though occasionally a nod is given in the direction of language, linguistic complexities are never addressed as constitutive factors in the generation of literary texts. Basically what can be measured (taken into account) is real (literary historical facts). Similarly close-reading (of the ahistorical New Criticism variety) yields uncritical, univocal counters in a positivist construct; the reader moves with the text of poem or fiction without questioning its validity or his or her own presence in relation to it. Just as the construction of the survey often entails skill and a great deal of knowledge, so the close-reading involves sensitivity and alertness; and both are carried through with tact and eloquence.

Yet to what end? Do we understand how literature comes into being, acts on our imaginations and intellects, exists in relation to other forms of language and to cultural experiences that are non-verbal merely because we can divide up, list and juxtapose scores of writers, their books and schools of thought? Or because we can, no matter how elegantly, paraphrase verse into prose or fiction into expository propositions? Here is where I would have hoped to find some particularly Indian insights, and at best I have recorded only a few vague hints at different Sanskrit and similar habits of reading. Perhaps the outsider is not sufficiently alert to the implications of these seemingly marginal remarks and maybe there is a deeper, more incisive web of alternative readings going on in the essays. If so, the subtlety may need to be adjusted to aid the interested but naive foreigner.

There is another related critical approach evident

throughout the volumes that have come before me, and that is something we might call moralistic criticism, deriving from Matthew Arnold and confirmed by such pundits of high British culture as T.S. Eliot or F.R. Leavis; not that the Indian essayists necessarily profess Anglican tenets, but that there is the same concern with the higher seriousness, the unquestioned assumption of touchstones of taste, the phenomenology of objective correlatives and the implicit presence of a great tradition. Much that is most admirable about the style of the essays we are dealing with arises from the procedures adopted or adapted from these English moralists. Unfortunately, in the last quarter of the twentieth century, their faith collapses in upon the soft innards of unproved assumptions. Particularly in an Indian setting, these self-righteous *prounundamentos* ring hollow indeed! Language is too much of a game and literature itself a more involved, involuted, playful, teasing manifestation of the unspeakable, the unimaginable and the unthinkable to be reduced to the solemn intonations of Light and Goodness. Our grasp of civilization is now too eclectic to find agreed-on general standards of normality, and our belief in the easy equivalence of culture to justice and humanity fell apart, as George Steiner pointed out, when those who read Goethe, listened to Beethoven and thought with Wittgenstein had no qualms about switching on the crematoria at Dachau and Bergen-Belsen. Our knowledge of psychology and the psychosis of whole cultures also disallows smooth discoveries of equivalence between the figurative language of poetry and the essential truths of the mind. Feminists and Foucaultists have also broken the spine of the great tradition, and what is or is not literature again, as at the end of the seventeenth century, streams past us in colourful confusion.

In probably the best of the anthologies—best in terms of consistent high academic quality and real diversity of points of view—C.D. Narasimhaiah's *Commonwealth Literature: Problems of Response* the deficiencies of the average Indian critic seemed to be made good, perhaps because the subject is more focussed (problems of response), perhaps because the contributors are more enthusiastic about the topics set to them. Whatever, it may be, what is revealed here is that actually having to confront their relationship to other literatures in similar but yet distinct situations the Indian critics can engage the texts, the historical situation, and the linguistic and generic problematics with finesse and real critical direction. Moreover, rather than relying on positivist models or the implicit morality of the Anglican pundits (and gurus), the contributors have to discover in themselves, as Third World, Commonwealth, Developing Nation persons the ways in which they are like their fellows in other parts of the Commonwealth, the ways in which they are different, and the reasons for these differences and similarities. What they cannot do—or at least what they are not doing in Narasimhaiah's anthology—is pretending to be members of the old Scrutiny contingent or latter day prophets of Victorian self-righteousness.

The reference to the Commonwealth reminds us that the English language is more than just the language of Great Britain, and that though it is essential to be aware of the great literatures England, Scotland and even Ireland have produced, English now belongs to many non-European peoples, and not just American or provincial nations like Canada, New Zealand and Australia. It has become a medium to express traditions which have their own ancient literate heritages as well as their dynamic oral creativities. We cannot see that Indian Literature in English is other than an Indian Literature and Indian English an Indian language. All that, and it is also an English literature and an English language, and no study of it can escape the need to address the essential complexities, involved and confusing as they may actually be. English neither exists in a vacuum nor is impervious to the presence of other languages within the social or psychological environment of the authors dealt with by the critics we are looking at. We see this at once as soon as we open a novel by Raja Rao or Salman Rushdie or begin to read the poems of Jayanta Mahapatra or Nissim Ezekiel.

While the overseas reader like myself (particularly because

of the New Zealand base I work from) suffers from limited access to Indian literature, not just because the books are hard to come by, but because our reading comes from the outside, without the resonance and dissonance of the great diversity of languages, cultures, and literatures which make up India as a whole, the Indian critic, needs the integrity and the wit to encompass the wholeness of his or her experience. If not just for the sake of Indian readers, then for ours; please. And in so doing, I would further suggest, something more than an understanding of Indian literature in English or Indian literature as a whole will be accomplished; that "more" is a revaluing, nay, re-siting of the perspectives by which we—all of us, Indian and European—encounter any and all literatures whatsoever. Our engagement with your enterprise, like yours with ours, enlarges the critical enterprise, directs us towards more critical awareness of each one's interdependencies and differences and hones our perceptual faculties.

The position I have tried to enunciate here derives from what I call the mentalities—approach, and this, in its synthesis of several contemporary schools of European thought, such as Deconstructionism and Psycho-history, essentially questions the assurances of older Eurocentric critical theories, the very ones, I fear, seemingly entrenched in Indian criticism. The paradox, then, is that, while I would not under-value the European contribution to world civilization, I do not see Civilization as equal to Europe or Christendom or—perish the thought!--the Anglophone World, and while I think the vastness, the complexity and the millennial complexity of India should allow it to play a major part in this enterprise, at the moment India through her critics is playing at best a passive and marginal role. Her critics seem, in many ways, as I have tried to show, to take a retrenched position in regard to the very theories which Europe and North America are viewing increasingly as outmoded. The new more open way of reading literature itself is stymied without greater awareness of alternative traditions, and here is where the Indian contribution could be so obviously useful. The promise already exists, as does the substance.

Critical Works Referred to

Das, Bijay Kumar; *Critical Perspectives on Relationship and Latter-Day Psalms.* Bareilly: Prakash, 1985.

Dwivedi, A.N., *Kamala Das and Her Poetry,* Delhi: Doaba, 1983.

Naik, M.K. (ed.), *Perspectives on Indian Prose in English,* New Delhi: Abhinav, 1982.

—, *Perspectives on Indian Poetry in English,* New Delhi: Abhinav, 1984.

—, *Perspectives on Indian Fiction in English,* New Delhi: Abhinav, 1985.

Narasimhaiah, C.D., *Commonwealth Literature: Problems of Response,* Madras: Macmillan, 1981.

Rahman, Anisur, *Form and Value in the Poetry of Nissim Ezekiel,* New Delhi: Abhinav, 1981.

Srivastava, Ramesh, K. (ed.), *Perspectives on Anita Desai,* Ghaziabad: Vimal, 1984.

4

Notes on Literary Methodology

P. S. Sastri

The methodological problem for the study of Indo-Anglian literature or for a close scrutiny of literature in Indian languages is a serious one. It needs to be formulated at least in its broad outlines. British critics have been formulating down the last four centuries principles of literary criticism largely based on the Greek critical theories. They forgot that the Greek theories were derived from a study of Greek texts. Later they borrowed some principles based on the works of Horace, Quintilian and others. The latter gave rise to Neo-Classicism which ruled the roost for sometime in Britain. When these theories were amended or supplemented by Colèridge and others, many sub-species of critical schools emerged. The basis re-mained in Greek-Latin theories. As the British critics came to look, upon the literatures in other languages,. they started applying their theories as standards of judgement. This is typical of British insularity. The theories did not originate in Britain, and yet they considered those theories as their own. The modified tradition became the standard of evaluation. The Latin ethos was fairly well represented by Horace, Cicero and Quintilian, and it was modified by Vico and Croce. This is totally opposed to the Anglo-Saxon—originally Greek—insistence on the organic unity of form and content. Intuition and expression identity and a new interpretation of the past came to the fore. While the modified British literary ethos ran into the Platonic and Aristotelian modes and then got transformed by the native empiricist tradition, the Latin ethos ran counter to it. The result is a chaos of literary standards.

In India the ethos was said to be determined by the Vedic tradition. This is unacceptable. Lotus, which plays a major role in Classical Sanskrit literature, and in the Hindu and the Buddhist art, has no place in the Vedic texts. The Vedic transition was disrupted long long ago. The only tradition of literary evaluation that we have in India is the one enunciated by Bharata. Thus, there arose the schools of *rasa* (aesthetic experience), *Guna-dosha* (dualities of literary style), *Riti* (nature or form of style), *Alankāra* (figurative language), *Vritti* (modes of style), *Aucitya* (propriety), *Vakrokti* (oblique use of language), and *Dhvani* (suggestion). Six of these can be subsumed under *Rasa* and *Dhvani* which are the two major standards of literary evaluation. Abhinava Gupta has fused these two into *Rasa-dhvani.* If the European critics can judge our literature from the standpoint of their own theories, we can as well judge their works from our standards. In both cases there is an error. Are the literary-critical theories *a priori* or *a posteriori?* Just as grammar owes its rules and principles to standard, but changing and evolving, usage, so should the literary theories be based on the available literature of the country concerned. Let us take an instance. The Anglo-Saxon tradition insists on the unity of form and content. Croce speaks of their identity. The Indian concept of *Sahitya,* meaning togetherness, is misleading as far as the word is concerned. A correct meaning appears in the opening verse of Kalidasa's *Raghuvansa*--"Vāg arthāv iva sampriktau". The relation between the sound of the word—not the word as such—and its meaning is a peculiar one. They appear to be united or related to one another. It is not so. From one point of view the word is sound, and from another, it is meaning. In itself the word is both sound and meaning at the same moment.

Bhattanayaka observes that in the *Veda* the sound is important, in the epic it is the meaning, and in literature it is the two taken as one. It is not unity but identity. This is not exactly similar to Croce's theory of lyrical intuition. In Indian sculpture we have the images of *Ardha-Narishwara.* Half of the idol is masculine and the other half is feminine. This is a visual embodiment of a mental concept. In actuality, the same image has to appear as feminine at one time and as masculine at another. This raises a serious problem in critical theory. How to arrive at and evaluate this identity? Only for the sake of analysis or of convenience we can separate the two. Once we separate them we cannot make them one intellectually. The author of *Jayamangala,* a commentary on Vatsyayana's *Kāma Sūtra,* called it (word-sound and word-meaning unity) significantly as "bhāva lāvanya yojanam." It is the yoking of the idea with beauty. In our methodological approach we cannot accept either the Anglo Saxon form-and-content unity, or Croce's intuition-expression identity. It is beauty-sound identity or beauty-meaning identity that I plead for.

Like the British and American critics evaluating the literature in foreign languages, we are also guilty of employing double-standards. When we read Indo-Anglian works, we tend to apply Western literary standards; and when we study the works in our own languages, we apply the traditional standards of judgements. This is grossly unfair. A work like *Sāvitri* needs a closer understanding of the Indian ethos. Though the language is Victorian, the theme is Indian, going back to the Upanishads and the *Mahabhārata.* Here, the basic problem is to find out how the antiquated Macaulaysque language is fused with the content. The available interpretations of this poem emphasize only the content; and the result is not a literary evaluation, but a philosophical or a quasi-philosophical analysis.

In the case of the English version of *Gītanjali* the problem is not acute. The English text was amended by W.B. Yeats who understood the Indian ethos very well. The text thus achieves a certain measure of sound-meaning identity. In both these works *(Sāvitri* and *Gītanjali)* the central problem has a universality. They present the perennial problems of humanity. This is another problem that only methodology has to reckon with. Has the work a universal appeal? If so, it is an integral part of the human heritage.

Our next problem is the problem of tradition and individuality, ably mishandled by T.S. Eliot. In Eliot's hands it referred to tradition of literary works accepted by him and his followers. This refers to serious problems ignored by Eliot. Tradition in literature should always go hand in hand with the tradition of critical standards, not with that of the poets whom one likes for personal reasons or otherwise. In our country the basic critical traditions are those of the *rasa* and *dhvani* or *rasa-dhvani.* Within that tradition experimental variation is possible to reveal the individuality of the author. Kalidasa modified the *Mahabhārata* story in his *Abhijnāna Sākuntalam* and retained his individuality when he spoke of "Kalidasa granthita vastuna". But as a work of art, its value lies not in this amended story, but in the work itself. The entire drama is woven round the relation between the *sahakāra* (mango tree) and *navamālikā* (the jasmine creeper). A Telugu poet of the thirties described the Taj Mahal as the *mādhavi lata* (creeper) twining round the mango tree. A unifying image of symbol is necessary for a successful work of art. Thus Valmiki saw the whole *Rāmāyana* in the slaying of the male *kraunch* bird.

The second problem refers to the tradition of "broken images". If a work is "a heap of broken images", it fails to inhere into the literary tradition which emphasizes wholeness, not brokenness. It is wholeness that any work of art should reveal. Eliot's theory of tradition is based on Bradley's coherence theory of truth. A work of art should cohere, not correspond. Eliot's own work corresponds, it does not cohere.

Reverting to Indo-Anglian literature, we are faced with a series of problems which a methodology has to take into account. A writer like Mulk Raj Anand is, in a sense, uprooted from the Indian ethos. The influence of Marxist and Leninist ideology made him view the Indian situation from the standpoint of an alien ideology. This ideology may be relevant to the present Indian socio-economic conditions. It is the ideology that is emphasized in his work. But this ideology does not cohere with the artistic product. The same applies to our surrealists (originally French), Existentialists, and Absurdists. Such writers may, by birth, be Indians, but as writers of works of art they are aliens.

Raja Rao's *Kānthapura* has only a historical relevance. His *Cat and Shakespeare* has no substantial theme. Apart from the mode of presentation, the theme should be serious. It is in this sense that I interpret Bharata's "prakhyatam iti vrittam". As Bradley remarked, a pin's head and the fall of man can be the themes for a poet; but a major poet chooses the fall of man only. The theme can be from any sphere of human activity, but it should concern the basic human values. These values, however, should not be merely those of the artist's times. Bharair's *Kiratarjuniyam* may have arisen out of the then prevailing political situation. But the poem as such presents the conflict between the physical or brute valour and spiritual strength. This is a basic human problem.

Coming to the technical problem, what should be our tools? Are we merely to examine and analyse words, phrases, and clauses in a work of art? Irony, paradox, metaphor, and the like, are mere linguistic tools. When the meaning of a poem arises from the words employed by the artist, these tools may be useful. But in a good literary work we find that words emerge from the meaning. The verbal gymnastics of the New Critics and others lead us astray from the actual work. A part of the difficulty in *Sāvitri* is due to the words emerging from the meanings. A mere examination of the word is a case of *camatkāra* or wit. As against this, a major methodological concept is *dhvani.* It means suggestion. Bradley remarked that our atmosphere of infinite suggestion hovers round the best poetry. Ancient critics like Anandvardhana and his followers have arrived at a few thousand of varieties of suggestion. Along with this concept, the methodology should also include the Buddhist concept of *apoha.* According to this concept, the meaning of a word is primarily determined by what it excludes. *Determinatis est negatio,* said the God-intoxicated Spinoza.

Literary-critical theories are always amended and supplemented as time advances. The original theory of *rasa* stated by Bharata got diversified into various schools which were later unified into the theory of *rasa-dhvani;* and finally, an expanded meaning was given to *rasa* by Jagannatha. Within the framework of *rasa* we have to incorporate some principles which appear in Indo-Anglian literature. Thus, symbols, typologies, and archetypes can be included. Thus in Kalidasa's *Nalavikagni mitram* we have the artists with and without imaginative concentration. There is also the conflict between two types or archetypes of dancing, represented by Haradatta and Ganadasa, the latter appearing to be a symbolic representation of the poet himself.

Similarly, *karuna rasa* can be given an extended meaning in order to cover tragedies. Though there are tragic situations in our epics and literary works, they do not end on a tragic note. *Rasa* is the tragic experience as such, and its manifestations are the various *rasas.* Indian ethos, as illustrated by Abhinava Gupta, demands the culmination of any *rasa* in *Santa rasa—in* the peace that is beyond comprehension. This is the concept of total impression and in this light a work of art, has to be interpreted. In our multilingual country I find three literary traditions derived from *Rāmāyana, Mahābhārata,* and *Bhāgavata.* The first is in the east, north and Tamil Nadu, while the last is in Eastern India. The second covers the rest of the country. Accordingly, the Indian writer has, consciously or unconsciously, the corresponding ethos. If we keep this in mind, we can easily discover the related archetypes. In the light of these, an evaluation becomes comparatively meaningful.

The literary text is the given object. We can study it from the philological, philosophical, and literary standpoints inherited by the writer. But a pure historical or biographical approach has not been part of Indian critical tradition. The biographical method has not been followed by our ancients. It may be that we do not know the biographies of those writers; or the artists were not ego-centric. But it is interesting to speculate rare separation or bereavement in Kalidasa's life, as five of his works have this theme. The historical method has only a philological or contemporaneous interest, if it has not universal appeal.

Any methodology accepted by the Indian reader or critic should not forget the multiple layers of meanings. For instance, Kalidasa calls the Himalayas *"devatama"*. It is not because Shiva has his mythical or *puranic abode in the Himalayas*. The answer is to be found in *Kenopanishad* where the spirit appearing as *yakasham* is transformed into "Umā Haimavatī balu sobhamāna". It is because of Uma that the Himalayas are divine; and the fIrst eight cantos of the poem are about her.

But we should not stop with the multiple layers. Our tradition justly emphasizes the unity of the literary work in terms of *rasa*. The Indian creative artist and critic should be aware of the Indian ethos which is a perennial stream.

5

Indianization of English Studies: Some Tentative Reflections

G. S. Balarama Gupta

Moving Frontiers of English Studies in India – that happens to be the title of a critical work by C.D. Narasimhaiah.[1] Far from being fanciful or pedantic, the expressive phrase was intended to blast the myth of the monolythic concept of English literature as being just British literature. It was, in brief, an emphatic plea for a shift from English literature to Literature in English.[2] This was, of course, just the thing to be expected from a responsible professor of English of Narasimhaiah's calibre. It was his innovative perception as well as unflinching determination which was responsible for the introduction of American literature into the postgraduate syllabus of Mysore University, and a little later of Indian writing in English also. A pioneer that he was in many ways, he was then pleading for a study of Commonwealth literature. This ought to lead us to a realization of the need for altering the curricular designs of our postgraduate English studies with altering times. The trend is clear too. Most of our universities have either totally dropped or minimized the study of Old and Middle English authors. So have they done with exclusive studies of Shakespeare, Wordsworth and Tennyson. Instead, almost all Indian university English Departments today offer American literature, even if it is as a "compulsory optional" paper (this phrase is again Narasimhaiah's). Many, if not most, universities offer Indian writing in English, at least as an optional paper. And some provide for a study of Commonwealth literature (which sometimes includes in it Indian writing in English). And just a few Departments have a paper on Indian Literature in English Translation. But no English Department in the country seems to have considered the need for introducing Anglo-Indian Literature.

This paper is predicated on the assumption that any attempt to reorganise English studies at the postgraduate level in India should consider the advisability of laying enough emphasis on literature in English which has a positive relevance to the Indian context. It suggests that out of eight papers, three be devoted to British literature considered Age-wise or genre-wise, one to English language including Linguistics, another to Commonwealth literature (excluding Indian writing in English), and the remaining three be set apart for Anglo-Indian literature, Indo-Anglian literature or Indian English literature, and Indo-English literature (translations or transcreations of works in Indian vernaculars into English).

Wisdom lies in turning an accident into an advantage. The emergence of the Anglo-Indian race was the result of the historical accident of the encounter between Britain and India. So was the phenomenon of Anglo-Indian literature—a historical fact we cannot shy away from. It was the result of the impact of Western literature on a totally different culture, one nourished in India, an Eastern country. A community of men and women sprung from a land whose literature had made a distinct contribution to the advance of ideas in the world came face to face with Indian conditions with their ancient heritage and culture steeped in mysticism and dreaminess. It was natural that the sensitive among the British community could not remain unimpressed by the splendour and richness of India. Moved by the stimulus of India's romance, culture and beauty, these sensitive spirits have left records, some of them of unique literary value, and some others of fascinating historical interest. Thus was Anglo-Indian literature born. It is the outcome of the coming together of two cultural forces. It shows the dilemma of interaction between two bloods and cultures in a bid to locate the contours of identity and expression in local surroundings and familiar environments. It is not a totally dead subject either—as the recent interest in British Raj in the English reading public reveals. The romance of India which attracted the British in those days continues to be revived as the recent themes of *Jewel in the Crown* and *Far Flung Pavilions* show.

It is a pity that Histories of English Literature take but a scant notice of Anglo-Indian literature. And, though some isolated authors like Forster and Kipling are now and then fervently studied, it is a sad fact that this branch of literature as a whole continues, to suffer an undeserved neglect. There are several other writers like Meadows Taylor, L.H. Myers, Flora Annie Steel and Paul Scott who, along with several others of lesser or greater literary merit, should form a group of writers who can provide enough texts to form a viable course. For an Indian student of English literature, *Bhowani Junction* should prove itself to be a more palpable text than *Cakes and Ale*. The theme, the conflict, the locale; the characters, the fancies and images would be familiarly Indian and so would be the tone, idiom, and texture of language, moderated by Indian exigencies rather than distanced by British modes. For a proper understanding of India's political and social history during the British rule, a study of Anglo-Indian literature is valuable. In the modern concept of Integrated Education, where literature is not expected to be removed from other subjects, specially history, the study of Anglo-Indian literature at the postgraduate level must be considered essential. And from the point of intrinsic aesthetic merit also, there should be enough Anglo-Indian literary texts which can be subsumed under one paper.

And, then, the prescription of Indo-English literature or Indian literature translated or transcreated into English can be of great importance and import. We cannot afford to neglect our regional literatures in the snobbish pursuit of international literature. An Indian student of English literature should not deny himself a knowledge of the great works of literature produced in different Indian languages. Epics like *Rāmāyana Darshanam* of Kuvempu in Kannada and *Kāmāyanī* of Jayshankar Prasad in Hindi, *Jnaneswari* of Jnaneswar in Marathi, *Mahāprasthānam* of Sri Sri in Telugu are just a few instances of lofty literary masterpieces which we cannot afford to neglect. Also, there are several literary works which are unique in the sense that the like of them are not to be easily found in other *literatures* – *vachanas* in Kannada (a sample of them are to be found in *The Speaking of Siva* (rendered into English by A.K. Ramanjuan), *abhangs* in Marathi and *dohe* in Hindi (Kabir's *dohe* have been done into English by Tagore). All this in addition to works in other genres also, like drama and fiction.

A study of Indo-English literature ensures the use of English for the national purpose which it is meant to serve – that is, to break down the barriers of regional isolation and unite them into a national whole by increasing the area of intimacy and understanding between different regions. And then this kind of discipline would serve the great cultural purpose of facilitating a sympathetic appreciation of different lifestyles and literary imaginations converging upon creative products. This would also ensure a sharing of conflicts and dilemmas, and resolutions and reconciliations that are native to us. An increasing study of Indo-English literature can be expected to result in more and more of translation work. Then, English, as a language, will be gradually shorn of its British and Western affiliations, and will become more and more nativized and moulded to local use. Rendering of moods, feelings, emotions, similes and tones of native hue into English would make English pliable to Indian psyche, its vision and aesthetics. This will enable us to appropriate English to our use and purpose and not *vice versa* as is the case today. And we would be presenting to our students models of English which are addressed to Indians and their milieu. This kind of literature would present a changed vista of the whole aesthetico-semantic nature and texture of words, word usage, idiomatics, connotative shifts and metaphoric extensions of expressions and statements against the background of Indian poetics and imagination. One, therefore, will not have to seek the approval of our English from the British or England-finished academicians. Our norms of correctness then would be native, not foreign. The debates on the idiomatic use of English would be local, not dictated by the British sanction It is our engagement with Indo-English literature which will help create and formulate the true Indian variety of English potent and polished for our native use and purpose, much after the African variety of English.

Today none except the incurably chauvinistic would shut his eyes to the merits of the considerably substantial body of Indian writing in English which is being nourished and sustained by writers like Anand, Raja Rao, Narayan, Rushdie, Chaudhuri, Anita Desai, Kamala Markandeya, Nayanatara Sahgal, Ezekiel, Dom Moraes, Kamala Das, Keki Daruwalla (to mention just a few names), most of whom have elicited international appreciation and recognition. Indian English is hardly any longer a term which elicits ridicule: it is an authentic variety of English, "different from English English. Not *very* different, but different........"[3] It is now increasingly realised that English does not mean British English alone but that it can be Australian English or Caribbean English just as it can be Indian English also. It is high time we stopped feeling apologetic about Indian English and Indian English literature. It is in fact gratifying that the opposition to the inclusion of Indian writing in English as a paper at the postgraduate level in our universities is becoming less and less vehement, though whining and moaning is still not inaudible in some conservative academic quarters.

A study of Indian writing in English would give our students an idea of the change that English language has undergone at the hands of Indian writers to suit their cultural and experiential needs. In other words, it provides a historical perspective on the nativization of English.[4] It also reveals the extent to which the Indian imagination has been coloured by the use of English as a vehicle of creative expression. And it is also likely to inspire our creatively-inclined students to undertake writing in English some of which may prove worthy of recognition. The pursuit of an international outlook and integrated vision is bound to remain a chimera unless one's feet are firmly rooted in one's own national milieu and culture. Naturally, therefore, it is necessary that our advanced students of English literature should study Anglo-Indian literature, Indo-English literature, and Indian writing in English, without necessarily sacrificing a study of all other literatures in English—British, American, or Commonwealth.

Notes and References

1. C.D. Narasimhaiah, *Moving Frontiers of English Studies in India* (New Delhi: S. Chand,1977).
2. For an illuminating introductory study of different Englishes, see Narsu K. Nihalani, "English in the Third World: Changing Attitudes," *Journal of Indian Writing in English,* Vol. 13, No.1, January 1985, pp. 24-30.
3. Alastair Niven, in an interview with Anita Kuryan and Annie Chandy Mathew, *Literature Alive,* Vol. 2, No. 2, September 1988.
4. For a scholarly investigation of this problem, see Braj B. Kachru, *The Indianization of English* (Oxford: Oxford University Press, 1983).

6

Study of Poetry: A Linguistic Model

R.S. Sharma

Much literary criticism of the past directed towards the understanding of poetry was centred around either the poet or the reader. The poet-oriented approach emphasized the need to know in detail the life and circumstances of the man who composed the poem. This resulted in a good deal of discussion around the poem, and gave rise to much information, but little aesthetic experience, in the mind of the reader. This also led to the image of the poet as a fully integrated and logically consistent personality with a philosophy of life and set responses to beauty. Consequently, variability of mood, and changes in approach were often overlooked, if not "disallowed", and every poem by an author was understood in the light of his image built by critics. Some critics have emphasized the need to study the process of "making". They have claimed that the task of the critic is to retrace the footsteps of the poet, to recapture for the reader: the original mood of the author. This task requires an exercise of poetic imagination and demands creative talent in every genuine critic; a good critic must also be a poet himself. This tends to place the art of literary interpretation beyond the reach of many professed critics, not to speak of the common reader.

On the other hand, I.A. Richards and those who draw their inspiration from his theories give primary importance to the reader's reaction to a poem. A poem is treated as a kind of stimulus to which the reader is expected to make a satisfactory response.[1] This implies two things: a close study of the text, and a psychological consideration of the effect on the reader. The critic engages himself in considering the meaning of the poetic language from a general psychological perspective and studies the reader's adjustment to the poem. This approach leaves out one aspect of the process—the poet—and may lead to interpretations far removed from the original intentions of the "maker". The original aesthetic mood of the poet resulted from a particular and socio-cultural interaction which is reflected in the poem. A reader can never hope to gain the full intended impact merely by paying close attention to the text unless he limits himself to contemporary and familiar authors, or gains knowledge of the context by study. Even a close linguistic study confined to the text will not be adequate. Recognising the value of literary scholarship, Enkvist makes a pertinent point: "Only the literary scholar can tell us all that is implied in Milton's making Comus the son of Circe by Bacchus. The full implications of Comus' sinister ancestry do not emerge from a linguistic analysis of the whole corpus of English literature. Yet they must be understood for a proper appreciation of Milton's poem".[2] In extreme cases, this method may lead to serious errors of interpretation. Judged from the contemporary reader's perspective, a daily tool of the ancient man may appear to be an object of beauty, or an utterance intended to, arouse pathos may be mistaken for an example of humour.

The main problem with these two approaches, with a number of intergradations, is that they are inadequate and incomplete; they do not take account of all the essential factors involved. A poem must be treated as a special type of communicative act whereby the poet attempts to transmit a unique experience to others. Although the elements of self-expression and release always accompany poetic performance, no poem is composed without a receiving target in mind. We need not be misled by the assertion of the Hindu poet Tulsidas who claimed that he wrote the *Rāmcharitmānas* for self-satisfaction, since the very fact that he chose the language of the masses implies a desire to communicate, apart from the other clues found in the work itself. Similarly, G.M. Hopkins, who was imbued with the spirit of self-surrender and regarded his poetry as a way of worship, also enter-tained a hope for the publication of his verse and expressed it in a letter to Bridges. There is nothing unnatural or ignoble in this. Indeed the entire edifice of human culture is based on an innate urge to share our experience with others; it is the first condition of collaboration and cooperation.

The sharing of poetic experience through the medium of language involves the writer, the hearer or reader, and the linguistic code with its systems of sound, grammar, and meaning. The poet's message is a difficult one. He must consciously or unconsciously struggle with language in order to encode the content of his aesthetic experience, which is far more intractable than ordinary cognitive matter.[3] The reader is expected to decode the message correctly if he is interested in its true import. But language is far more complex than a simple deliberately constructed code. In the latter case, encoding or decoding are more or less mechanical; the code itself has little creative possibility and no range beyond its specific purpose. Language, by contrast, is a living medium organically related to the communicants; it lives and grows and changes with us, it pulsates with our innermost feelings, emotions and moods, ideas, thoughts and meditations, dreams, reveries and introspections. It is both social and personal making for a fine correspondence between individual and community, speaker and hearer. It is both a vehicle and a hindrance; it facilitates and blocks expression, it involves ease as well as struggle. The total meaning (including feeling, mood, and ideas), which a linguistic symbol has for a particular individual, never. completely coincides with that of any other individual in the community, but in ordinary social intercourse, difficulties in communication are seldom felt because the central area of meaning (central for general practical purposes) is commonly shared by all the users, although, even conversation, we occasionally find ourselves struggling with words.

Poetic communication is of a special kind.[4] The experience communicated is unique and uncommon—I find no contradiction in saying that truly universal experience is also unique and uncommon inasmuch as it clearly differs from conventionally shared experience. It is deeply rooted in the personality of the author both as a unique consciousness and as a member of the society. The poet must therefore wrestle with the medium, manipulating it and forcing it to get his message across; it is by his peculiar handling of the code that he is able to transmit his experience. The totality of meaning present in his mind is at considerable variance with that of the reader, and the latter must endeavour to know both the code and the encoder in order to gain access to the poet's meaning. For these reasons, a satisfactory model for interpretation must take into account all the three factors: encoder, code, and decoder. The totality of the situation includes the poet, the poem, and the reader. It is necessary to consider the relation between poet and reader in time and space, and to know relevant facts about the writer and his milieu. The language of the poem is certainly of crucial importance; it contains information about the man who composed it, and it is the chief source of the aesthetic enjoyment. "In considering. the language of poetry", writes Mrs. Nowottny, "it is prudent to begin with what is 'there' in the poem—'there' in the sense that it be described and referred to as unarguably given by the words.[5]

Another question of importance is whether poetry is to be addressed to the general mass of readers or to a select few. No doubt, the full enjoyment of a work of art demands varying degrees of effort on the part of spectator or reader, but this is quite different from the specialist demand which tlis common reader can only satisfy by making literature his main occupation. The outstanding figures in literature from

Homer down to Shakespeare and Dickens evidently offered their work to the general public who responded enthusiastically, although some understood them better than others. Great writers of literature have generally directed their productions towards the society as a whole and this has in fact, been responsible for the universal element in their writings without which no work can survive for long. It accounts for an important modality in the language used. There has certainly been a widespread belief that literature is a means of mass education in higher human values and in fine perception. According to a famous Sanskrit verse a man unfamiliar with literature, music, and art is an animal devoid of tail and horn.

In the third and fourth decades of the present century, poets and critics, particularly in England and America, created a powerful impression that the society in modern times has become so materialistic that the majority of men are not interested in arts and literature, nor prepared to take pains for their sake, that the writers and lovers of literature live in isolation, and that it is no longer possible to address one's work to the general public. It was also suggesed by implication that those interested in literature are the pursuers of higher values and constitute the aristocracy of the intellect. The poet is under no obligation to accommodate the majority, which no longer cares for art and is satisfied with commercialised forms of entertainment. It was further argues that since our modern society is complex, its literature is bound to be so. These ideas were employed to elevate the work of such writers as T.S. Eliot, later Yeats, and William Empson. The Auden Group, which emerged during the thirties, also composed poetry which was difficult to interpret (although the difficulty came from a different source) and the neo-Romantics of the forties with their knowledge of new psychology and the "use" of unconscious proved to be quite complex. The deliberate attempt to write difficult poetry must be regarded as a deviation, for it runs counter to the broad social aim of common enjoyment and makes aesthetic experience the concern of an elite: it also falsifies the original role of poetry.

It needlessly involves poetry with philosophy, theology, mysticism, and science: the result is a kind of verse analogous to an over-rich dish, out of reach for the majority, and a source of luxury for the constipated minority. From a communicative point of view, the common consciousness able to touch only the fringe of what the poet wishes to convey.

What is being attacked here is not that poetry may involve complexity and may not yield its full impact immediately to the common reader, but the theory that poetry is bound to be complex and that the poet need not consider the common mass of humanity to be his audience. It is possible to suggest normative limits of deviation or manipulation in the creative use of the language system (as well as cukure). In a defence of what may be called populist poetry Rosenthal has stated: "Poets are the verbal antennae of a people. The awareness they distil and convert into the dynamics of language is somehow present in the populace at large. We neglect it at our peril."[6] The communication chain is bound to snap at a certain point of incomprehensibility, beyond which the poet ceases to serve as the antennae of the speech community, and may be said to be using a purely personal code. It would be interesting to consider this point in the perspective of the work of Korzybski [7] and Hayakawa.[8] I also suspect that the cult of difficulty has yet another source. The early part of the present century saw the rise of a new kind of worker, the specialist. Specialization is supposed to command much respect in the field of knowledge; every intellectual would secretly like to be called a specialist. Some poets, who were convinced that no one is interested in poetry, probably thought that they could at least attract a minority by resorting to what may be broadly called specialist poetry. But this kind of infection, though justifiable in literary criticism, is self-defeating in poetry, and runs counter to the communication principle.

In considering the nature of a poem I am chiefly concerned with its dynamic structure and its distinction from a painting or a statue. In painting and sculpture, we do not have to watch the artist at work in order to see how he handles his tools and materials until the finished work appears; we do not have to reconstruct the process in our mind. In contrast, a poem takes place as an event in time; its essence is in the making, or growing, where, as some poets have admitted, the "made" led the maker the poem was born in spite of the poet. "The overriding property of texts is linearity: speech occurs linearly in time, and writing, imitating speech, occurs linearly in space."[9] The pattern emerges, the mood builds up as you read the poem. Here, you must first follow the sequence of words as they roll out one after another and modify and gradually give shape to the experience. A poem has dynamic construction in this sense: we have to watch the deft touches which the poet gives his material from beginning to end. It is only after we have seen the last line, that we can contemplate the pattern and symmetry which is the source of deeper satisfaction. It is this distinctive fact about the growth of a poem which should be kept in mind when interpreting a poem.

Now we can turn to the making of a poem. There are two basic processes involved in building a poem. First, the poet starts with a broad, general area of experience and proceeds to chisel out the exact mood or "thought" by skilful modification, specification, or concretization. Each word and grammatical structure that is added gives a new turn to the thought, and the theme emerges continuously into a clearer shape. We have to be watchful of each linguistic turn, and a sensitive response to structural modulations is what is required for a perception of the creative process. Here the distinction drawn earlier between painting, or sculpture and poetry ought to be recalled. In a poem it is not the final shape alone which matters, but the whole succession. Our theoretical position calls for an adjustment in the use of what has been called stylistics, or to be more precise "new stylistics"[10] (although I would prefer to call this branch of applied linguistics simply "literary linguistics", just like psycholinguistics and socio-linguistics). Linguistic study can give us insights into two related aspects of poetry: the poet's fundamental view of life—his personality, and the dynamic design of his poem. Literary stylistics as practised today apparently has failed to take the dynamic nature of both life and art into account. As far as its application to language varieties is concerned, as in the work of Halliday *et al.*.[11] or David Crystal and Derek Davy,[12] stylistic approach is perfectly valid and quite useful, but in literature, to hold that a person's use of language is as individual as his fingerprints[13] is going too far. There is no doubt stylistic study can reveal the "epistemic choices"[14] a writer makes, but the possibility that such choices may alter as a result of growing experience must also be accommodated in a good model.

I am not pleading for a total rejection of the current approach. What is needed is the recognition of linguistic choices related to the developing theme of a poem, in addition to those induced by realistic context of situation on the one hand, and stable traits, wherever present, of the personality of the author on the other. In a successful poem, choices of the first category are inevitable, while the latter two may or may not be present; if they are, a study of the first will offer us clues to the period style, and of the second, to the individual style (hence the epistemological stance) of the man. E.L. Epstein clearly recognises this kind of distinction within literary style when he introduces the concepts of what he calls "the public game" and "the private game".[15] The kind of discriminations I have proposed will take care of both convention and idiosyncracy, and aesthetics and personality.

II

In Part I above, we have outlined in its essentials, a linguistic model for the study of poetry. We shall now proceed to present [16] an analysis and interpretation of the Hindi poet Jaya Shankar Prasads's well-known poem *Kāmāyanī*, adding the phonglogical and discoursal dimensions to the above framework. Within the scope of a single article, the study is bound to be partial, yet it is hoped the applicability of the theory and its usefulness will emerge clearly in the course of our discussion. As already stated, a linguistic approach to poetry focusses attention on the text—"what is unarguably given by the words"—rather than the bio-graphical, social and literary background. This attitude may be (and has sometimes been) misunderstood to mean that the background information has no relevance to the study of a poem. In this regard there has been a mutual reinforcement between the New Critics and linguists, leading, in the field of teaching, to statements like the following: "In the lesson we have just watched we notice the absence of introduction. It begins with the reading of a poem not with a statement of who wrote it, and certainly not with a mine of information about why, where and when he wrote it and how it relates to the rest of his work. If all this is not in the poem then it does not matter at this stage of literary education, nor, we suspect, at many other stages."[17]

This extreme position will not accord well with a linguistic theory which takes a functional view of language, because a linguistic text, or message, is never totally independent of its context of situation; on the other hand, its thought, feeling and purpose are revealed only with the help of its context. Therefore, we may take it as a fundamental assumption that an idea of the context is necessary for the full understanding of a poem. But the context of a poem must be determined along linguistic lines so that (as is often the case) the teacher, or interpreter, does not involve himself in unnecessary or irrelevant discussion, or graft his own preconceived notions on the poem. As a matter of fact, the poetic context, as compared to the ordinary linguistic communication, is quite complex. In my view, there can be, at the most, three kinds of context to a poem. First, we have the real context, or context of situation, in which the poet communicates his message directly to the reader or hearer. For example in:

Carana kamala bandaū harirayi
Jākī kṛapā pangu giri langhai andhē kō sab kuch darasāyi

(I adore the lotus-feet of Lord Hari by whose favour the lame crosses the mountain and everything is visible to the blind).

The poet of the Bhakti period often declares his identity in the poem itself and indicates by discoursal means whether he is communicating as addresser or as narrator or as observer.

In the above lines, the poet speaks in his own person. The verbal inflexion in *bandaū̃* establishes an exophoric link with the outside world and we come to know that the poet Sūrdas is praying to Lord Hari. This is a characteristic method of the romantic poet. When we read the following lines in the light of their context of situation, we gather that the first person pronoun used in them refers to Wordsworth and Shelley respectively:

My heart leaps up when I behold
A rainbow in the sky.
O World! O Life! O Time!
On whose last steps I climb

The second type of context is imaginary. This context, even though it does not negate the real one, is independent and free of the constraints of the latter. This does not mean that it is situated in a vacuum because, in some way or other, it does establish contact with the context of situation through exophoric reference, which a close analysis alone can reveal, Makhanalal Caturavedi's following lines illustrate this kind of imaginary context:

cāha nahī̃ main surbālā kē gahanō main gūtha jaun
cāha nahī̃ prēmī̃ māla main bindh pyāri kō Ithlaun

(There is no wish that I be threaded in the ornaments of a divine maid. There is no wish that being beaded in the lover's garland, I tempt the beloved.)

Here the first person pronoun does not refer to the poet himself; it stands for the flower in the poet-created context. More completely, in the following lines by T.S. Eliot, both the first and second person pronouns refer to the imaginary character named in the title of the poem:

Let us go then, you and I,
When the evening is spread out against the sky

Like a patient etherised upon a table.

The third kind of context is the one whose source lies in another text and with which the poem being interpreted is hooked up by paraphoric reference:

Ūdhau jāhu tumahī hama janē
Syāma tumahī hyā kau nahī pa!hayo tuma hau bīca bhulānē.

(Ūdho, go away, we have seen you. Syama hasn't sent you here, you have lost your way in the middle.)

Here, too, the flrst person pronoun has been used, but it refers to the Gōpis in the legend of Krişna; Ūdho and Śyām are also part of the same story. In the same way, we have paraphoric cohesion in Eliot's "The Waste Land", which is set within the legend of the Holy Grail; needless to say, the full meaning of "The Waste Land" is beyond grasp without an understanding of this paraphoric context. It is important to note that where all the three kinds of context are present they are joined through cohesive devices and the direction of cohesion is always outward. The relationship can be represented in the form of a diagrm given on p. 69.

Another aspect of poetic communication is that it is connotative in its impact, the purpose being not to transmit information, but to convert facts (real or imaginary) into feeling, mood and emotion: poetry, when it is genuine, produces a multidimensional insight into life and its working, which goes beyond data-based knowledge. The process of conversion of denotation into connotation takes place in all the components of the text's language: sound, form, syntax and vocabulary. We have already noted in Part I that the text of a poem is experienced in the form of a sequence of occurrences in time: in normal reading, a poem unfolds itself bit by bit as the eye moves from one end to the other or as the ear receives impression after impression. A poem is therefore a cumulative experience and ought to be approached

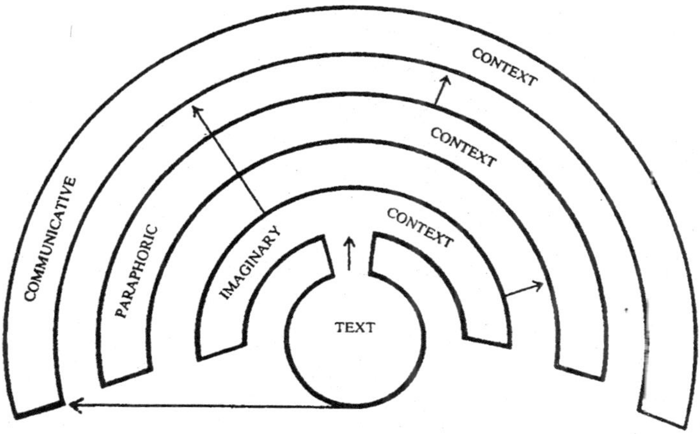

as such.

Finally, a word about the psychological status of a poem. On the psychological plane, a poetic text is to be thought of as an artistic organisation of verbal stimuli. These linguistic stimuli cause a complex of responses which gradually mature into a rich experience in the form of an aesthetic mood or emotion.

So far we have been dealing with the theoretical aspects of poetry in the light of which we propose to analyse *Kāmāyanī*. We begin by recalling that a poem *happens* to the reader as a series of events in time. In reading a poem, therefore, we first take hold of the context and then are confronted by the title of the poem. We have to pay attention to the form and content of the title and explore all its implications in terms of morphological structure, syntactic possibilities, denotation and connotation. We have also to see whether and how the title is relaled to the contexts. Gutwinski[18] has dealt with cohesion in literary texts, but he has not thrown sufficient light on how the poet (specially the modern poet) sometimes suspends or suppresses cohesion with a view to arousing a transitory feeling of suspense, eagerness and disappointment.

From the title, we move on to the first line and thereafter

sentence is added to sentence until we have reached the last sentence of the poem. We shall treat the sentence as a unit for our analysis, but it should be noted that rhythm has its own units which sometimes run parallel to the syntactic progression and sometimes proceed by cutting across it and this interaction between syntax and rhythm may be productive of very rich poetic experience. After we have completed our reading of a poem, we are in a position to look at it (as a linguistic construct) as a whole. For this, we have to examine the statistical position of the various linguistic categories employed in the poem, for example, the proportion of verb phrases or noun phrases, or content words and within them the strength and distribution of sub-categories, *i.e.,* stative verbs, mass nouns, etc. This operation will enable us to specify the qualitative impact of the poem as a single object.

Now we turn to the poem under study. By way of context, it is enough to say that Jai Shankar Prasad is a modern Indian poet who is regarded as a precursor of Romanticism; he had a profound knowledge of Indian philosophy and religion. He was also aware of modem scientific thinking. He was keenly interested in the ideology of Indian Renaissance.

Next, we attend to the title, *Kāmāyanī* which is derived from the stem *kāma.* As a linguistic stimulus, *kāma* covers a wide area of meaning ranging from sublime love and mystical experience of union to lust and sexual activity. Its associations involve longing for the beloved, attraction to beauty, union and creation. It gives rise to pleasurable and sweet feelings. Being the only contentive part in the title, it is in the focus of our mind. Its pure Sanskrit form raises expectations of an exalted style or composition. But in the absence of any other collocation and syntactic frame, it is difficult at this stage to ascertain the specific meaning and intent of the word. After the title, we read the poet's "Preface" in which the theme is briefly explained and the specific meaning of the word *Kāmāyanī* is given. We gather that the word is derived by adding *-ayan,* in the sense of descendant, and the feminine termination and that the word has been used in Vedic literature for *sraddha.* A little thinking makes it clear why the poet, after inscribing the word *sraddha* in the brackets, finally chose *Kāmāyanī* as the more appropriate title. In the mind of the reader, the word would also, perhaps, suggest *kama* + *ayana.*

The beginning of any poem is of special significance. The manner in which a poet opens his poem and connects the opening with the title and various types of contexts produces a unique effect on our mind and heart. Therefore, before we study the opening lines of *Kāmāyanī*, we will do well to look at some famous openings. Since *Kāmāyanī* is a poem with epic dimensions, we choose three epics and two long poems. Homer's[19] *Iliad* begins thus:

> Sing, O Goddess, the ruinous wrath of Achilles
> Son of Peleus . . .

The work begins with an imperative sentence modulated to a request or prayer in which the goddess of poetry is asked to 'sing' the anger of Achilles. In this, there are two things to be noticed. First: there is no clear cohesion with the title because the story begins in the middle: the device, which later became a convention, helps in arousing our curiosity. Secondly, this beginning indicates the factor of divine inspiration. The ancient Greeks believed that sublime poetry is composed under the guidance of a divine power: the word *enthuse* means "to fill with god". Later the question-answer pattern is used to achieve cohesion and thus the text proceeds:

Q: Which of the gods caused two such men to contend?
A: The son of Zeus and Leto.[20]

Milton,[21] too, follows the same method in *Paradise Lost:*

> Of man's first disobedience and the fruit
> Of that forbidden tree whose mortal taste
> ... ...
> Sing heavenly Muse. . .

Milton asks two questions and with the answer to the second the story begins:

Q: Who first reduced them to that foul revolt?
A: Th' infernal Serpent.

In Kalidasa's poetry, the structural variety of the openings is admirable. In the first sloka of *Raghuvansam,* the poet genuflects to Parvati-Samkara:

vāgarthāviva sampraktau vagarthapratipattayē,
jagataha pitarau vandē pārvatīparmēsvaru.

(For the perception of Word and Meaning, I adore the world's parents Parvati and Siva who are united like Word and Meaning.)

The first person pronoun, which is understood, relates the text to the communicative context. The beautiful simile used has implications for the nature of the proposed text. The deep-set cataphoric cohesion in *vāgarthapratipattayē* gives a broad hint to the theme. In the second sloka, *kva Sūryaprabhvo vansah* (where the Sun-generated race) is instrumental to semantic cohesion: the poet has repeated one part of the title *Raghuvansam* and rendered the other with a descriptive adjective. Thus, this cohesion has a dramatic effect on the mind. From slokas 5 to 9, the communicative situation becomes clear: *sō-aham raghunā-manvayam vakchyā* (that I sing of the race of Raghus) ..., and the story is begun in sloka II.

Kumārasambhavam begins with a description of Himalaya and there is no apparent cohesion with the title. Later in sloka 21 a light, semantic connection is secured through *bhavapūrvapatnī* (Siva's former spouse) when we take *Kumāra* in the specific sense, "son of Siva". In the third work of Kalidasa, *Meghadūtam,* the poet as communicator is absent and there is no direct link with the communicative context. In such texts, a close stylistic analysis alone can disclose cohesion with the real context. In *Mēghadūtam* the story appears before us independently. But there is internal cohesion: the relation of *megha* in sloka 2 relates the text to the title and in sloka 4 the situation becomes clear.

We shall make a small digression at this point in order to consider the concept of "semantic field" which is of special relevance to cohesion in literary texts. Hans Hoermann[22] has mentioned three approaches to the subject. According to one of them, the lexicon of a language is divided into semantic fields comprising words arranged on a vertical scale. For example,

(i)	*prapitamaha*	great-grandfather
	pitamaha	grandfather
	pita	father
	putra	son
	pautra	grandson
	prapautra	great-grandson
(ii)	*daurana*	run
	kūdana	jump
	calana	walk
	rēngana	creep
	sarakana	slide
(iii)	*mēdhavī*	intelligent
	samajhadār	sensible
	cālāk	clever

According to the second, a semantic field is a collection of words (as units of meaning) which raise expectations about one another:

(i)	*likhanā*	write
	kalama	pen
	kāgaza	paper
(ii)	*vyāpār*	business
	pūnji	capital
	munāfā	profit
	ghātā	loss
(iii)	*chanda*	stanza
	mātrā	quantity
	gaṇa	foot
	yati	pause
	laya	rhythm

The third approach, mainly concerned with semantic analysis from a psychological point of view, may also be considered. It holds that two words, which as stimuli do not recall each other, may, each of them, call forth the same words in response by association. Thus *piano* by association does not bring *symphony* to our mind and *vice versa,* but both of them call to our mind *music, note,* or *orchestra* as associated words. Since this matter is subject to psychological experiment, I shall say no more about it, but it must be pointed out that ordinary processes of associative thinking about meanings can also help in discovering concealed relationships on the semantic plane in a literary text and thus throw some light on semantic cohesion. The technique will be use in the study of Eliot, Dylan Thomas, or the surrealists.

We now return to our analysis of *Kāmāyanī*. After "Preface" our attention is drawn to the title of the First Book. *Cinta* has a negative connotation; it arouses the feelings of mental pain, anxiety, fear, etc. How this connotation is expanded and transformed is a matter for a later stage in our experience of the poem. The word also precludes any clear connection. But it certainly agrees in gender with the title of the whole book, *Kāmāyanī,* and this may not be superfluous, because, in the structure of the whole text, gender-meaning has an importance of its own. Also, when we recall the "Preface", we find the word *manana* used significantly and this leads to a very faint cohesion. With this stock of ideas and feelings, our reading proceeds. The basis of the text is the edition prepared by Ratnasankar Prasada.[23]

Himagiri kē uttung sikhara para baith sila ki sitala chahā
eka puru a bhīgē nayanō sē dēkha rāhā thā pralaya
pravāha.

(On the high peak of Himagiri sitting under the rock's shadow, a male human, with wet eyes, was looking at the all destroying flood.)

These lines present an independent description and there is no obvious sign of cohesion. The strong connotation aroused by *Cinta* receives a mild setback; the expectation is not fully satisfied. But we should not regard cohesion as missing, because *bhīge nayana* (wet eyes) and *pralaya pravāha* (all-destroying flood) are associated respectively with sorrow and fear, which, in terms of semantic field, are related to *Cīnta*. In the "Preface", the word *jala plāvana* (flood) is used, which is synonymous with *pralaya pravāha* (all-destroying flood), and as Halliday and Hasan[24] have pointed out, synonymous words are a means to cohesion. In this way, through the "Preface", the needed intertextual cohesion is achieved. The level of vocabulary employed in these two verses, constituting the first sentence of the poem, points to an elevated style and serious theme, and creates a corresponding feeling in the mind. If we replace this vocabulary with conversational terms, the quality of our response will also change:

> *Himālaya, unci coṭī, caṭṭāna, thanḍhīādamī gīlī, ãnkhē, bhayōnaka, bārha, etc.*

(High peak, rock, cold, man, wet eyes tetrible flood, etc.)

Ignoring the rhythm for the moment, if we rephrase the verses in the following form, the difference in effect can easily be perceived:

> Himālaya kī ūnci cōṭī para bai ha cattanō kī chāva
> ēk manuja gīlī ānkhō sē dēkh rahā thā pralaya bahāva.

From the standpoint of sentence-structure, the first sentence of the poem is periodic. The first line, consisting solely of adverbials, creates suspense and an impression of a lofty utterance, for periodicity is associated with the sublime style. It should also be noted that the two noun phrases used in these lines are symmetrical·

Noun	*Post-Position*	*Adjective*	*Noun*
himagiri	kē	uttunga	sikhara
silā	kī	sitala	ċhāha

This kind of equivalence has a distinctive beauty and has been regarded as the main organising principle in poetry.

In the second line, *ēk* (one) in *ēk Punṣa* (one male human) is to be treated as an indefinite article. In Hindi, *ēk* can be used either as an indefinite article or as a numeral adjective, and each use has its distinctive meaning and effect. By using the indefinite article, the poet has allowed the feeling of curiosity to persist: had he introduced the word Manu at this point, we would have recognised a clear connection. The word *Puruṣa* also requires explication. Semantically, it is gender-distinctive, and gender-meaning, as we have suggested earlier, is quite important in this text. It may be added that the role of male and female elements and their mutual relationship form a major plank in the structure of *Kāmāyanī*; they are reflected in the language of the text. *Puruṣa* is the first example of this motif; it cannot be replaced with *mānava, manuṣa, manuja,* because they are not gender distinctive and are generally used to mean both men and women, or mankind. The second verse has the following structure:

Subject + Adverbial + Verb Phrase + Object

The' adverbial, coming after the subject, creates a minor arrest, although this kind of foregrounding is not as striking in Hindi as in English. Compare, for example,

I live in this house. *(maĩ is ghara mē rahatā hū.)*
I shall see you tomorrow. *(maĩ āpasē kal milūga).*

In the English versions, if the adverbial is moved to the second position, the effect will be quite marked:

I, in this house, live.

I, tomorrow, shall see you.

On the other hand, the object *pralaya pravāha* (all-destroying flood) has been clearly displaced from its normal position. On account of this shifting and on account of occupying the end-position in the sentence as well as the line, the word strikes our consciousness with great force and establishes the cataclysmic flood as a major element of the poetic thought.

We shall now consider sound-patterning and rhythm in these lines. Sound-effects in poetry should not be treated as confined to similarity and onomotopoeia alone; they go deeper than that, and in subtle ways help the meaning and feeling crystallize; they also impart a physical dimension to the thought: its movement, force and quantity. Strictly speaking, the human speech apparatus is not calibrated to reproduce exactly the sounds made by animals and things. For example, *gurrinla* (snarling) in *kuttā gurrāyā* (dog snarled) is not a re-creation of the original noise; it is, as a matter of fact, an interpretative translation by our nervous system made in terms of our speech apparatus. Therefore, it is more appropriate to say that in artistic organisation of speech sounds (involving, of course, time, juncture and pause), the poet, consciously or unconsciously, seeks to build up, through sound and rhythm, an auditory image of the phenomenon being dealt with by him.

While considering the lines under discussion, we must note that the First Book of the poem is printed in two different layouts. In many editions, such as the one by Bhārati Bhandār[25] the stanza is printed in four lines, whereas the poet's son, Ratnasankara Prasada, following closely the author's manuscript, has printed the stanza in two lines in his edition 1985.[26] We have followed Ratnasankara's layout, which is, indeed, the author's. The two-line stanza is quite in keeping with the title and the content of Book I. If we divide the stanza into four lines, the rhythm loses in speed and creates an atmosphere of leisurely thinking, which is contrary to the mood expressed by words in the lines. Secondly, the four-line stanza requires pauses where the other form would have juncture or transition, which, again, is incompatible with the state of mind being represented. By comparison, the two-line stanza ensures the speed and tightening of rhythm which can adequately represent the anxious thinking going on in Manu's mind. Furthermore, this disposition of lines gives us, an easy access to the subtleties of the theme. Let us suppose that we want to present the image of a peak on which there is nothing:

Himagiri kē uttunga sikhara para
kaise pahūcē yahī prasna thā.

In this rhythmic sentence a long pause after *para* would be quite suitable and in keeping with the thought. But the lines under analysis do not contain such an idea, and therefore, an end-p use after *para* would fail to convey the desired effect. Similarly, a pause after *bhige nayanō sē* will not only slow down the speed, it will also affect the contour of the images. Regarding the layout and punctuation, which are a key to the oral delivery of the poem, we shall do well to give a serious thought to what Ratnasankara Prasada has said on the matter:[27]

āja bahudhā iṇa avākāsō athavā antarālō kō mudrana-sauṣthavā matra māna lenē kā bhrama hō raha hai. ataevā kāvya kē samucta anusīlana kē artha ina prakṛata caranō aura anucchēdō kō unakē maulika rūpa mē prastuta karanā avasyaka hō gayā.

(Today, these pauses or intervals are mistakenly taken to be only matters of presentable printing. Therefore, for a proper pursuit of the poetic meaning, it has become necessary to present the natural lines and sections in their original form.)

The first line begins with an image of the high peak of the Himalayas, treated in Hindi as a single mountain and not a plural being as suggested by the English form of the word. Read with the adjective *uttuṅga* (high), the expression creates a sensation of mounting, of elevatory movement. We have to see how his connotation is transformed into sensation with the help of sound-patterning. Let us first examine the deployment of consonants and the points of articulation activised. They are ,as follows:

glottis —> teeth —> velum —> alveolus —> velum —> teeth —> teeth (nasal) —> velum —> alveolus —> lips —> alveolus —> lips —> palate(higher) —> palate-alveolus —> alveolus-velum —> palate-alveolus —> teeth —> alveolus —> palate-alveolus —> glottis.

It is clear from the above that the articulatory activity, beginning at the lowest point of the speech-mechanism, proceeds irregularly to higher points and then descends in the same manner until it reaches the initial low position. If we combine with this description the arrangement of the vowels, manner of articulation and the printed contour of the line, we will find that the figure of the mountain is traced skilfully on the canvas of our mind and it is in terms of nervous stimulation; the peak is formed by *uttuṅga* (high) which begins in a fairly high region in (u) and rises still higher in (n), involving the nasal cavity, the highest region, and then declines to (g) on a still relatively high point.

Let us now look at some special features of rhythm, because it is closely related to image reception and foregrounding. We may read the first line thus:

Himagiri kē/uttuṅga sikharā para/ baitha silāl kī sītal chāta

In this manner of reading, the image of *uttuṅga sikhar* emerges prominently as a distinct aspect:

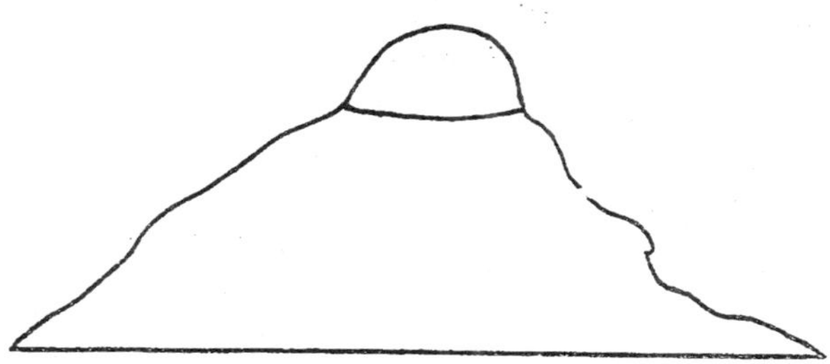

If, on the other hand, we do not apply the short pause, we get the following figure:

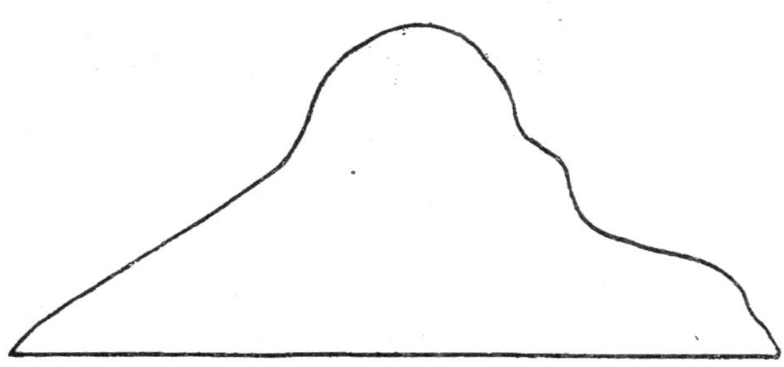

There is a subtle difference between the two images: in one the peak is taken to be a distinct part, in the other, an extension of the mountain.

In the second line, Ratnâsankara Prasada provides a comma after *ēka puruṣa,* which means we have to make a short pause here in reading. If we follow this manner of articulation, the image of a lonely man comes to the fore and *bhīge nayanō sē* (with wet eyes) moves close to the verb in its true adverbial function: On the other hand, if no pause is made, the movement is speeded up, and we see the image of a man with his wet eyes. We now proceed to the next two lines:

> *nīce jala thā upara hima thā, ēk tarala thā ēk saghana*
> *ēk tatva kī hī pradhanatā – kahō ouse jada yā cetana.*

Here *nice* and *upara* function as deictics to relate these lines to the first two and *ek* links up line four to line three. *Tattva* as a superordinate of *jala* and *hima* also helps in cohesion. The syntactic structure truly repeats the difference and unity of water *(jala)* and ice *(hima)*. *Pradhanatā* (prominence), as compared to other words in these lines, is the longest word; it makes us feel the expansiveness of water. The deviant use of *celana* (sentient) is also worth noting. The dash after *pradhanatā* requires a good pause forcing us to ponder on the philosophic comment that follows.

The first four lines that we have studied are marked by one special feature. Thc proportion of the verbs is very small — 41:8, when every word is counted irrespective of repetition and every auxiliary verb is counted as a separate item. There are only three lexical *verbs – baitha* (sit), *dēkha* (see), *kahō* (say). In these verbs, too, the activity element is very weak. Apart from *cetana* (sentient), the adjectives are also devoid of dynamic content. As a result of this lexical position, this portion as a whole produces a static rather than dynamic impression. All the activity is inside the protagonist's mind and that is reflected in rhythm and syntax. This observation will be better appreciated if we place by the side of these lines another text abounding in dynamic verbs:

thumukī calata rāmacandra bājata paijaniyā
kilakilāya uthata dhāya girata bhumi latapatāya
dhāya māya gōda lēta Dasaratha ki raniyā

(Ramacandra walks lurchingly, foot-ornaments make music; laughing gleefully (he) rises, and running, falls to the ground being unsteady. . .)

Here the proportion of the verbs is 2:1 – half of the words are verbs and all of them lexical-dynamic.

Before we complete this partial study of *Kāmāyanī*, I should like to comment briefly on some discoursal and thematic aspects of the work. The first of these is use of direct speech in a special way:

O cinta ki pahali rekha, ari visva-vana ki vyali
jvalamukhi sphota ke bhisana prathama kampa si matavali.

(O the first stroke of anxiety, or the she-serpent of the world-forest/Mad, uncontrollable, like the terrible first tremor of a volcano burst.)

In the preceding lines, the poet does not indicate whose utterance or loud thinking this is. We are only told:

nikala rahi thi marma vedana karuna vikal kahani-si,
vaha akeli prakrati suna rahi, hasti-si pahacani-si.

(The heart-rending pain was issuing like a restless tale of pathos/There only Nature was listening, as if laughing, as if familiar).

We certainly gather from the context that these thoughts arise in the mind of Manu, yet the special discoursal style has an important effect: the direct speech, before we recognise it as the expression of an individual's state of mind, appears to us as a universal or philosophical statement, or the outburst of the human mind in a reflective state. This device employed at several other places in the poem can be seen to have a crucial importance in the structure of the theme.

Secondly, the theme of *Kāmāyanī* is compounded of three strands. The first is the historical-imaginary legend of Manu, Sraddha, Ira, etc.; second, a dynamic treatment of the different tendencies of the human mind – the structure of human thought; and third, the ascending stages of Hindu mystical *sadhanā*. The question is, by what means have these various strands been brought together and wound in a unified whole?

If we regard *ċintā*, Sraddhā, Ira, Kāma, etc., as the different states, urges or elements of the mind, then *Kāmāyani* may be treated as organised on a hyponymic principle. Hyponymy, as already shown, will also account for intersectional cohesion. It is possible to join the other strands with the main hyponymic structure and represent the thematic construction of *Kāmāyanī* by means of the following diagram, but this is no more than a suggestion in need of verification and specification. The mystical strand in the diagram is symbolised by the relative height of each division: thus *ċinta* is the lowest stage and *ānanda* the highest.

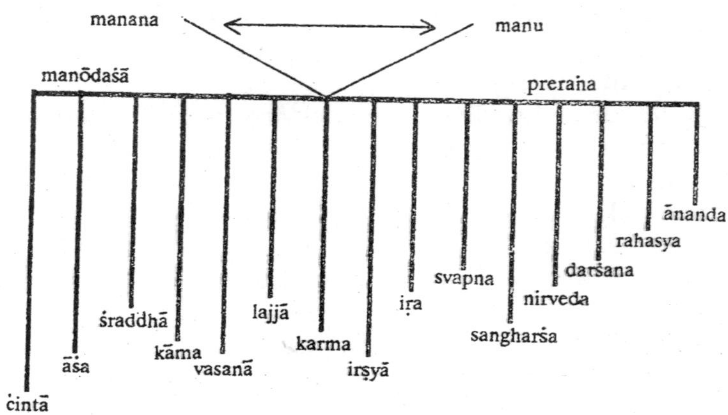

Notes and References

1. I.A. Richards, *Principles of Literary Criticism* (London: Routledge, 1925).

2. Nils Erik Enkvist, John Spencer and Michael J. Gregory, *Linguistics and Style* (London: Oxford University Press, 1964), p. 4.

3. Randolph Quirk has produced the testimony of poets themselves in the chapter entitled "The Intolerable Wrestle with Words" in his book *The Use of English* (London: ELBS, 1972).
4. On ordinary and poetic communication see John Lyons, *Semantics* (London: Cambridge University Press, 1977), I, Chapter 2. .
5. Winifred Nowottny, *The Language Poets Use* (London: Athlone, 1962), p. 1.
6. M.L. Rosenthal, "Foreword", *Poetry and the Common Life* (New York: Oxford University Press, 1974).
7. A. Korzybski, *Science and Sanity: An Introduction to Non-Aristotelian Systems and General Semantics* (Lancaster, Pa: International Non-Aristotelian Library, 1933).
8. S.I. Hayakawa, *Language* in *Thought and Action* (New York: Harcourt, Brace, 1949.
9. Geoffrey N. Leech and Michael H. Short, *Style in Fiction: A Linguistic Introduction to English Fictional Prose* (London: Longman, 1981), p. 211.
10. Leech and Short, *Style* in *Fiction,* p. 1.
11. MAK. Halliday, Angus McIntosh and Peter Strevens, *The Linguistic Sciences and Language Teaching* (London: ELBS, 1970), pp. 87-92.
12. David Crystal and Derek Davy, *Investigating English Style* (London: Longman, 1969).
13. *Ibid.,* "Foreword" by Randolph Quirk.
14. Richard Ohmann, "Prolegomena to the Analysis of Prose Style "in *Contemporary Essays on Style,* ed. Glen A. Love and Michael Payne (Glenview: Scott, Foresman and Company, 1969), pp. 181-82.
15. E.L. Epstein, *Language and Style* (London: Methuen, 1978), Chapters 3 and 4.
16. Most of this part is the author's translation of his paper, "Kamayani: Bhasika Sanracana evam Kavyanubhuti", read at a seminar organised by the Central Institute of Hindi, Agra.
17. Bright, JA and G.P. McGregor, *Teaching English as a Second Language* (London: ELBS, 1970).
18. Gutwinski, *Cohesion in Literary Texts* (The Hague: Mouton, 1976).

19. Homer, *The Iliad,* Tr. E. Rus (Indianapolis: Babbs-Merril, 1977), 3.
20. *Ibid..*
21. Milton, J., *Paradise Lost,* Ed. G.H. Cowling (London: Methuen, 4th edn., 1950).
22. Hoermann, H. *Psycholinguistics* (Berlm: Springer-Verlag, 1971), pp. 164-73.
23. Jayasankar Prasad, Kāmāyanī, Ed. Ratnasankar Prasād (Varanasi: Prasad Prakasan, 3rd edn., 1985).
24. Halliday, M.A.K. and R. Hasan, *Cohesion* in *English* (London: Longman, 1976), 278-91.
25. Jayasankar Prasad, *Kamayani,* (Allahabad:Bharati Bhandar, 1964). – *Kamayani.* (Facsimile of the original manuscript) Allahabad: Bharati Bhandar, 1971; – *Kamayani.,* Ed. R Prasad (Varanasi: Prasad Prakasan, 3rd edn., 1985).
26. Jayasankar Prasad, *Kāmāyanī,* Ed. Ratnasankar Prasad, *op. cit.*
27. *Ibid.*

7

Mahāvākya: The Indian Theory of Literary Discourse

Kapil Kapoor and Ranga Kapoor

The conception of "grammar of narrative" is well-established in modern, Western literary theory as a model for analysing the structure of content, particularly of prose-fiction, and is associated chiefly with the French theoretician Greimas (1971), with its intellectual sources in Propp (1928) and Levi-Strauss (1958). The theory is concerned with "how the infinite variety of stories may be generated from a limited number of basic structures" (Rimmon-Kenan 1983:10) and with the logical relations among elements in a story. The term "grammar" is used variously in this theory to mean either the linguistic grammar or the general principles of organisation. There are, in fact, three grammars of discourse—of content, of expression, and of meaning. They are not really independent and can be worked out only with reference to each other and all the three complement each other in the description and interpretation of a text. But the strict domain of each can be easily identified. Thus, the grammar or structure of content deals with *types* of elements (*i.e.,* characters and events), types of arrangements (the relations among elements) and types of movement or developments that the characters undergo and that generally emerge from the whole narrative. The grammar of expression is what the familiar linguistic analyses are concerned with—the type of lexis, the type of syntax and the type of imagery. The grammar of meaning analyses the lexis and the structural patterns to arrive at the patterns of meaning and the world-view implicit in the narrative. The "grammar of narrative" as it has developed in modern Western literary theory has chiefly been a grammar of content in the sense outlined here.

In the Indian tradition, while *pada,* the morphological structure, is the object of study in *vyakarana* (the science of grammar), *vākya,* sentence, is the subject-matter of *Mīmānsa,* a philosophical system dealing with the interpretation of *Vedic* sentences. It is understandable that in the course of the analysis of the meaning of sentences, the *Pūrva-Mīmānsa* should confront questions of larger-than-sentence units, that is the concept of discourse. *Mīmānsa* was the first to use the term *Mahāvākya* technically for longer-than-sentence discoursal realitics and gradually it came to be used for units ranging from a collection of a few sentences to the whole epic such as the *Rāmāyana.* The term *Mahāvākya* evidently has complex denotation. In its more familiar sense, it refers to the key equative sentences of Indian philosophy—*Aham Brahmasmi* (I am the Brahman) and *tat tvamasi* (Thou art that). In fact, this is the unmarked sense, and when it is used to mean "a unit of discourse", it has to be explicitly noted. Technically, *Mahāvākya* is "a group of sentences which are interconnected and serve a single purpose or idea. . ." (Subramanyam, 1986). This discoursal entity is identified on the basis of two-fold unity—of syntax *(Ekavākyatā)* and of sense and purpose *(Arthaiktva* or *Ekārthībhāva).* Though *Mahāvākya* is defined by different parameters to suit the needs of different philosophies and different disciplines, these two requirements—those of unity of meaning and of syntax—are constant. So just as *varṇa,* sounds, together constitute a new entity, "the word", and the words together constitute the entity known as "the sentence", the sentences together constitute *Mahāvākya,* provided they fulfil the requirements of sequence *(krama),* mutual expectancy *(akānkṣa)*, compatibility *(yogyata)* and spatio-temporal contiguity *(samnidhi)*, besides the syntactic unity, a kind of textual unity expressed through linguistic items, and a unity of sense and purpose directed towards communicating a single overall meaning or *bhāva*. It was easy for the poeticians to extend the thus defined concept of *Mahāvākya* to refer to whole literary works, the *kāvya*, themselves. Bhoja in the eighth chapter of his *Ṣmgāraprakāṣa* calls *Rāmāyána* a "Mahāvākya", treating as it does the character, and conduct of Rama, which is its *ekārthībhāva*. The unity of literary texts, *prabandaikya*, is recognised as early as Bharata who talks of both the aesthetic unity and the narrative unity. And *Sāhityadarpana* explains its definition of *kāvya*, literary composition, as a *Māhāvakya* that has a unified aesthetic experience.

The Sanskrit poeticians' application of this construct to whole literary texts has much significance. They are thereby propounding a theory of the structure of discourse. To a large extent, the abstract principles of this structure are the compositional principles—*akānkṣa*, etc.—that govern sentence-building. But there is more to it—true to the tradition of aphoristic statement, the *implications* that are left unexpressed have to be seized upon. If a literary composition is a *mahāvākya*, an extended analogue of a sentence, then like a sentence, *vākya*, it has an internal grammar—in fact, its grammar is essentially an extension of the sentential grammar. In other words, it is possible to describe the structure of a literary composition by using the categories of grammar. The claim is founded upon the major assumption of the Indian grammarians, discussed by us elsewhere, that "grammar" is a system of conceptualisation, an abstract framework in terms of which we make sense of, and structure, all experience, not just the universe of language (see Srivastava and Kapoor, 1988a). How the categories, operations and principles of the Pāṇinean grammar serve just such an epistemological framework has already been described and discussed (see Kapoor, 1988b; 1989). Therefore, if the structure of a literary narrative is to be analysed in a grammatical framework. and we need to have a grammatical model, it is logical in the Indian context to adopt the Pāṇinean framework which will be a natural fit for Indian habits of thought.

The Pāṇinean grammar has a powerful simplicity. We present the broadest outline on p. 89.

This broad outline does not capture the extreme richness and complexity of categories that enables Pānini uniquely to devise an exhaustive description of the Sanskrit language. By substituting *kavya* for *sabda* we transform a linguistic model into a discoursal model. We will now, by way of example, illustrate this discoursal model by applying it to a modern Indian short story—R.K. Narayan's *The Astrologer's Day.* We will restrict ourselves only to the general, higher level categories that appear in this outline, and some that do not, to show, without claiming either exhaustiveness or ultimate value for this abbreviated model in the hope that it would suggest the lines of investigation and indicate possibilities of finer and richer analyses that can be reached by applying finer and deeper categories and sub-categories of this model of grammar.

Pāṇinean grammar, as the outline suggests, is essentially a *dynamic* model—it takes abstract elements, such as the *pratipādika* (a nominal base) and transforms it into a living referential reality by subjecting it to various catalyctic elements *(pratyaya,* affixes) and processes (derivation, agreement, etc...). The whole process is called in the tradition, *siddhi,* which literally means "to make real by investing with a particular form". It is a grammar of process, of movement. Secondly, it has a pyramidical structure that ends in a single construct, *sabda,* an *ekārthībhāva* (to apply the term metaphorically). The immense variety and multiplicity of phenomena is organised and arranged to create in the minds the cognition of a single, well-coordinated entity. Both these characteristics of the Pāṇinean grammar give it the necessary mobility to move out of the strict, local domain of language and become sorts of global framework that accounts for, among other things, the literary narrative, which we feel is a dynamic arrangement of texts and events, and is at the same time designed to evoke

KAVYA

(For our grammar of discourse, we replace *sabda* by *kavya*)

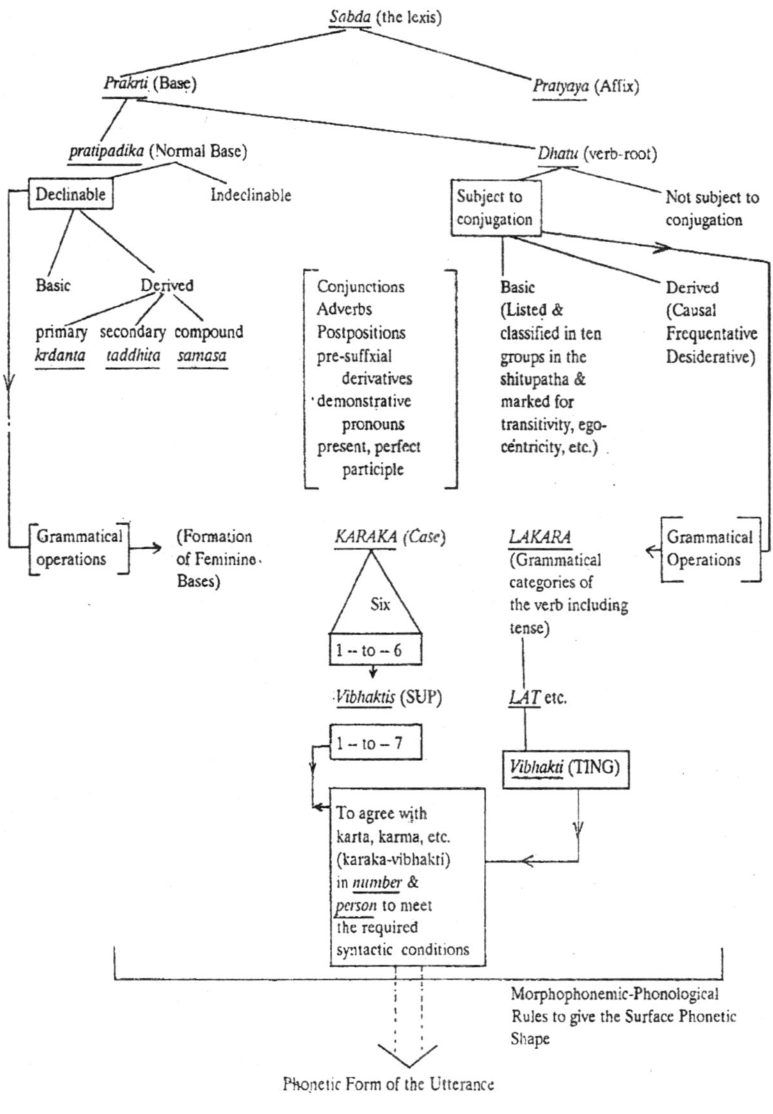

in the reader's mind a single *bhāva.* R.K. Narayan says in his 1981 introduction to his collection, *Malgudi Days:* "I discover a story when a personality passes through a crisis of spirit or circumstances" (p. 8). This crisis comes in the life of the astrologer when he recognises Guru Nayak and realizes that the man he had supposedly killed in a fit of anger is very much alive to his great relief. This recognition is followed by a restoration of the original harmony in the life of the astrologer.

The movement in the story, like in other stories of R.K. Narayan, is a movement from Being to Being:

Being—Disturbance or Action (generally disturbing)—Being. This evolution from one state to another with an intervening "disturbance" is an expression of the essential Indian world-view which takes Harmony as the basic condition, a harmony that is disrupted by human action, and the restoration of which is the goal of the ideal human conduct, and also a condition of human happiness. In this world-view, objects co-exist in a state of harmony; then, act and are acted upon; and, finally achieve a new order of co-existence. The Pāṇinean grammar, in its overall structure, provides a key to this central theme—the given *pratipādika* (the nominal status corresponding to objects) co-exist independent of each other; they then interact with *dhātus* (the verbal roots, corresponding to acts and actions) during which the objects contract relationships (such as Agent and Object), and this results in a surface structure, a "sentence", which represents a new order of co-existing objects, a new harmony. In the case of *The Astrologer's Day,* this new harmony is of the disengaged Agent and Object—the astrologer and Guru Nayak come together, interact, and then disengage, *i.e.,* get out of the Agent-Object nexus, and co-exist again dependent though transformed objects, each at peace with his respective self. The formal grammar of The *Astrologer's Day* is thus, in fact, a dissolution of arrangement —the "nouns" become *intransitive* Beings, rid of their "case-markers" *(kāraka-vibhaktis). This* insight into the world-view, or "philosophy" implicit in the story, is to be gained and validated, by looking at it through the framework of grammar.

A grammar, *i.e.*, a grammatical theory, is made up of elements, their mutual relations and arrangements, and various operations. Each of these can function as an interpretive construct for the narrative structure. We can talk of *discoursal function* of a grammatical category* just as we talk of its grammatical function. The discoursal function of a category stems from its *content, i.e.,* the substance, the class for which it is a variable. Thus that a "noun" formally takes postpositions in Hindi is a fact of grammar but that it potentially refers to some entity, is the substantial fact that pertains to discourse. The category of "tense" has formal grammatical properties but it is also the discoursal perspective on the actual time of the events. "Case" has some grammatical attributes but by virtue of its semantic content, it becomes a very appropriate principle to identify the relationship or function of different characters in a story. Again, the transformational operation known as "permutation" relocates an item in the linear order. In discourse significant spatial relocations of characters can be understood as discoursal analogues of "permutation". The categories of grammar need to be reinterpreted, in this manner, to suit the needs of narrative analysis.

Consider now the outline grammar. A series of binary oppositions hold the categories together in a system: *(i) prakṛiti* (base) versus *pratyaya* ("affix"); *(ii) pratipādik* (nominal base) versus *dhātu* (verb-root); *(iii)* declinable (subject to change) versus indeclinable (not subject to change); *(iv)* basic versus derived. These are useful categories for a rather straightforward classification of elements in a narrative.

---

* We are using the term "category" to include all the units of grammar—"parts of speech", "declension" and "conjugation" classes, and strict nominal and verbal categories like "tense", "aspect", "number" and "use", as also syntactic types operations such as "declarative", "complex", "transformation". Grammatical categories are the grammarian's construct, as Bhartrihari noted so long back, and have an abstract reality and an explanatory function.

Characters and events constitute the class *prakṛiti* – they are "the given" in a story. Guru Nayak, the astrologer, his wife, the auctioneer, the nut-vendor, a passerby, gambling, migration, search, meeting, recognition, warning, return, are some of "the given" in *The Astrologer's Day*, the *prakṛiti*, and they are of two sorts – characters and events, the *pratipādika* and *dhātu*. In themselves, both the characters and events are abstract. The *pratyaya* are affixes – elements that happen to be *prakṛiti*, the bases. It is the *affixes* that invest the *bases* with reality, particularise them and give them an identity. The affixes act like catalysts and change or transform the objects to which they are attached. Thus the entire paraphernalia of the astrologer functions like *pratyaya* in creating the unique identity of the astrologer – ". . . a dozen canine shells. . . a square piece of cloth with obscure mystic charts. . . a notebook and a bundle of palmyra writing. . . . sacred ash and vermilion. . . a saffron coloured turban". These are the *pratyayai* – affixial elements that externally identify a given character. "Events" *(dhātus)* are similarly particularised – consider, for example, the astrologer's "astrologising" or the astrologer's transaction of his business, as R.K. Narayan puts it. Now this is a major motif in the story. But it is no ordinary astrologising; it is very particular, defined by several "affixes" such as the astrologer's "perception", his "working analysis of mankind's troubles", the crowded contest, the patient listening that precedes the foretelling, the highly general nature of questions and advices, the flattering criticisms offered, etc.

The third opposition between elements that are subject to modification and those that are not helps us to isolate the dynamic constituents that evolve in the course of the story. Thus, the auctioneer, the nut-vendor, the wife and the passerby are the four static elements – the only dynamic constituents are the two main characters – the astrologer and his friend Guru Nayak. The fourth opposition – basic versus derived – helps us to identify independent as against the dependent constituents. Thus the *wife* is a derived, *i.e.*, dependent constituent in that her significance in the story derives from her relationship to the protagonist. The nut-vendor and the auctioneer are also dependent though their relationship to the astrologer is oppositional rather than subordinate as in the case of the wife. In the case of events, this opposition invites us to separate the contingent events from the independent events. Thus the astrologer's migration follows his mistaken belief that Guru Nayak is dead. Similarly, Guru Nayak's search follows upon his sense of treachery by his friend. One can, with the help of this principle, draw up a chain of causality among events, which has implications for interpretation of the events in terms of free-will, responsibility and fatalism. In this story, for example, all that happens to the astrologer follows upon an unpremeditated act and a mistaken belief.

This part of grammar so far is called morphology, *pada-siddhi,* which is concerned with generating fully inflected forms. In the *discourse,* as we have seen so far, its analogue is the full identification of characters and events which is achieved by filtering the text through a series of oppositions. The terms in these oppositions, *pratyaya* for example, are variables for classes of elements and also names for processes. The *pratyaya,* for example, represents the principle of affixation, adding something to something, besides the entire class of affixes. This part of analysis not only achieves a *classification* of objects and events but also an *ordering* of these constituting elements with respect to each other. This enables us to recognise the abstract type of characters and events and also enables us to group several facts around those characters and events, as we noticed in the case of the astrologer and his paraphernalia.

Consider now the second part of grammar—the syntactic part, how the different elements relate to each other, what in grammar amounts to building of sentences. A sentence is a configuration of given number of nouns in relation to a verb (see Kapoor, 1985). Thus: "*Rama* killed *Ravana* with an *arrow* from his *bow*" has an arrangement of four nouns which functionally relate to the event of "killing" as agent *(karta),* object *(karma),* instrument *(karana)* and ablative *(apadana)* respectively. It is possibJe to transform the *karaka*-structure to a whole narrative and see how different characters cohere mutually. Thus in *The Astrologer's Day,* we have a very simple *karaka-structure,* an agent-object structure. The other characters are ancillary and cluster around the two main characters:

```
{The wife          }
{The auctioneer    }→  The Astrologer     Guru Nayak  ←  (The passerby)
{The nut-vendor    }         |                 |
                          {Agent} ——————— {Object}
```

This is a very simple story about two persons one of whom is always acting upon the other. The "story" consists in the fact that the victim is all the time *free,* while the agent is all the time compelled to act and is without peace of mind. This suggests an opposition between "freedom of will" and "freedom of spirit". Guru Nayak has no "freedom of will" but enjoys a certain freedom of spirit—the astrologer has the freedom of will but lacks the freedom of spirit. The distinction is very "Indian" and important. The *kāraka*-structure based on the six *kāraka* relations provides the finite abstract structure from which infinite variety of stories may be generated. This, however, is a subject-matter for a separate study.

We can also examine the mutual coherence of a character and the events in which he participates. This would reveal to us "the theme of a character"—what happens to him or her in the course of the story and how he changes in response—to what, happens. The first thing we notice is that almost all the events concern the astrologer. Only a few—being left for dead, occasionally going out of the village to look for his enemy, satisfaction at the supposed death of the enemy—relate to Guru Nayak. The wife is overjoyed, expectant and shocked—all passive predicates. The auctioneer "creates a din" and the vendor of nuts gives his work a fancy name everyday. That is all—all the rest is about the astrologer. So this is not even a story about two persons; it is about *one* person, and this is what R.K. Narayan also asserts—"a personality passes through a crisis of spirit or circumstances". Examine also the predicates associated with the astrologer:- they are mostly *transitive* in which he appears as an active, volitional agent—he "*transacted* his business", "*said* things. . .", "had *left* his village. . .", "saw a man...", *pressed* his invitation. . .", "*caught* a glimpse...", "*flung* the corns. . .". Only a few predicates are stative or passive—he "felt uncomfortable", "shivered", "a great load is gone. . ." Besides, there are a few existential statements about him—"his forehead was resplendent. . .", "he was as much a stranger to the stars..." etc. Thus the astrologer is a man of action—one who controls and shapes things—all his acts are careful, meditated acts, except the act of stabbing. That single act changed him into a *careful* doer.

An important aspect of arrangement of events is the temporal and spatial ordering in the narrative as against the actual temporal and spatial location of the events. Thus the stabbing which ontologically comes in the beginning is presented near the end of the narrative in the story. If we chart the order of presentation and compare it with the actual order of happening, we see the presentational structure of the story, its craft. If we take the straight line as the line of chronology we can present structure roughly like this--

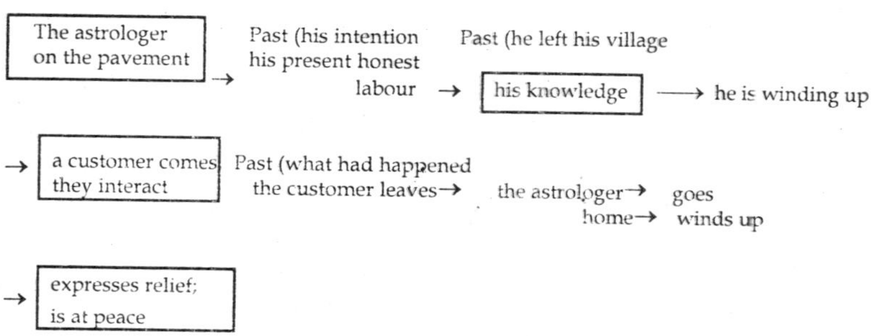

The square boxes represent static points where things happen before the narrative moves forward again. We notice that the narrative is interrupted at three points to take us back into the *past*, and what comes first (the stabbing) is presented near the end. So the reader is kept glued, in suspense. Albeit, the structure is not complex. And, significantly, there is no projection into the *future.* It is the *present* that is of interest and the *present* is a product of the lived past. Life is essentially a recollection, a memory. That seems to be part of the message.

Let us now turn to the *operations* of grammar. There are two kinds of operations in grammar—*(a)* morphological, and *(b)* syntactic. *Affixation* is the central morphological process, and we have already taken note of it above. *Affixation* explains in discourse the incorporation of the ancillary by the dominant character or event--

(1) The wife
(2) The nut-vendor

The Astrologer

(3) The Auctioneer

It also explains modifications of an object by details—for example, the astrologer identified by the details of his appearance.

The syntactic operations are essentially transformational, *i.e.,* processes that bring about a change. The transformations *are – lopa (deletion), agama* (augment or appearance), and *vikāra* (change or modification). These exhaust the dynamics of the changeful world. Under *vikāra,* we also subsume "substitution" which is in fact "disappearance of X" and "appearance of Y in its place". Transformations can be observed in the narrative in three domains—*(i)* the temporal, *(ii)* the spatial, and *(iii)* the personal. Thus this story is narrated in the narrative span of twelve hours—from mid-day to midnight—and as hours pass, we are given an account of events that have taken place over a number of years, but which exist within the narrative span of twelve hours and are located in the mind of the astrologer though they actually happened in different places. These are major transformations in the temporal and the spatial domains and their effect is to render a physical reality into a reality of the mind. In the same manner, a change comes about in the two major characters—they both move from "agitation" to "peace with the self". And this again is a profoundly Indian movement—the search ending in peace with the self. One would think that R.K. Narayan has at the back of his mind or in his subconscious, the Sāṃkhya-Yoga philosophies. We begin to understand why R.K. Narayan's stories are called "very Indian stories by a very Indian writer".

Finally, there are three syntactic relations that have significance for the *Mahāvākya* as *well—akānkṣā* (mutual expectancy), *yogyata* (compatibility) and *samnidhi* (contiguity). Of course, like the above elements of grammar as pointed out above, these too have to be suitably re-interpreted for discourse. Guru Nayak's search, according to the laws of expectancy, can only end in his finding the object of his search, as it does in fact. But he does not know that he has found what he has been looking for. And that is an element of irony in the story. Presence or absence of these relations—and when they are present, their nature—create what is called "the story-interest" in the parlance of the film-world. The pertinence of all elements of grammar, cannot reasonably be displayed with reference to one short story, just as not all elements of grammar may be pertinent for the analysis of narrative structures. Like in all other critical frameworks, much depends on who is handling the framework—a sophisticated student of both literature and grammar can perhaps find critical use for a very large range of grammatical constructs. Several problems no doubt suggest themselves. How would one, for example, analyse a long narrative such as the epic? Would it not be necessary in such a case to posit frames within a frame, to see successive structures embedded within one another or distinctly coordinated one to the other? That is a distinct possibility, and one that needs to be investigated and illustrated. The principles of organisation remain the same for the sentence, the short story, and the epic.

To sum up: this model is based on Sanskrit grammar.

It has three parts—elements, arrangements, operations (and relations). It allows us to describe the structure of a narrative in terms of characters (objects) and events both in their typological and their particular identities. It describes patterns of coherence of these characters and of the characters and events. It describes the "theme" of each character. It also describes the general themes (by a typological analysis of the meanings of all the verbs). It also describes the overall movement of the narrative. Much is being made these days of the structuralist poetics and the semiotic approaches in the modern western literary theory. This preliminary study is also a submission of the fact that Indian students of literature do not really need to go out of the tradition for structuralist-semiotic frameworks.

Notes and References

1. Greimas, Algirdas Julien "Narrative Grammar: Units and Levels", *Modern Language Notes,* 86, 793-806, 1971.
2. Kapoor, K. *Semantic Structure and the Verb,* New Delhi: Intellectual, 1985.
3. Kapoor, K. and Srivastava, R N. "Semiotics in India", in *The Semiotic Web* Sebeok and Sebeok (ed .), Berlin: Mouton de Gruyter, 1988.
4. Kapoor, K. "Vyākarṇa aur Jñāana-Mīmāṁsa" Paper presented at the *Annual Conference of Akhil Bharatiya Darsana Parisad,* Baroda: M.S. University, 1986. "Forms in the Ocean: The Indian Conception of Language and Reality", paper read at the National Seminar on *Hindu Grammatical Thought and Contemporary Linguistic Theory,* Bombay: University of Bombay, December 1-2, 1989.
5. Levi-Strauss, Claude (originally in French) 1958, *Structural Anthropology,* New York: Doubleday Anchor Books, 1968.
6. Narayan, R.K. *Malgudi Days,* Penguin Books, reprinted 1986.
7. Pratt, Vladimir (originally published in Russian), 1928, *Morphology of the Folk-Lore,* Austin, Texas: University of the Texas Press, 1968.

8. Sriramamurti, P. *Discourse Analysis in Sanskrit Tradition*, Visakhapatnam, Matrvidya, 1978. "The Concept of *Mahavakya* according to *Mimansakas*", Paper read in the Delhi session of the *All India Conference of Linguists*, 1979.

   "The Concept of *Mahavakya* according to *Vaiyakaranas*", *Prof. Kuppuswami Sastri Birth Centenary Volume*, Part III- KSRI, Madras, 1985.

9. Subramanyam, K. *Mahavakyavicara*, Visakhapatnam: Sherwani Printers, 1986 (in Sanskrit with Introduction in English by P. Sriramamurti).

8

Towards the Development of a Hermeneutical Model for Understanding Traditional Religious Literature

Javier Ugaz Ortiz

The relevance of a literary approach to religious, mystical, metaphysical and related texts is twice established, first, when having in consideration that in a broad sense of the term "literature", they are comprehended into literature's scope (along with any other piece constituted by word-construction), and, second, understanding "literature" in a narrow sense—that literature's contents, as well as its reservoir of construction-material, are drawn from that common pool or strata of human-psyche which nourishes the oniric, imaginative, mythico-religious, esoteric, and artistic activities. This fact is to be established most especially in the face of the clear irrelevance of current analysis of religious literature from two sides, that is, from the side of philosophy-specialists that concur to the understanding of the religious text with a strong linguistic-philosophic bias, as well as from those who disclaim any capacity of literary analysis or criticism to help throwing light on the *meaning* of "religious" discourse.

In a manner, they could be characterised by saying that the first approach commits the fallacy of ignoring too much of the difference between secular and religious discourses and hermeneutical strategies, and the second, of maximising differences between them.

The average procedure reduces the text to its explicit semantic level and tries to codify it in terms of a formal logic which would make evident the validity or otherwise of the claim of the "religious" statement. This amounts to the replacement of a formulation from a codal "annotation" to another codal "annotation" which would place the logical structuration in focus. This standard procedure commits the errors of, firstly, reducing the "religious" statements, noted for their semantic polivalence, to simply their surface-meaning level; secondly, of ignoring the historico-anthropological, and the deep psychological imports of the "religious" text, so necessary for its proper comprehension. In other words, it sets aside the placement of the text in its exterior and interior contexts from which they draw sustaining meaning; and, thirdly, of neglecting to have in consideration the wealth of exegesis and hermeneutics ascribed usually to the "religious" texts in the form of commentatorial corpuses. Indian traditional disciplines concerning proper understanding of mythological, religious-philosophical, and literary discourses, are deep and diverse. They range from specific "religious" exegesis to criticism of "secular" literature. The chief integrating discipline which transfers all these diverse reading strategies into a continuum is the indigenous philosophy of language to be taken along with its mystical and metaphysical overtones. This would include Indian aesthetics which endeavours to lead the savouring of the flow of aesthetic relish *(rasa)* to its merger with its metaphysical source through a percourse by the archetypal images embodying the essence of different psycho-cosmic "states", "feelings", "moods". This abolishes the profane-sacred, secular-religious dichotomy as well, tapping a continuum of experience and reality which has broken off only in human thought. The transaction is performed by a paradigmatic "universalization" of the aesthetic emotion—a process which is concurrently replicated in other mystico-esoteric environments, ritual and meditational. It is, however, not our claim that the task of a contemporary hermeneutics of "religious" literature is tantamount to a repetition of the traditional exegesis of the text. Our position is not tautological in terms of what the text respects (as it would be in current linguistic or analytico-philosophical approaches), nor literally traditional in terms of what the commentatorial, tradition affirms. The approach here is to have a feeling of the sense (emanating out of a "religious" text) which goes beyond its own times, and immediate contexts opening doors to universal values and transcending all forms of thematic and stylistic provincialities. "Real" literature, thus, is characterised by the access to, and employment of, those universal constituents which define the humanness of mankind. This is surely the achieved or unachieved endeavour of any literary creation.

A contemporary hermeneutics of religious literature should certainly not ignore. traditional exegesis; it should, however, be inspired by its spirit than by its literality. The contemporary hermeneutics should acknowledge the freedom of interpretation, amounting to a real personal transcreation of the text which results in a plurality of interpretations from a variety of standpoints. Tradition acknowledges, implicitly or explicitly, a space of semantic permissiveness in the interpretation and understanding of "religious literature" which unfolds itself as a creative imaginative activity twined with a close reading of the text. The "religious" text, thus, becomes a source of inspiration for a personal and creative re-enactment of universal contents; it is no more an univocal provincial legal-code to be blindly repeated, followed, and applied, because of divine sanction. A hermeneutics, which, while claiming faithfulness to tradition, fails to understand the complex and creative features of it, falls short of its spirit, and could only be called "literalist". Religious text, in this sense, becomes a guide to the meditative-hermeneutic process which attempts to produce a personal transcreation of a given text. This transcreation is possible because both the reader and the text draw support from a transtemporal and trans-cultural platform—modalities which intersect with cosmic and metaphysical domains. The sequence of myths, very much part of the humanness of human cycle, seems to close with a disclosure of the simultaneous ambivalence of reality when merging creative and dissolutive modalities in the grand "transformational" act (which finally evolves into a doctrine of the moment-to-moment re-creation of an instantaneous reality). However, the mythical cycle, in fact, only "closes in" for man to acknowledge that his attempt to escape the imperialism of myth and word is in its turn the enactment of another myth: myth engenders itself unceasingly, un-endingly, having swallowed even the silence into its domain, as says Paul Valery: "Unbeauvers renait indefiniment descenders, il redevient,—comme l'effet de son effet,--cause harmonique de soi-meme". It is for this reason that this article selects Abhinava Gupta's concepts of *guhā* and *hṛd-guhā*—concepts which synthesize life and interiority and bring out universal values of *Tantric* Saivism.

Introduction

Keeping ourselves within the perimeter of Hinduism, we shall briefly refer to the presence of the same symbolic compound in Vedāntic commentators, notably Śamkara.[1] This should be read as a hermeneutical attempt[2] to relate symbols and images employed in this Saivism to the larger Hindu canvas to which they belong, in a step towards the recovery of the universal value of the symbol concealed behind local or sectarian employments. Our search, then, is for the basic intuitions wrapped in different yet equivalent modalities of symbols and images. We intend to search for the essentials, and try to discover the final intentions and meanings to which symbolic and metaphoric deployments are instrumental.

A General Hermeneutic of Hrd-Guhā and Guha

Phenomenology of hṛd-guhā. Under the formula *hṛd-guhā*

is to be enclosed a variety of symbolic equations which related *hṛdaya* and *guhā* their synonyms, and the meanings they stand for, in Upanisadic, Āgamic, and Tantric literatures where the mystic or esoteric charcter is prominent. 'Heart' *(hṛd,* and sometimes *pumḋarika,* etc., *suṣumṇā,. madhya, ċakra,* and also *guhā)*[3] expresses mainly man's interior centre. 'Cavern' *(guhā, gahvara:* also 'cavity', 'hole': *dahara, suṣi, chidra),* a sacred, secluded 'space' in general (ākāsa, vyoman, sūnya). *'Hṛd-guhā,* therefore, refers to the 'mysterious inner space of the heart. Also *kha-cakra, kha-madhya,* etc., indicate the interiority or hollow of the 'centre' in general, corresponding to the semantic function of *hṛd-guhā* in the symbolic cluster of hardayą. On most occasions the formula *hṛd-ākāsa vyoman* stands for or implies, *hṛd-guhā.* As in the case of *haṛdaya* and *guhā ākāsa (vyoman, nabhas, kha,* etc.) encloses an independent symbolic cluster. But whereas *guhā* connotates a secluded, hidden space, *ākāsa* refers to the ether space as the foundation of the positional space, as well as to its pervasiveness.[4] Thus understanding *hṛd-guhā* to be a designation of the 'sacred enclosure of the heart', we encounter a large variety of modalities referring to this 'concealed central space', all of them coinciding in what is meant by the interior dimension and workings of consciousness. These modalities place the emphasis in one or another of the senses connotated by this symbol: its interiority, mysteriousness, hiddenness, or in its being a dwelling, container, enclosure. Besides, in Kasmir Saivism occassionally the referent is the 'heart' of Bhairava or cosmic 'heart'. This being so, the values of cosmic creativity are ascribed to that macrocosmic 'heart', and by extension to the 'cavity' of that 'heart'. In contrast to other symbolic equations clustered around *hṛdaya,* as *prakāsā, trikoṇa,* etc.,[5] *hṛd-guhā* lies as dominant note the notion of concealed process, of a space dynamism;[6] the notion of *guhā* then encompasses the occurrence of the void and the occurrences in the void.

Theory of guhā (1). The formulas *hṛd-guhā, hṛd-vyoman, antar-vyoman,* etc., consequently, introduce us in the domain of the interior sacred world, where the operations of the deliverance process occur. They designate the entrance, path, and goal of the road towards deliverance. Hence their polysemia. Deliverance in this *Śaiva* context is correlated to the reabsorption of the apparent exteriority into the resting ground of the Transcendental Subjectivity. The emergence of *pūṃna-ahaṃbhāva* is, therefore, coeval with the submergence of *idaṃtā*. The process may be described as one of successive 'dissolutions' or mergings into more and more pervasive principles *(tattvas)*. Terms like *guhā, ākāsa, tamas,* etc., here do not have a single value. They carry all the nuances of meaning given in the philosophical, cosmological, and literary settings, which are here applied to the esoteric *yogic* process of re-absorption *(saṃhāra, laya, viśrānti)*. In Kaśmir Śaivism also, along with most if not all non-Śaiva Hindu literature, the term *guhā* and are synonyms is also employed when referring to *māyā*. There is a conceptual continuity that travels from the archaic notion of the cavern as place of origination, womb, dwelling, to the cave-temple, and to the cave-womb in the temple. Moreover, cavities in general are mentioned in the ritual prescriptions on altar building, sacrificial sites, and holy enclosures. In *guhā* we can distinguish two main values: (1) it is a concealed sacred enclosure, (2) it contains something. Both values are shared with the symbolism of the sacred space in general. The diverse functions of *guha* can therefore be summarized as follows:

		as locus of origination (emergence)
	cosmic	as locus of display (preservation)
		as locus of withdrawal (submergence)
guhā		
	mystic	as locus of disclosure (mystery)
		as locus of concealment (secret)

They correspond to *sṛṣṭi, sthiti, saṃhāra,* and *anugraha* and *tirodhāna* of the *pānca-kṛtvas,* and therefore to *unmesanimeṣa saṃkoca-vikāsa,* the *mantras ahaṃ* and *ma-ha-a,* and other polarities in this circular dialectics.

Theory of guhā (2). The conception and experience enclosed in the equation *hṛd-guhā* indicate the transposition of the concealed sacred space designated by *guhā,* to the domain of man's interiority, which is what *hṛdaya* indicates in the mystic context. The archaic correlation between the cavity of the heart—cave of the mountain—cosmic centre, precludes the classic correspondence between body—temple—cosmos.

Guhā indicates a particular, secluded space. It can be considered to be a delimited, self-consistent, field or net of forces. In this sense it implies that which, while distinguishing, creates a space from the rest of the chaotic undifferentiation. It indicates the foundation, establishing or marking of a qualitatively separated space. In this respect *guhā,* and *maṇḍala, cakra,* are equivalents.[7] The trace which shapes *guha* is a bound, a demarcation. It liberates and creates through measurement.[8] Hence its simultaneous two-fold value: it creates, and therefore identifies, reveals, exposes, yet it also envelops, covers, hides.[9] Because it is secluded, that space is protected, secure, inaccessible.[10] Its inaccessibility implies imperturbability and stability, non-expositionness,[11] as well as its being in a latent, potential state. Because it is concealed it is non-evident, untangible.[12] However, it is simultaneously a defined totality: a voidness amidst compactness, a voidness which expands into compactness, as well as the voidness which keeps compactness together.[13] In its vertical value it is the immutable and fixed pole or axis, the 'hollow reed', the ancillar vacuity which maintains everything in its proper place in a differentiated space or texture.[14] As a sacred emplacement its entry requires discarding of all exteriority or profanity. This vision, paradoxically, implies darkness and silence, in short negation, as articulative and creative nods or nucleus, giving origin to the life-affirmations, to the differential light of multiplicity, which is the night of delusion from the point of view of the adept. Yet, darkness, and silence are also images of the omni-devouring voidness, the night and vacuum of lack and hunger.[15]

Etymologies, Antecedents, Parallels

Etymologies, Definitions, Derivatives. The word *guhā* is derived from the *guh,* conveying the ideas of 'covering', 'concealing', 'hiding', 'keeping secret'.[16] It is similar to *gup,* applied to whatever is not manifest to the exterior; it corresponds to the Greek *'kryptos'*, whence the word 'crypt', a synonym of caverns, and 'cryptic', meaning secret, mystical.[17] The dictionary meaning of the word provides us with the following definitions: a hiding-place, cave, cavern, and figuratively the heart; a pit, hole in the ground; intellect.[18] The term *guhahita,* of abundant occurrence in Vedic and Vedantic literatures, is translated as 'placed in the heart', or 'lodged in the heart'.[19] *Guha* is rendered as 'being concealed, covered, or kept secret, private; secret, solitary, retired; mysterious'. *Guhyam* gives the following meanings: 'a secret, mystery; a privity, the male or female organ of generation'.[20] In Vedantic literaturre there are some synonyms of *guha* of frequent recurrence, such as *dahara* – which usually designates the small hollow of the *heart – gahana* and *gehvara; susira, chidra,* etc.[21] In the context of the symbolism of the wheel we find *kha,* related to Greek *'chaos',* which generally means a cavity,[22] and in the *Ṛg Veda* 'the hole in the nave of the wheel through which the axle runs'.[23] It should be noted that terms as *sunya, akasa, vyoman,* which are indicated to denote zero,[24] are also applicable in reference to *hrdaya.* Among personal names of divine beings constructed from the *guh,* we find some which belong to the mythology of the underworld, being their personifications, or that are hyposthasis of the mystic and occult knowledge. We encounter among them: *Guha,* which is a name of Siva, as well as, more commonly, a name of Siva's son, Skandha or Karttikeya. *Guhaka* and *Guhavaktra* mean Skandha's heads or faces. *Guhesvara,* 'lord of caverns', is the name of one of Siva's attendant. *Guhyakali,* is a form of Durga, *Guhyaguru,* is a name of Siva. *Guhyapati,* 'lord of the mysteries', is a name of *Vajradhara* in Buddhism. *Guhyesvari* is Prajna in Buddhism. *Guhyaka* is 'a name of a class of demi-gods' who, like the *Yakshas,* are attendants of Kubera (the god of wealth) and guardians of his treasures (they may have received their name for living in mountain caverns),[25] and mines, because *guhera* means not only a guardian but also smith. *Guhyakodhipati* or *Gultyakesvara* are names of Kubera. In this context it is important that the word *gudhartha,* comes from the same root and means a hidden or mystic sense.[26] It is in *guha* where three of the four parts which constitute *Vak* are hidden.[27] This notion of concealment *(guhanihita,* or *hrdaye ahitam),*[28] is the same as the one of veiling, covering, enveloping, measuring.[29] The veil is conceived of as darkness or night.[30] From another point of view darkness is as a womb which contains potentially what it conceals.[31] These associations are later concretized in the philosophic concept of *maya,* one of whose functions is precisely to conceal, obscure. It is through this *maya* that the Vedic Indra assumes different forms.[32]

Upaniṣadic Doctrine of the Cavity of the Heart. The term *hṛdaya's* conveyance of the image of shelter, of sheltering, and of the notion of stability, is illustrated in the older Upaniṣads (cf. *Bṛh Up,* 2.4.11,4.1.7).[33] It is by 'entering' into the 'heart' that one acquires stability *(sthitatā).* The acquisition of a stable 'position' *(āsana)* is a prerequisite for the more complex contemplative or meditative practices *(upāsanā);* and this is achieved through an entrance into and establishment in the 'heart'. In this manner the internalizing 'movement' is a prelude to the 'ascentional' one. The secret of the heart is its interior *ākāsa,* where the *manas* goes having discarded the distractions of the sense objects.[34] The classical description of the *'dahara vidyā'* appears in the *ChUp,* 8.1.1.ss.; placing it in the 'city of Brahman' *(brahmapura).* The symbolism of the city pertains to the wider category of the symbolism of the sacred space.[35] The heart is described as a lotus, and the subtle aperture which is *ākāśa* is in its interior.[36] Another interpretation says that the lotus is symbolic of the intellect, and the heart of the centre *(guhā)* of the *buddhi. Ātmān* has gone into and is hidden in that cave (cf. *KaUp,* 2.20, 1.14;' *SvUp,* 3.20; 2.1.10; *TUp,* 2.1.1). Examination of the employment of expressions such as *guhā-granthi (MuUp,* 3.2.9), and *hṛdaya-granthi* (as in *ibid.,* 2.2.8), makes clear synonimic of the terms *guhā* and *hṛdayain* this upaniṣadic context. The knots which bind the soul are conceived to be all in the *buddhi,* physiologically signified in thetext by the physiological image of the innumerable nerves creating a sort of network inside of the heart, through which the soul gets entangled with exteriority.[37] Samkara, and after him most if not all of the Advaita-Vedāntic tradition, makes it clear in different occasions that by *hṛdaya* is meant *buddhi* (cf. Samkara's comm. to *BrhUp,* 4.4.7, 4.3.22; *AUp,* 3.2).[38] The process of the *dahara-vidya* consists in, first, entering in the *brahmapura* through one of the 11 or 9 gates of the city. These gates mean the senses. That is to say, in withdrawing the mind from the sense-objects, catching hold of a sensory stimulation, or the breath, and following its course until the *buddhi* or heart, is attained according to the Vedāntic theory of perception. In other words, the access to the mystic city is accomplished when the gross object is taken as a sign of, and a way leading to, its archetypal or subtle form, when it is dissolved in its basic constituents. Then, having penetrated into the inner abode of the heart through one of the five heart-gates, the five petals of the heart-lotus corresponding to the four quarters and the zenith and to the vital breath, the object reaches the *ākāśa* inside the heart. Finally, beyond the *ākāśa,* one reaches the centre of being, the dweller *(BrhUp,* 4.4.20; *virajah parākāsai).*[39] It is on this imperishable being that *ākāśa* is supported *(ibid.,* 3.7.12, 3.8.11).[40] The *KaUp,* similarly, teaches that the *ātmān* iṣ hidden *(guḍhotma)* in all beings. It is covered by *avidyā, i.e., māyā,* and therefore does not appear *(na prakāśate)* as the self.[41]

The Heavenly Cave: Tai Up, 11.1.2, *and Commentaries.* Commenting on *TaiUp,* 11.1.2: 'who knows the one hid in the cave in the highest heaven...' *(yo veda nihitam guhāyām parame ryoman),* Saffikara and Sureśvara give different interpretations of the word *guhā.*[42] (1) *guhā,* derived from the *guh,* meaning 'to hide', means the intellect *(buddhi),* which is designated so because in it are hidden the triad of the knower, knowledge, and the knowable. In fact *cave-buddhi* is the highest heaven, or the highest akasa, the Unmanifested *(aryākrta).* (2) 'cave' is the *aryākrta-ākāśa* itself, *i.e. 'guhā'* is the 'highest heaven'. Cave-heaven is the cause which contains all things. In it Brahman is hidden. (3) by *parame ryoman* is to be understood the *hṛd-ākāśa,* or *hṛd-vyoman.* In this *hṛd-*

The Five Gates of the Heart lotus and their Correspondences, *(ChUp,* 3.13.1-5)

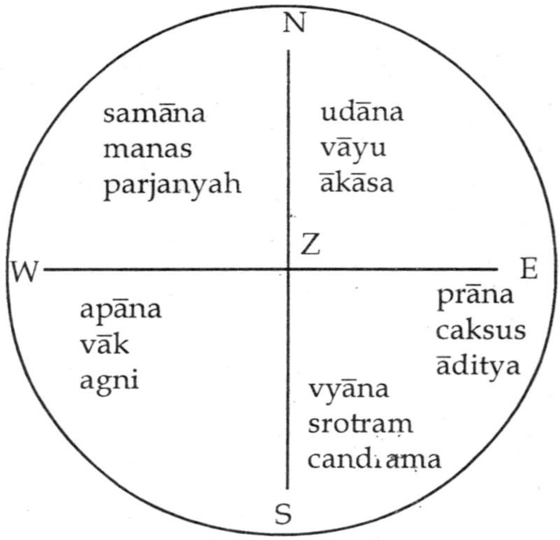

vyoman there is a 'cave', which is the *buddhi,* and in that *cave-buddhi* is hidden Brahman. It is pointed out that in the first .case *guhā* and *parame-vyoman* are understood as *vyadhikarana,* referring to two different things, one *(parame-vyoman)* placed in the other *(guhā-buddhi),* as the cause is present in its effects. In the second case, they are taken as *samonadhikarana,* meaning the same thing.[43] In the third case, according to Sathkara, they are taken as a *Vijnanaanga,* as an auxiliary to Brahman knowledge. The definition of *guhā* given by Vidyaranya when commenting on the first of the interpretations given above is noteworthy. Quoting his Pañcadasi, 3.2, he says that the 'cave' is the aggregate of the five *kośas.* The seris of the gross-body, *prana, manas,* the agent, and the enjoyer, one. behind the other, is the 'cave'.[44]

The Interiorized Pilgrimage. 'Cave of the heart' often designates the holy site. It belongs, in this sense, to a symbolic inner geography. It is the centre of it, the central city, castle, or island.[45] It means, historically, the culmination of the process which internalizes the exterior path to the shrine, or which corresponds to it.[46] It implies, philosophically, that man's essential dimension is a source of sacrality, as well as that, in his immanent dimension, he is its vessel and carrier. *Hṛd-guhā,* therefore, is the cipher of the consecration of autonomy, the incidence being placed in one's own deeper self, and not in the 'cave in the mountain'. In this sense *hṛd-guhā* is the sign of a turn towards the interior, of its victory over an externally centred religiosity. It constitutes also part of a discovering of that hidden and subtle dimension of the corporality which embodies. the pilgrimage through the stations until the shrine. The cave of the heart is the centre, or even the end of the pilgrimage, and entrance into it takes place after the ritual circumambulations. Pilgrimages and circumambulations relate to laby-rinths.[47] Taking in consideration different esoteric systems, *hṛd-guhā* is both, the end of pilgrimage through exteriorities, and the beginning of the interior, underground, circumambulation and ascension.

The Cave in the Temple: guh and garbhāgṛha. Guhā also finds its place in temple architecture. It is a synonym for *garbhāgṛha,* the *sanctum sanctorum,* or it designates a second sanctuary, an underground one, axially connected with the *gṛha.* It also designates a category of temples.[48] The process of deliverance takes place through multiple ritual paradigms which are homologized in an effort to synthesize orders, because they coalesce in fact at a deeper symbolic layer. The choice of paradigms or symbolic structures depends on the particular tradition or path which is being followed; nevertheless, within a given frame particular paradigms or symbols are also selected because a particular point is better exemplified with one type of symbolism than with another. The initiation drama happens through a symbolic topography. It corresponds not only to the pilgrimage to the shrine in the mountain, it is also re-enacted in the steps to enter into the shrine or temple, while crossing the threshold to encounter the indweller. The temple is the architectural embodiment of the *yantra,* as the body is its physiological embodiment, all being supports of the consciousness which inhabits them. In this context we should remember some aspects of temple symbolism: (1) the existence of a *guhā,* underground crypt, whose quality is *tamas,* darkness, and the descending tendency.[49] (2) The coincidence of the door (entrance) and the indweller (the god), from a certain angle.[50] (3) That the sum of all possible cavities *(guhā* and *garbhāgṛha)* is like a hollow reed.[51] (4) the existence of the guardians of the threshold *(āvaraṇadevatās)* and the required transformation to enter.[52]

Abhinava Gupta's and Kaśmir Śaiva's Concepts of Guhā and Hrd-Guhā

The Cosmic Cavern: Guhā as Māyā. In Kasmir Śaiva context *guhā* also means *māyā: guhā māyā'.*[53] *Guhā,* strictly speaking, refers to *māyā-tattva,* one of three *māyās* technically differentiated in Kaśmir Śaivism, without referring to a general, non-technical use of the term. Abhinava Gupta precises that this *māyā-tattva* is beyond the cavity of *māyā (māyā-bilam,* here meaning *māyā-granthi,* the third *māyā,* standing for the *māyic* world or the production of *māyā.* It is the matrix of the universe, also called *yoni* or *bhaga.*[54] These schools differentiate three *māyās* or three levels of *māyā:* gross *(sthūla),* subtle *(sūkṣma),* and supreme *(parā).* They are also called *māyā-granthi, māyā taṭtva,* and *māyā-śakti,* respectively. Other technical terms which designate the *māyās* are, correspondingly, *māyā-bilam, guhā* or *nisā,* and *vāgiśvarī* or *māyā-devi,*[55] *Māyā-granthi* is defined as non-discrimination *(aviveka)* of the *taṭtvas,* taking as identical those which are considered to be separate.[56] It is said to be an extension of the primal ignorance of reality *(sa māyā taṭtva khyātimāyāh prapancah, ibid.).* It is cancelled by the process of absorbing, the various *taṭṭvas* in the body.[57] It is in the context of this *māyā* that mention is made of the terrible *śaktis* which push the soul into further enmeshment and entanglement.[58] This *māyā-granthi,* Abhinava Gupta precises, is *māyā* in a state of unbalance, a disturbed *māyā.*[59] Abhinava describes *māyā-taṭṭva* as being all-pervasive, deep, formless, the place of dissolution of all things.[60] It is the undisturbed *māyā,* and is called the cave *(guhā).*[61] The *MV,* 1.26, describes this *māyā* as one, all-pervasive, subtle, undivided, source of the universe, beginningless, endless, auspicious *(siva),* Lady of the world, unperishable.[62] This *māyā* seems to be the one that Abhinava Gupta refers to as 'night', or the 'supreme night' *(parā-niśā)* in *TA,IX.* 149b-152a. It is said to be the first manifestation of the differentiation, containing in itself all distinctions. This night is characterised by insensuality *(jaḍa).* The night is *māyā* as the primary cause of all limited manifestations. As obscuring power he refers to it as *'moha': 'māyā vimohini nāma* *(IPv,* 1.35). The effect of *māyā* is also spoken as *māyā.*[63]

Correspondences, Divisions, and Names of Māyā in Kaśmir Śaivism

Aśuddhādhvan	*sthūla-māyā*	*māyā-granthi/māyā-bilam/prakrti*
Śuddluāsudhādhvan	*sukṣma-māyā*	*māyā-tattva/yoni,bhaga/ guhā,niṣā, parā-niṣā*
Śuddhādhvan	*parā-māyā*	*māyā-śakti/māhā-māyā/vāgiśvari/ māyā-devi/Śuddha-vidyā*

To Abhinava Gupta *māyā-śakti* is *maya* as goddess, the one which confuses the creatures. She is a power *(śakti)* of the God of the Gods, his capacity of pèrforming the most difficult task.[64] She is the Supreme Autonomy of Śiva, as well as the veil which covers the Self of Śiva.[65] She is identified with *Vishewshawari.* In fact, it is explained, *māyā* is *śakti* operating at three levels simultaneously: at the level of the *śuddhādhvan* it is known as *māhā-mayā,*[66] then, as *māyā-tattva;* then, as *prakṛti.*[67] According to Abhinava Gupta this *prakṛti,* considered to be a further grossification of *māyā-tattva,* has the following names: the forest, dwelling of the *puruṣa,* the root, principal element, the unmanifest, cause of the constitutive elements.[68] Abhinava's *māyā* has two functions: it conceals *(āvaraṇa)* and it projects *(vikṣepa) (IPv,* III.L7-8). They correspond to the *tirodhāna* or *nigraha,* and *sṛṣṭi-kṛtya,* functions of the Supreme.[69] It is a noticed tenet the correlation between *māyā-śakti, ajñāna* and *avidyā,* etc., which Abhinava in *TA,* IX.84b-86, gives as names of defilement *(mala).*[70] The *MV,* 1.17a, says that one ought to flee from them, because one implies all the others.[71] To Abhinava this ignorance is the primal defilement *(aṇavamala)*. He categorizes it in two kinds, the well known animıcal and mental ignorances *(pauruṣajnāna* and *bauddhājnāna)*.[72] Ignorance, he elaborates, is cancelled only by *dikṣā* or *śuddha-vidyā*, also named *mahā-māyā*.[73] Also one of the *kañcukas* or contractors which finitize the soul into a particle or atom *{aṇu)* is called *māyā*. *Ānavamala* consists precisely in this contracting. In Abhinava Gupta's thought the cessation of the contraction of the heart is the illumining of one's own nature *(TAX.213-216)*. The root of all defilment, he thinks, is the wish of the Lord to obscure Himself *(ibid., X.110-112a)*. *Māyā* is as well the name of one of the defilments, *māyiya-mala*, the defilement which accounts for the feeling and notion of exteriority, that something exists separated from us. *Māyā* is also said by Abhinava to be a net *(TA.1.7)*, or is the name of one of the four 'eggs' *(anīda)* or spheres which constitute the cosmos: *śakti, māyā, prakṛti*, and *pṛthivi andas*.[74] Abhinava Gupta bundles the last three into a triad.

The Darkness of the Cavern. According to the *PT*, 2, the energy dwelling in the heart is both secret and non-secret, a mystery and a non-mystery.[75] In his short commentary Abhihavagupta indicates that this reality is obscure *par excellence;* great, that is pre-eminent; non-occult, that is to say, auto-effulgent.[76] Continuing his commentary Abhinava refers to *Sambhu*, one's own self, saying that it has the power to obscure and illuminate His own self.[77] Two values must be noted from these quotations: (1) the coexistence, side by side, of the obscure and luminous in relation to the divine energy of the heart, and to the divine in general, and (2) the line of correspondences which links obscurity, occultness, non-evidentness *(aprakatva)*, etc. This copresence of light and obscurity or darkness in the bosom of the divine is exemplified in a number of occurrences. As in *VP*,22, it is said the never setting self-shines and manifests itself as being embodied in light and darkness.[78] Unambiguously the text affirms: 'in me, the One, light and darkness are comprehended' *(antaḥ sthito mamāntasteāmsi tamamsi caikasya, ibid.)*. Or, in the *PTlv*, stanza of introduction, 1, Abhinava praises the supreme flavor where the lights light and the tenebrae obscure, and where light and darkness are together.[79] Similarly, Kṣemarāja in the *SvNir,* makes the heart formed by *prakāsa* and *vimarśa;* the pair, is illustrated by the images of light and darkness, which are compared to a cave.[80] Corresponding to that, we have mentioned it above, is the co-existence of the secret and the non-secret in *PT, 2a*. We find it again mentioned by Mahesvarananda in *MM,67,* for instance when he says that this glory is more occult than the occult, and more evident than the evident.[81] Abhinava Gupta also, in *PTlv,* introduction, in a play of words with his name, speaks about the supreme heart which brights by itself in a supreme irradiation, depicting it as being 'new and occult, ancient and known by all'.[82] In his doctrine of the day and the night, Abhinava presents an alternation between these two terms, assimilables to the alternatives of *unmēṣa/nimēṣa,* etc. Night, he says, is the inclination of consciousness towards the subject, while day is its inclination towards the knowable, the exterior world. Night is rest, beatitude, whereas day is light, consciousness. Both, day and night, are merged in the fourth state.[83] This identification of night with beatitude is clear enough: it indicates at Sakti,[84] this is ratified by noticing the usage of the term 'great night' *(paraniśā)* in relation to *māyā-tattva,*[85] *māyā* is an aspect of Śakti, and is related in various ways to darkness, obscuring, concealing. It is here that we encounter, then, a negative connotation attributed to this cluster of concepts and images. This indicates a shift in the point of view. Whereas the coexistence of light and darkness in the Ultimate is a purely meta-physical vision, as well as the alternation of night and day, and their merging into the fourth, have a practical, initiatory value, similarly the negative value realized in the night of *māyā* is from the point of view of the profane. These are gnoseological and psychological darkness, which are better identified with the day of *ahorātravāda,* in the sense of prominence of the knowable.

The negative darkness is referred to by Ehaṭṭanārayana in his *STv,* p. 58. as a hostile darkness prayed to be destroyed by *Śambhu* with the lamp of love which comes from that of his knowledge.[86] Abhinava also speaks of that darkness, saying that it is as blindness, and of consisting in the wrong imagining that there is no self in modalities which however are not distinct from the self, since they are revealed by the conscious light.[87] *Timira* is another term used in this sense. *Timira* is an optical defect which accounts for delusions and mirages,[88] as in *PS*, 25, where it is spoken of as the blindness of ignorance *(ajñānatimira)*, by which is perceived a multiplicity of subjects and objects, while there is only One; or in 31, where it is mentioned as the blindness arising out of blindness *(timiradapi timiramidam)*. The negative value of darkness is implied in Ehaṭṭanārāyana's reference to the contemplation of the deep cave, to which the supreme light, having dispelled the tenebrae, beautifies in its interior.[89] Again, in [Pv,I.V, intrd., Abhinava mentions Śiva illumining the multiplicity of objects lying in the great cave *(mahā-guhā)* with the lamp of the power of knowledge.[90] As can be noted, the theme of the lamp or of a light illumining the cavern is a constant. And this refers us to another motif: the treasure lying in the cavern and revealed by that lamp. To Kṣemarāja that treasure is the multiplicity of objects kept in the cave of the heart,[91] or the universe which is accommodated, as in a cave, in the heart.[92] However, in a veritable tantric attitude, this *timira* is not simply rejected. It is turned into a means or support *(dharaṇa)*. As in *VBlz,87*, where it is a prescribed meditation on darkness, in a dark night, in the dark fortnight, to attain the nature of Bhairava.[93] It is named *'bahya timirabhāvana'*. It is followed by a contemplation on the empty space as dissolving in one's own head. This empty space is understood to be dark. The peculiarity of this *dharaṇa* being that, dealing with the akasa full of darkness, its fruit is the light of the supreme form.[94]

Tāmas is a quality of the *tri-guṇas*. It is the obscuring, descending quality. *Kriyā-śakti* is said to be of the nature of *tamas*.[95] This *kriyā-śakti*, in a process of increased contraction, assumes the names of *suddha-vidyā, kalā-tatṭva, karmendriyas;* the zenith of the contraction of *kriyā-śakti* is the five *bhutas* and the five *tanmatras* (gross and subtle elements).[96] This is how process or operation of *nigraha,* the obscuring aspect of the divine, takes place.

Utpaladeva mentions also a mystical night, the night of Śiva *(Śivarātri),* whose radiant essence expands its own glare. It is in this mystical night that the moon and the sun, as well as all other luminaries, merge to rest.[97] The night of Śiva is mentioned in the *bhakta* literature. In this night, Utpaladeva says, there is not the least sign of light, and is where the entire universe is deeply asleep.[98] "When the sun disappears the moon shows herself, when the moon vanishes only thought remains, when thought also goes then nothing remains. Where are the earth, sky, ether, all gone?", asks the mystic poetess Lalla. After everything has vanished only darkness remains, the supra-luminous, trans-cosmic darkness.[99] Utpala also refers to a night of *Lysis,* "of the heroes dance, when the hero is inebriated with the wine of love, surrounded by the *vetala.* Śiva's troop, in a circle of joyous mysteries".[100]

A Hermeneutics of Abhinava Gupta's and Kaśmir Śaivas Symbols of the Central Domain

Terms for the Central Domain. As we have seen, the formula *hṛd-guhā* refers predominantly to the inner, concealed domain.[101] We have also mentioned that Kṣemarāja explains this *hṛd-guhā* as being of the nature of *prakāsa* and *vimārśa,* and as being as a cave, containing, or being an entrance into, the whole of the universe.[102] We have noted the recurrence of certain motifs as the lamp or the light illumining the cave, and the treasure which lies in the cave, which precisely is revealed by the kindling of the lamp. In a variant to the theme of the light in the cave, Abhinava employs the image of the fire of the great Bhairava which burns in the cavern of the heart *(hṛd-guhā) (TA, V.22.23).* The space of the heart is also called *'mahā-guhā'.*[103] Abhinava also refers to the treasure accumulated in the extremely secret interiority of the heart,[104] and Kṣemarāja precises that is the treasure of knowledge what is kept in the cave of the heart.[105] Abhinava also mentions the multiplicity of objects placed in the great cavern; *mahā-guhā*, here, would designate Śiva, or his heart.[106] In *Phr,18,* Kṣemarāja gives a different paradigm of the heartcave equation: in this case the lotus of the heart rises in cavity or cavern, dispelling the blinding darkness *(hṛdayapankajasyodare udetietat daritāndhatamasah)*. There are also other formulas designating the hidden interiority of the heart. Prominently among them are *hṛd-ākāśa, antar-vyoman,* etc. For instance, *VBh,35,* refers to the inner firmament or vacuity of the middle channel, which is placed in the middle *(madhya)*.[107] This central artery *(suṣumnā)* is mentioned to stay in the centre of the heart.[108] The *antar-vyoman* is of the form of *cidākāśa,* where it is all *sūṇya*.[109] Similarly, in *SpNIR,*I.23-25, Kṣemarāja refers to the meeting of the sun and the moon at the stage of the heart *(hṛdayabhūmi),* and their merging in *suṣmnā,* which is called *brahmanāḍi,* to finally reach the great firmament. *Hṛdayākāśa* is mentioned in *VBh,* 49, as the place where are to be merged the mind and the senses, to enter into the centre of the two lotus-bowls which constitute the coffer-like heart.[110] This merging of the mind and sense in the space of the heart is comparable to the recollection of the mind in the heart of Vasugupta's S, 1.15,[111] which is explained by Kṣemarāja in the Vimarśini as being *cit prakāśa.* It is also similar to *'hṛdaya Ilihitacittaḥ',* prescribed in the first means indicated by Kṣemarāja in *Phr,* 18, for *madhya-vikāsa.* It is also in the *hṛd-vyoma* where Bhairava in the *PT* places the energy *kula,*[112] and Abhinava adds: "which, residing in the ether of the heart, is known as that which is the heart".[113] In another important occurrence *(PTv,* p. 271) Abhinava indicates that the heart, vibrating in the form of cosmic creation, is to be worshipped inside the heart of the *suṣumnā,* which is the union of Śiva and Śakti.[114]

The *PT* mentions again this interiority of the heart when saying that in the interior of the *hṛd-padma* resides the seed *(bijā)* without beginning or end.[115] This *bijā,* Abhinava elaborates, is called the supreme heart, which should be meditated inside one's own heart, characterized by consciousness, which, as a lotus, is engaged in the play of its expansion and contraction. He adds that it should be meditated that this supreme heart enters into one's own heart, and that expands everything, expelling by force all contraction.[116] The interior dimension of the heart is implied, or indirectly referred to, in a number of instances. In some places the emphasis is placed rather on the function performed by the heart's space, or in the indweller, or, as in the case of *ākāśa,* etc., on its universal extension or all-pervasiveness, rather than on the concealed interiority, secrecy, or mysteriousness. As in the case of PT, 2, where it is spoken of as the energy *(śakti)* which dwells in the head which is said to be *kaulini* and *kulānayikā.*[117] Abhinava explains that this energy, which is absolute consciousness, is *svātantrya.*[118] He understands its *kula* (family) to be the circle of perceivers, perceived, and perception, which is originated by it. Therefore, he says, it is called *kaulini*. The *iv* affirms later that this *kaulik* reality is placed in the heart of Bhairava, in identity with consciousness.[119] In the same text Abhinava also says that Śiva fulgurates as the perceiver in the interior of all heart.[120]

The Cavern and the Mystery in Abhinava Gupta's Commentary to PT.2. We have referred above to the expression *mahā-guhā,* as employed by Abhinava in *IPv,* IV, intr., or in *PTv,*p.55.[121] In this latter one, happening in the explanation of *PT,2,* he also mentions *guhā,* which he defines as being māyā. Secret *(guhyā),* Abhinava says in the Vivarana, is what is kept in the cave *(guhā), i.e.,* what is unapparent, non-exposed, concealed.[122] In those words Abhinava Gupta explicitly links the symbolism of the cave with that of the secret in Kasmir Śaivism: *Guhā,* then, is the locus of secrecy and mystery, the archetypal place of the hidden things. It is known only by the *lingam.*[123] It is in the very formulation of the *PT,* 2, that is synthesized the dialectic of concealment and disclosure as understood by the Trika authors. The sentence *'etad guhyām mahā-guhyām'* is read as *'etad guhyām mahā + aguhyām'* or *'etad guhyām mahā + guhyām'*. Abhinava, in the Vivaraṇa, elaborates on both. *Anuttata,* he says, because of its un-exposedness, is called secret, mystery *(guhyām).* It is un-exposed because concealed in the cave. Simultaneously, he explains, it is the great non-secret *(mahā-aguhyām)* as far as it constitutes the nature of everything.[124] He continues by saying that the triangle which constitutes *śuddha-vidyā* is known as *mahā-guhā* when its angles *(pramatṛ,* etc.) are concealed by the solemn non-differentation. It is identical to the trident. That, which in the form of a self-tasting, Abhinava elaborates, is in this great cave *(mahā-guhā),* which is the *'mahā-a'* (the formula of dissolution or withdrawal), is the secret, the mystery *(guhyām).*[125] According to another interpretation freedom *(svātantrya)* is the secret *(guhyam),* the supreme secret *(ati rahasyam*).[126] Abhinava Gupta adds that the phoneme *A* which resides in *'ma-ha-a'* is the secret or mystery *(guhyam),* which is also the great mystery *(mahā guhyam),* or the womb of the universe, as well as the great non-secret *(mahā aguhyam)* bccause of its being a universal experience.[127]

While commenting on the word *'mama'* (mine) he precises that the secret or mystery to which that refers is the I, here called *'ma-ha-a.'*[128] Abhinava's exposition is understood as being enounced from three different levels: Śiva, Śakti, and Nara planes. (1) From the Śiva plane, the compound is broken as *'mahā + a + guhyam',* where the stress is placed on *'a', Anuttara,* which is the *'guhyam'*. (2) From the point of view of Śakti it is understood as *'mahā + guhyam',* this is the cave of *māyā,* and the source of entire universe. (3) From the point of view of Nara it is split in *'mahā + aguhyam',* meaning that it is known to every living creature as the union of the masculine and the feminine, and as the continuously experienced taste of enjoyment arising from the union of the knowing subject and the perceived objects.[129]

Conclusion: On the Model of Abhinava Gupta's Hermeneutical Enterprise

The philosophic-religious work of Abhinava Gupta is many-sided. Yet, its dominant charactcristic is the synthetic function it performs in the frame of Hindu Thought, especially by its bridging philosophy and Tantra. This task is accomplished not only in the building of an overall, inclusive, conceptual construction, where each and everything fmds a place and an explanation—a scholastic *Summa* keeping along with the medieval spirit of his e—, it is also fulfilled by discovering in the old symbols and gestures, attitudes, unapparent and superior layers of meaning which release their potentialities of a more abstract, higher philosophical value, as well as of deeper spiritual realizations. Moreover, this endeavour is realized not through simple rationalizations of symbols and images, but rather while dealing with reality and with traditional symbols—Vedic or Tantric—in symbolic ways.

Abhinava Gupta's elaborations, as shown especially in its commentaries to the Paratrimsika, are exemplary hermeneutical exercises which display the different sematic potentialities contained in those basic concepts, symbols, images. The display of the different lines of meaning-potentials occurs in a universe openly acknowledged as symbolic, *i.e.*, as a polidimensional reality where everything is given in everything else, and hence becomes the sign of everything else. It is configurated, consequently, a non-describable universe, which however is not a chaos. The dictum of everything in everything else would constitute, therefore, the central principle of a symbolic viewing in reality. Nothing being confined in itself, everything being interrelated, goes along with another principle, which reads that the subtler or deeper the level we get into anything, the most present all the rest in it. Unlike the spiritual aloofness of the Samkhya-Yogins, or the discrete phenomena of the Buddhists. Consequently the most intimate the level of something the most interrelated it is, because of the convergence of the essences. Language, conceptual or symbolic, becomes with Abhinava Gupta an accurate tool to the conveyance of those intuitions. In fact, Agamas and Tantras are considered to be literary embodiments of revelation. Language, to those schools of thought, is not an inert but an active conveyor, an effective evocator. Since archaic times, to nominate means to evocate. The closer is the utterance to the nature of the nominated, the more effective it is, until the sound-essence of that being is reached. Finally, we should keep in mind that a realm in which everything reflects everything else, as in a gallery of different kinds of mirrors, is necessarily a realm of allusions, not of limited concreteness. Being by its very nature is inexhaustible, we cannot expect that somebody, not even an Abhinava Gupta, could exhaust it. Abhinava's teaching is an invitation to a personal hermeneutics where the subtle ontologico-semantical levels of symbols, images, would disclose themselves existentially.[130] The discourse, with Abhinava Gupta and the general tantric tradition, becomes, therefore, a living embodiment of those intuitions, which attempt to effectively evocate while conveying them.

Notes and References

1. Key 10 abbreviations":

			PTlv	:	*Parātriṃṣikālaghuvṛtti*
AUp	:	*Aitareya Upaniṣad*	*PTv*	:	*Parātiṃśikāvivaraṇa*
Bth Up	:	*Bṛhādanyaka Upaniṣad*	*PS*	:	*Paramārthasāra*
ChUp	:	*Chāndogya Upaniṣad*	*SpNir*	:	*Spandanirnaya*
IPv	:	*Isvara Pratyabhijnā*	*Ss*	:	*Śivasūtra*
		Vimarśini	*SSiv*	:	*Śivastotrāvali*
KaUp	:	*Kātha Upaniṣad*	*SSv*	:	*Śivasūtravimarśini*
MM	:	*Mahārtha Manjari*	*STTS*	:	*Satiriṃsattavttvasandaha*
MV	:	*Malini Vijaya Tantra*	*STv*	:	*Stavacintāmaṇi*
MaUp	:	*Māṇdūkya Upaniṣad*	*SvUp*	:	*Śvetāsvatara Upaniṣad*
OLP	:	*Prinetalia Lovaniensia*	*TA*	:	*Tantrāloka*
		Periodica	*TaiUp*	:	*Taittiriya Upaniṣad*
Phṛ	:	*Pratyabhijnāhṛdaya*	*VP*	:	*Virupaksa Pancasika*
PT	:	*Parātrisika*	*VBh*	:	*Vivhina Bhairava*

2. "A hermeneutics, syas M. Eliade, "is the search for the sense, for the meaning or meanings that a given idea or a given religious phenomena have acquired in course of time... Hermeneutics is the discovery of the deepest sense of these (religious) expressions". Eliade calls it creative, "for two reasons.—he says-. .. It is creative first of all for the very hermeneut. The effort to decipher the revelation present in

a religious creation...to understand the sense, the function, the object, this effort enriches in a singular manner the consciousness and the life of the researcher. . . There is a second sense,—he continues—, in which a hermeneutics is creative: it reveals certain values that were not evident on the plane of the immediate experience. . . The hermeneutic enterprise reveals the latent meanings and the becoming of the symbols. . ." This lucid and encompassing description of the hermeneutical endeavour in a religious context was given by M. Eliade in an interview by C. H. Rocquet, published under the title M. Eliade, *La Prava del labirinto, intervista con* C. H. Rocquet. Edizioni Jaca Books, Milano, 1980. pp. 119-20.

3. If *guhā,* in many occasions, is to be understood as referring to *hṛdaya,* the opposite also happens: *'...guheva hṛdayam; māśa,* 11.2.6.5. Also the mantra *'hrm',* in Śakta Tantra, indicates *'guhā',* cr., *Devi Up,* 14, in Warrier, *Śakta Upaniṣad-s,* p, 80, fn. 1.
4. Considering the symbolic compound *'hṛd-akasa'* different from *'hrd-guhā',* although being a semantic area of mutual intersecting and overlapping, we have dealt with *'hṛd-ākāsā'* separately, in another work.
5. For an appreciation of the symbolic equations *'hṛd-prakasa'* and *'hṛd-trikona',* refer to our *Symbolic Meaning of Light and Its Relation to Heart* in *the Śivaism of Kāśmir and Vedāntā',* in *OLP,* 14, 1983, pp. 276-92, and to *"Triangle and Triad and Their Relation to 'Heart'in the Sivaism of Kāśmir and Vedāntā",* in *OLP,* 17, 1986, pp. 209-30.
6. As the symbolic compound *'hṛd-spanda'* conveys the notion of a time dynamism.
7. "The *Viśva* also says, *cakra* means city, hamlet, town and abode'. And the commentator of the *Sūtra* '(13) of Gauḍapada interpreted the word *Śripura* to mean *Śricakra.* 'One may enter the city *(Nagara)* without knowing the *Rsi;* the city *(Pūr) of Devas* is impregnable; the city is surrounded by nectar, etc'., in these and other *Śrutis,* city *(Pūr* or *Nagara)* mean *cakra;* (vide *TaL Ār.,* 1) and *Nagara* and *Cakra* are one and the same". *(Saubhagyabhaskara,* comm. on name 56, cr. *R. Anantakrishna Sastry, Lalitā-Sahasranoman with Bhāskararāya commentary,* Madras, 1951, p. 65); *(cakraṁ ca sadanam agāram guheti viśvakhyokteh 'kagajadasāre' Iyādi gandapādiyasture śripurasya*

cakraparatvena tadbhāsye vyākhyānacca, naitamrism viditvā nagarām pravisei, 'devānām pllra yodhyā' amrtenavrtam puri mityadisrutisu nagarādipdānām cakre prayogadarsanācca nagara-cakra-ityādi-rudrayāmalāt). (cf. *Lalitā Sahasranama,* Nirnaya Sagar edition, p. 40). Also, quoting the same *Viśa,* says in the commentary to name 895: "pur (city) means wheel *(cakra),* own house, room, cave"; *(cakram puram ca sadanam agārah* na *guhā strivām);* cf. Sastry, p. 367, and the Sanskrit text happens in the Nirnayasagar edition, p. 79.

8. "The *sunya* has no form until encircled by *māyā*", it is mentioned while commenting on "of *Nirākāra-Brahman,* understand *Māyā* to the *Akara*" *(nirākāra-brahmer-ākāra dekha māyā),* in J. Woodroffe, *Hymns to the Goddess,* p. 280, fn. 1.
9. It can be differentiated on the following traces or circunscriptions: (1) the creative trace: (2) the limitative or negative trace: (3) the liberative or protective-trace.
10. This refers us to the 'quest for secrecy', for initiative purposes mentioned bŷ St. Kramrisch, *The Hindu Temple,* p. 171. while speaking of the *guhā* in the temple. It can be compared to *'ckanidam',* a single place of rest, as mentioned in the *Maha-Narayanopamsad,* 1.14-15. in proximity with *guhā* (cf. SW Vimalananda. *Mahā-Nārāyanopaniṣad,* Madras, 1957. SW. Vimalananda comments: "*...nida...* has the sense of resting place, a bird's nest in which the young ones live together or the inside of a vehicle where the occupants remain together. The idea of safety and togetherness is implied in these meanings". In Kāśmir Śaivism *hṛdaya* is also the place of rest *(visrānti).*
11. "What is stability?.. the heart is stability... the heart is the abode of all creatures ... in the heart all creatures are supported ... The heart ... is the Supreme Brahman". *BrhUp,* 4.1.7 (cf. SW. Madhavananda. The *Brahādaranyaka Upaniṣad,* Calcutta, 1972)"*...ka sthiatā ... hṛdayameya ... hṛdatan vau...sarveām bhutāmāyatanam ... hṛdaye hyeva ... sarvāni bhutāni pratisthāni bhavani ... hṛdayam vai ... paramam brahma ...* "(cf. *Ten Principal Upanisad with Sankarabhāsya,* Motilal, Delhi, 1978, p. 856.)
12. *Aprakata* and *suksmatā.*
13. As the *guhā* of the temple or the hub *(kha)* of the wheel.
14. One of the meanings of the word *tentra* is, precisely, texture, which relates to net *(jāla,* as in *nādi-jāla, māyā jāla,* cf. *TA,1.7).*

and the spaces of a net. The universe is a texture of living forces. It is to be remembered here that the term *guṇa* of the *tri-guṇas,* substances or tendencies which constitute the cosmos, means literally 'thread'. It wouldn't be out of place tc conceive the net of *nāḍis* that envelops the *ātmān* in the heart, as a particularization of this cosmic texture. In its negative aspect it becomes the bonds *(pāśas)* and knots *(granthīs)* which entangle and tie down the soul to one state.

15. This aspect is mentioned in the symbolism of Tara, called the 'Night of Anger' *(krodha-rātrī,* in the context of the *Daśa-Mahāvidyās.* (cf. A Danielou, *Hyndu Polytheism,* Routledge Kegan Paul, London, Bollingen Foundation, New York, 1963. p. 274-77). The devouring void is also the devouring fire of consciousness, the *agni which cries (rud)* to be fed. This privation is also spoken about in different contexts: as in *Phṛ,* 4, when referring to the state of *sūnyatisūnyarmataya,* which precedes the cosmic manifestation. *Anāśrita Siva* is another name of this state. This *sūnya* may be equivalent to the *śūnya* experienced by the subject, aparailled with the emergence of *māyā-tattva,* mentioned by K. C. Chatterji, *Kashmir-Shaivism.* Srinagar, 1962, p. 79 & 84, or to the *sūnyatisūnyarnpa,* a highly potentialised 'void' which is *'sakti-tattva* (cf. D. Sen Sharma, *STTS,* p. xviii). On Kṣemarāja's understanding of *sūnyatisūnya as mahāmaya* in *SvT,* VIII, 57, or Śiva as *śūnyāti-śūnya* in *Phṛ,* 4. which is Siva about to create, see J. Singh. *VBh.* introduction, p. xxiv-xxv. Also *madhyamā* have been called *śūnyātisūnya (Ibid).*

16. cf. M. Monier-Williams, *A Sanskrit English Dictionary,* Motilal, Delhi, 1986. Also St. Kramrisch, *ibid.,* fn. 108.

17. *Concise Oxford Dictionary,* p. 295. The *Webster's New Collegiate Dictionary,* Calcutta, 1985, gives as secondary meaning of crypt "a single gland, glandular cavity, or tube...follicle" *(Ibid.,* p. 272). For follicle it gives: "a small anatomical cavity or deep narrow-mouthed depression ... a small nymph node ... Graafian follicle". *(ibid.,* p. 442). The terms *hṛdaya, guhā.* and *hṛd-guhā* are of abundant use in *Ayur-Veda* texts. In that context. *guhā* in relation to heart means the small ventricle or chamber of the heart. We leave as matter of a future work the considerations about the relations between these terms according to their employment in Upanisadic, Ayur-Vedic, and Yoga-tantric settings.

18. M. Monier-Williams, *ibid.,* p. 360.
19. V. S. Apte, *Sanskrit-English Dictionary,* pp. 409-10. See also A. C. Bose, *The Call of the Vedas,* p. 3: "the term *guhā-hita* or *guhā-nihita* (literally meaning 'hidden in the cave') has often been used in the Vedas to indicate a mystical truth", see also pp. 152-61.
20. V.S. Apte, *ibid.* The *TA,* XV, 278b, quoting the *Matangatantra.* says that the *wordvāma'* designates *'guhya'.*
21. For the occurrence of these terms in Upanisadic literature. see G.A Jacob. *A Concordance to the Principal Upaniśads and Bhagavadgitā (upaniṣādāk-yakośāh).* Motilal. Delhi. 1963. We find some of these terms again in Ayur-Vedic context: "the term *chhidra,* 'aperture', is used in Ayurveda for the openings of the body". But in Kashmir Śaivism Abhinava Gupta says: ". . . *chidram ākāsa ucyate*", *PTv.* p. 236. On the anatomical meaning of the terms *puram, guham, bilam, guhā, kanda, guhya,* cf. S.C. Srivastava, *Nervous System as Described* in *Vedic Samhitās and* in *Early Upaniṣads;* in *Studies* in *History of Medicine* (journal), New Delhi, December 1982. pp. 290-300. The *TA,* VII.65b-68a, gives the relation between cavity *(susi)* and channel *(nāḍi):* 'the extreme degree of materialization of the movement of consciousness is the so-called cavity *(susi),* which assuming the nature of channel *(nāḍi)* connects together this our body': *(yaduktam prāk citspandaprānavṛtināmantyāyā sthūla tā sūṣih. sa nāḍirūpatam-etyadeham santānayedidam',* says Jayaratha in *TA,* VIII, 283, quoting VII.66) , *(ITA,* p. 211).
22. "A more general term denoting any aperture, hole or cavity in the body, internal or external, is *kha.*" B. Walker, *Ibid.* In the *Amarakọsa* the terms *Kuhara, Suṣira, bilam, chidra,* all of them denoting cavities or holes, are given in the section dealing with *pātāla loka,* along with *timiran, tamah, śesa, ananta, kuṇḍali.* Another name of *pātāla* is *nāgaloka* (cf. N.G Sardesau-D.G. Padhye, *Amara's nāmalingānusāsanam* (text). Poona Oriental Series N. 69, Poona, 1969). On the 'plan of reflection between hell and body' in the Orphic religion, and its vinculation with the "old Indo-European theme of migration and reincarnation", see Paul Ricoeur, *The Symbolism of Evil,* Beacon Press, Boston, 1969, pp. 283-89.
23. M. Monier-Williams, as quoted in A.K. Coomaraswamy, *Selected Papers,* vol. II, pp. 220-21.

24. Cf. AK. Coomaraswamy, *ibid.* For *kha* as zero and its relation with ananta, see A.N. Singh, *Scientific Thought of Ancient India* (in *'Zero and Infinity'*, in Mathematics Section). S. Radhakrishnan, Ed. *History of Philosophy Eastern and Western,* Vol. I. Allen & Unwin, London, 195f. pp. 441-44. The Indian traditional defintion of zero is given as "the sum of two equal and opposite quantities", *ibid.,* p. 441.

25. M. Monier-Williams, *Ibid.,* p. 360.

26. *Ibid.,* pp. 360-61. Among Hindu Tantric texts bearing names derived or related in meaning to *'guhā'*, *'guhya'*, etc, let's mention *'Guhyacakra'*, one of the sixty-four Bhairava Tantras, belonging; to the *'cakrastaka'*; *'Tantragunya'*; from *'gahvara'*, *'Matagahl'am-pañcāsitikā, Kulagahvara'*.

27. *Rg Veda,* I. 164.45. See comm. in V.S. Agrawal, *The Thousand Syllabled Speech* pp. 104 and 108. It should be remembered that *ākāsȧ* is considered to be the medium of sound, or the cosmic ending of a correspondence which has hearing through the ear's cavity at the other end. In puranic context: "The principle of *Akāsa* is a kind of vacuum *(chidram)* which in the precreational stage of *principio* was turned towards the centre *urdhvam* but in course of time attains a hollow condition *(vivarakrti)* which has an opening outside. That comes in contact with the cosmos and becomes the world here below which in other terms is known as *Rasarala* . . . Since the Golden Egg was floating in the primeval Ocean its cavity was filled with a golden liquid which became frozen as the Golden Mountain *Sumeru* . . ." V.S. Agrawal, *Matsya Purāna, – a Study (Matsyapurānānusilanam) (an exposition of the ancient Purānāvidyā),* All-India Kashiraj Trust, Ramnagar, Varanasi, 1963, p. 309.

28. A.K. Coomaraswamy, *Ibid.,* pp. 83-4 (vol. 1).

29. On veiling and covering, cf. V.S. Agrawal, *The Thousand Syllabled Speech Ibid.;* on measuring and enveloping, see his *Sparks from the Vedic Fire,* Varanasi, 1962, pp. 63-4. The author designates this doctrine of concealment as *āvaraṇavāda,* which is said to be already contained in *Ṛg Veda* X. 129.1.

30. Refer to V.S. Agrawal. *The Thousand Syllabled Speech* p. 104, which refers to the symbolism or the kind of darkness. *Svayambhū* and *parameṣthi.* mentioned in the *Naṣadiya Sūkta.*

31. *Ṛg Veda*. I. 35.1.

32. *Ṛg Veda*. VI. 47.18. And in Śaivism *Māyā* stands for Śiva's capability to perform the most difficult tasks.

33. G. Mukhopadhyaya, *Studies in the Upanisads*, Calcutta, 1960, p. 198 ss.

34. *Ibid.*

35. About this inner city, cf. *KUp*, 5.1; *SvUp*, 3.18, *ChUp*, 3.13.6 with *Śamkara's Bhasya*.

36. *Daharavidyāprakāsika*, p. 8, as quoted in G. Mukhopadhyaya, *Ibid.*, p. 200.

37. G. Mukhopadhyaya, *Ibid.*, p. 201.

38. Samkara, while commenting the *BrhUp*, clearly states the logic involved in the employment of the term *hṛdaya* meaning 'intellect': "The heart is the lotus-shaped lump of flesh, but being the seat of the internal organ, intellect, it refers to that by a metonymy, as when we speak of cries of the chair meaning persons occupying them" (SW. Madhavaṇanda, *BrhUp*, 4.3.22); *"hṛdayasya hṛdayamiti puṇdarikākāro mamsapindastat-sthamanatahkaranam buddhih hrdayamityucyate, tatsthamancakrosanavat"* (*Ten Principal Upanisads*, p. 894) And, again Samkara: 'within the heart' ... heart is primarily the lotus-shaped lump of flesh; here it means the intellect, which has its seat in the heart. The expression therefore means 'within the intellect'. (Madhavananda, *Ibid.*, 4.3.7); ". .. *hṛdyantariti hṛcchabdena puṇdarikakāro māmsapindh tātsthyāt buddhirhrttasyām hṛdi buddhau antariti buddhivrttivyatirekapadarsanarthan* . (*Ten Principal Upanisads*, p. 868). In the *Amarakośa hṛdaya* is given as a synonym of *citta, cit, mānasa, manah,* in 1.3.31. It is followed by 1.4.1. which gives the names of *buddhi*. See also *AitUp*, III. 1.2: *"yad etad dṛdayam manas caitad sanjnanamajnanam vijianam prajnanam medhā drstirdhrtirmatirmanisa jutih smrtih sankalpaḥ katurasuḥ kāmo vaśa iti, sarvāṇyevāitāni prajiāinasya nāmadheyāni"*- "That which is heart, this mind, that is consciousness, perception, discrimination, intelligence, wisdom, insight, steadfastness, thought, thoughtfulness, impulse, memory, conception, purpose, life, desire, control, all these, indeed, are names of intelligence". (Radhakrishnan, *The Principal Upanisads*).

39. G. Mukhopadhyaya, *Ibid.*

40. *BrhUp,* 3.7.12: "He who, dwelling in space, yet is other than space, who space does not know, whose body space is, who controls space from within-He is your Soul, the Inner Controller, the Immortal". (trans!. of Hume, *The Thirteen Principal Upanisads,* Oxford University Press, Madras, 1965. p. 116). *Ibid.,* 3.8.11: "Across this Imperis able is space woven, Wrap and woof'. *(Ibid.,* p. 119).
41. *KaUp,* I. iii. 12, and Satbkara *BhGsya.*
42. cf. *The Taittiriya Upanishad, with the commentaries cf Sri Sankaracharya, Sri Suresvara, and Sri Vidyaranya,* translated by AM. Sastry, Madras, 1980, pp. 275-84.
43. A.M. Sastry, *Ibid.,* p. 281.
44. *Vedānta-Pañchadaśi,* in *Ibid.,* p. 279.
45. The Supreme City of *Sri Vidya,* placed in the Isle of Gems *(maṇi-dvipa),* in the Ocean of Ambrosia, outside and beyond the countless myriads of gross world systems; this Isle is in the red eight-petalled lotus *(ānandakaṇda),* which exists in the middle of the *Bana-Linga* within the *trikoṇasakti* (inverted triangle) of the pericarp of the lotus of the *anāhata-cakra.*
46. On 'pilgrimage', see S.W. Aghehanandabharati, *The Tantric Tradition,* B.I. Publications, New Delhi, 1976, pp. 85-92. On shrines along the Vitasta (actual Jalum) river, near the bank or source of which was Abhinava's paternal home, see K.N. Dhar, *'The Selpentine Vitasta; Glimpses of Kashmiri Culture (GKC),* 1976, II Srinagar, pp. 59-81: also c.L. Sapri, *Pilgrim-Spots of Kashmir, (GKC),* 1976. II. Srinagar, pp. 59-81; also c.L. Sapri. *Pilgrim-Spots of Kashmir, GKC.* 1979, pp. 33 to 43; on the *Nilamata Purana's* account of the ancient geographical conception of Kashmir., cf. 1.I.K. Jailai. *The Nilamatapuranam and Kashmir, (GKC).* 1979, IV. pp. 1-8: also V.K. Ghai. *The Nilamata Purana', GKC.* 1977. III. pp. 31-41.
47. "The person who travels through the labyrinth ... is finally able to find the 'central place', which is from the point of view of initiatory relization his own centre ... If we consider the case in which the labyrinth connects with a cave, the latter, which is surrounded by the labyrinth's winding and is its final goal, thus occupies – in his overall pattern – the most interior and central point. This corresponds very well with the idea of a spiritual centre and equally well with the equivalent

symbolism of the heart". Rene Guenon. *Symboles Fondamentaux de la Science Sacrce,* pp. 216, and 392, as quoted in A Danielou, *Shiva and Dionysus,* m, New York, 1984, pp. 122-23.

48. S. Kramrisch, *Ibid.* p. 171. Here we should remember that "the influence of Western architecture is clearly to be seen in Kashmir ... which gives the Kashmir style an almost Gothic appearance. Most famous of Kashmir's early temples is the temple of the Sun at Martand, dating from the 8th century ... The standard type of Hindu temple, which has persisted from 6th century to the present day, was not fundamentally different from that of the ancient Greeks. The heart of the temple was a small dark shrine-room *(garbhagrha),* containing the chief icon". (Basham, *The Wonder that Was India,* Rupa & Co., New Delhi. pp. 357-63). Let us mention here another famous Sun Temple, the so-called Black Pagoda at Konarak (1250), built by the Ganga kings of Orissa in the Orissan style of the Medieval North India architecture which flourished from 8th to 13th centuries, and contemporary to the emergence and development of the Kashmir Saiva philosophico-religious schools.

49. S. Kramrisch, *Ibid.,* p. 172.

50. *Ibid.,* pp. 313-17.

51. *Ibid.,* p. 174. On the symbolism of the 'reed'. cr. V.S. Agrawal, *Matsya Purana,* pp. 70-1 and 255-57.

52. S. Kramrisch, *Ibid.,* pp. 313-17 and 338-40.

53. *VP,* 49, and Vidyācakravartin's comm. in H. Lenaerts, *A Study of the Pratyabhijña Philosophy of Kashmir,* thesis. DHU, 1971. Also, for instance, Jayaratha's comm. to *TA.* IX, 138: *'guhāgahanam māyāgarbha',* or Abhinava Gupta in *PTI'.* p. 53: *'guhāyām ... aprakaṭam'.*

54. *TA,* VIII. *307-09: 'māyābilamidamuktam paratastu guhā jagadyonih, yonivivareṣu nānākāmasamṛddheṣu bhagasarhijñā.*

55. On the three *māyā*: see 1. Singh, *Siva Sūtra.* Delhi, 1979. pp. 132-34. On *bilam,* etc., cf. R. Gnoli, *Luce delle Sacre Scritture,* Torino, 1972. p. 279. fn. 171, and p. 313, fn. 46. A different fourfold division of *maya,* in the context of Saktism, is mentioned by A.G. Krishna Warrier, *Sakta Upaniṣad-S,* p. 29, note to "By means of the fourth and final *Māyā* has the supreme Brahman been indicated..." of the *Tripurātāpilli Upaniṣad.* 5.2 The note runs like this: "The four *Māyā-S* or forms of the Power of

Illusion are 'error' or *avidyā,* knowledge or *jñāna,* specialized knowledge of *vijñāna,* and right knowledge or *samyagjñāna.* The last alone is related to the fundamental Reality or Brahman".

56. Cf. SS. III. 3: *'kalādināṁ tattvānāmaviveko māyā'.*

57. *Ibid.,* III. 4: *'sarire saṁhāraḥ kalānām'.*

58. *SpNir.* I. 20.

59. *TA,* VIII, 321b, and Gnoli, *Luce,* p. 282, fn. 190.

60. *TA,* VIII. 322a: *'māyāttvanṁ vibhu kila gahanamrupam' samastavilayapadam.*

61. Gnoli, *Ibid.,* p. 279, fn. 171.

62. *MV,* I, 26: *'sā caikā vyāpinisukṣmā niṣkalā jagato nidhiḥ anādyāntāsiveśani vyayahina ca kathyate'.* (*cf.* Gnol *Ibid.,* p. 785).

63. K.C. Pandey, *Abhinavagputa,* Varanasi, 1963, p. 371.

64. *TA,* VIII, 332b-333: *'ataḥ parāṁ sthitā māyā devi jantuvimohini deva devaṣya sā śaktiratidurghatakaritā nirvairaparipanthinyātayā sramitabudhayah'.*

65. PS, 15: *'paramaṁ yat Svatantryam durghatasampadam maheśasya'.*

66. Gnoli, *Ibid.,* p. 279, fn. 171.

67. D.S. Sharma, *Saṁvimsattattva Sandoha,* pp. 15-8.

68. *TA,* VIII, 273;-274a: *'gahanaṁ purusanidhānaṁ prakrtirmulaṁ itam gunakāranamiryete māyāprabhavasya pāryāyāhi.*

69. In the context of the *Vaisnava Pancaratra,* the following list of *nigraha śakti* synonyms is found: 'illuśión, ignorance, great delusion, great gloom, darkness, bondage, and knot of the heart', in *Ahirbudhnya Samhita,* 17 (*cf.* F.Gllo Schrader, *Introduction to the Pancaratra and the Ahirbudhnya Samhita,* p. 133). Compare with advaitin Padmapada's synonyms of *avidyā: māyā, avyākrti, agrahoṇa, avyakta, tamaḥ, kāraṇa, laya, śakti, mahāsupti, nidrā, kṣara,* and *ākāśa,* in S. Dasgupta, *History of Indian Philosophy,* vol. 1, p. 149. In the *Yoga-Vāsistha,* as synonyms of the same concept, are given *avidyā, saṃsṛti, citta, manas, bandha, mala tamas (Yoga-Vāsiṣṭha,* III. 4.46, in *Ibid.,* vol. II. p. 234). While exposing from the same text Dasgupta comments: "*manas, buddhi, ahmkāra, citta, karma, kalpanā, saṃsṛti vāsanā, vidyā, prayatnā, smṛti, indriya, prakṛti, māyā* and *kriyā* are different only in name, and they create confusion by these

varied names: in reality, however, they signify the same concept, namely, the active functioning of *manas* or *citta*. These different names are current only because they lay stress on the different aspects of the same active functioning. They do not mean different entities, but only different moments, stages or aspects". *(Ibid.,* p. 238).

70. *TA,* IX-84b-86: "defilement is called, in the various texts, with various names, according to the meaning of its nature. Such as, for instance, desire, ignorance, *avidyā,* frenzy, absence of vision, defect of phenomenic existence, boat of the particla, illness, dryness, state of confusion, condition of 'I' and 'mine', sadness, power 'of *māyā,* veil, seed of defects, state of animality, cause of the sprout of transmigration". (After Gnoli, *Luce,* pp. 305-06*)*. The Sanskrit text runs as follows: *'malo bhilāsāscajñānamavidyā lolikāpratha* (84) *bhavadoso nuplavaśca glānih soyo vimūdatā aham namātmatā tankomāyā śakti-rathāvrtih* (85) *dosa bijam pasutvam ed samsārānkurākaranam ityādyanvarthasaṁ jnābhistatra tattaisa bhunmyate'* (86).

71. *MV,* I. 16-17a: "the defilment, *karma, māyā,* the entire māyic world: one should flee from all these". *(malah karma ca māyā ca māyiyamkhilam jagat. sarvaṁ heyam iti proktaṁ vijñeyāṁ vastu niscitam*).

72. *TA,* I. 22. ss.

73. K.C. Pandey, *Ibid.,* p. 376. Abhinava Gupta in the *TA,* XV, 29Th-303, while speaking of the symbolism of the trident *(triśula),* mentions that between the nod and the trident, one should mediate in the quadrangular base, which is in contact with the two veils. These two veils are interpreted by Jayaratha as being *māyā* which veils one's own proper nature, and *śuddha-vidyā* which veils *māyā.* This *mahā māyā* may be the one which Abhinava mentions in the PTv, p, 184, saying it to be greater than *māyā.*

74. On the four 'eggs'. see *MV,* 11.49 ss.

75. *Etad guhyam mahāguhyam'.* A similar sense has the Upanisadic teaching about light and shadow, both having gone into the heart.

76. *PTv,* 2a: *'ctad aprakatamarisayate manat urkrṣtamaguhym, svaprakāsm'.*

77. *'...acchādane svarupāsya prakaṭena ca prabhavanasia...; Ibid.*

78. *Ahamcko 'nastamitaprākāsarupo smi tejasām tamāsām', VP,* 22.
79. *PTlv,* intrd: *'yatra tejasi tejāmsi tamānsica tamāsāmsi ca tamāsyalam tejāmsi ca tamams etad vande jyotir anuttaram* (I).
80. *SpNir.* IV, 2: *Prakāśa vimarsātmakam hṛdayameva . . . guhā'.*
81. MM, 67: *'gudhād gudhataro bhabvati sputtād api sphutaraeṣaḥ.*
82. PTlv, intrd.: *'sadābhinavaguptam vat purānam ca prasiddhimathṛdayam tat prollāsaiḥ svayām sphurajaryallütraram.*
83. *TA* VI. 63-68.
84. In the *Saubhāgyabhāskara,* there is a quotation which says: "night is the Great Devi, and the day is Siva". (d. R. Anantakrishna Sastry, *Lalita Sahasranama,* p, 158): (Madras, 1970). Later the transl. identifies brightness and darkness with *prakāśa* and *vimarśa* respectively, cf. *Ibid.,* p. 194.
85. Vide *ante,* 'The cosmic cavern: *guhā* as *māyā.*
86. *Sn.* 58: *'hṛtodharatamas... madbodhadipikā me'stu nātha tvadbhaktidipikā.*
87. *PS. 30: 'ctad tad andhakāram yad bhāvesu prakāsamānataya ātmātirikteṣvapi bhavatyanātmābhhimano 'yam'.*
88. Cf. PS *of Adi* Śeṣa. p. xxii. edited with transl. and notes by S.S. Suryanarayana Sastri, All other references to the *PS* refer to the PS of Abhinava Gupta, except especial reference.
89. *Stv.* 12: *'api paśyema gambhirām pareṇa jyotiṣābhitaḥ unmṛṣtatamasam ramyā mantarbhavā bhavadguhām'*
90. *IPv,* I. V. intrd.: *'mahāguhāntamirmagnabhāvajataprakāśaḥ jñānasaktipradipena yah sadā tam stumaḥ sivam.*
91. *"...jñānadhānam hṛdguhānatarkṛtanihiteḥ (SpK.4.2).*
92. *SpNir, Ibid., '. . . hṛdayameva viśvānatah praveśāvakāsapradatvād guhā.*
93. *VBh.* 87: *'evam eva drniśāyām kṛṣnapakṣāgame ciram. taimiram bhāvayam rūpam bhairavam rūpam esyati'.*
94. *VBh,* 83, in Dwivedi's Hindi translation: *'is dhāraṇā ka yah adbhuta vyāpāra hai ki ismem ālambanā to andhakāramaya ākāśa ko banāyā jātā hai, kintu phai milatā hei param svarūpa ka prakāsa',* (p. 104).
95. *STTS.*.15: '. . . *tasya kriyātamomāya* . . .' (it corresponds also to *manas).*

96. *Ibid.*, pp. 13-14.
97. Utpaladeva, *SSv.* IV. 22: *'yatra so' stamayam eti vivasvams 'candramah prabhrtibhih sarvaih'.*
98. *Ibid.* XV, 17: *jyotir asti kathayāpi na kimcid visvam apy atiṣusaptam aseṣam. Yata nātha sivarātripade smin nityam arcayati bhaktajanastvām'.*
99. After L. Silburn, STv. For different rendering. cf. J. Kaul, *Lal Dev.* Sahitya Akademi, New Delhi. 1973. p. 116, n. 85. In the Upanisadic *jyotirsamjyotirvidyā,* similarly, all the luminaries, and after them *Vāk* which is equivalent to the thought of Lalla, go to rest. 'It only remains, after the disappearance of all lights, the luminous darkness, the foundation of them all. In Sakta literature is equally said: "She is dark with the refulgence of a million suns...". cf. Woodroffe. *Hymns to the Goddess.* p. 286. Also Samviduliasa: "The Saivite Reality is in a non-describable manner, nonchalance full of ardour, intense darkness identical to light, a void made of plenitude". *(udyogamayam ālasyam prakāsaikātmakam tamaḥ aśūnyani śūnyakalpam kim api śāmbhavam).* (quoted in L. Silbum, *MM,* 39, pp. 140 and 205).
100. Utpaladeva, *SStv,* XX. 20: *"tāvakabhaktirasāsavasekād iva sukhitamarmamandalasphuritaih nrtyati virajano niśi vetālakulaih kṛtotsāhaḥ'.* Cf. also *Ibid.,* V. is (Silbum, *STV,* p. 66).
101. See above: 'Phenomenology of *hṛd-guhā.'*
102. *SpNir,* IV. 2: *'prakāśavimarśātmakam hṛdayameva visvāntaḥ praveśāvakāsa pradatvādguhā'.*
103. A. Padoux, *PTv,* Paris, 1975, pp. 74-5.
104. *PS,* 59: *'atiguḍhahṛdayaganja prarudhaparamārtharat-nassañcayataḥi.*
105. *SpNir, Ibid.*
106. *IPv,* LV., intrd.: *'mahaguhāntarnimagnabhāva'.* The first interpretation is provided by KC. Pandey, in *Bhaskari,* vol. III, p. 54 (Allahabad, 1950), and the second is given by L. Silburn, *STy,* Paris, 1964, p. 28.
107. *'madhyanādi madhyasamstha visasūtrābha rūpāya ... antarvyomāyā...'.*
108. *'suṣumṇā nam ki madhyanāḍi hṛdaya ke madhya men rahti hai',* B. Dvivedi, *VBh,* p. 44.
109. *Ibid.*

110. *'hṛdayākāśe nilinakṣaḥ padmesamputamadhyagah...'*

111. *SS,* I. 15: *'hṛdaye cittasamghattād dṛsyāsvāpadarsanam'.*

112. *PT,* 4: *'kauliko yam vidhirdevi mama hṛdvyomnyavasthitaḥ'.* Correspondently, *'mama yonih' svarūpam,* is mentioned in *Devi Up* (Warrier, *Ibid.,* p. 78, fn. 2).

113. *PTlv,'... yah kaulikovidhiḥ sa mama hṛdayakase hṛdayatvena ca sadā viditaḥ . . .'* (corrections of the text after Gnoli, *Commento Breve,* Torino, 1978, pp. 109-23).

114. *'tathobhayamahānandasauṣumṇahṛdayantare spandamānanupāsit hṛdaym sṛstilaksanam'.*

115. *PT,* 34: *'ādyamarahitam bijam ...hrtpadmāntargatam...'*

116. *PTlv,* 34: *'. . . svasmin hṛdaye smvillaksane samkocavikāsalilāyogāt kamalarupe'ntargataṁ tāṁ , samvidaṁ , praviśya saṅkocahathapasaranakāritayā vikāsayat dhyāyet nityam'.*

117. *PT,* 2: *'hṛdayasthā tu ya śaktih kaulini kulanāyikā'.*

118. *'hṛdayasthā... hṛdaye saṁvidrūpe ya svātantryalakṣaṇa śaktiryasyāh'.*

119. *PTlv,* 5-9a.: *'evṁ' kauliko vidhir mama tāvad hṛdi saṁvidrūpatādātmyenavasthitah'.*

120. *PTlv,* 2.; *'grāhakarūpam sarvasya hṛdaye spurati...'*

121. *Cf.* above. 'The darkness of the cavern', and fn. 112.

122. *PTlv,* p. 53: *'ghuyam aprakatavat, yato guhāyam māyāyam, svarūpāparijñānamāyyām sthitamapi aprakaṭam'.*

123. "That which gives the knowledge of the hidden things is called *linga" (linam gamāyatityuktelinganirvacanam yataḥ,* MVV, p. 36, as quoted in Dvivedi, *Vijñāna Bhairava,* p. 204; he renders it in Hindi as *"chhipi hui vasm kā jñāna karā dene vālā lin ā kahalata hai").*

124. *'atha ca'mahad-aguhym' sarvasya cvmvidhacamatkāramayatvāt; Ibid.*

125. *'... śuddhavidyāiva trikonā ... aparijnāyamānatvāt, abhedamāhātmya-tirohitatat-tat-pramātrādi konatrayatvāt 'mahāguhā' — iti ucyate saiva ca vastutah pūjādhāma triśulam trikārthe* (Ibid., p. 54). *'tat... svacamatkārarūpena bhavati yan 'ma-ha-a'iti etat 'guhyam' (Ibid.,* p. 55).

126. *'...I'imarśarūpam Svātantryam... tad eva 'guhyam' atirahasyam'. (Ibid.,* p. 55).

127. *'mahe' ... 'a' iti rūpam, tadeva guhyam etadeva ca 'mahāguhyam' –*

jagajjan-anadhāma tathā ubhayasamāpattyā ānandena 'aguhyam' sarvacamatkārama-yam' (*Ipid.,* p. 57).

128. '..*yatguhyam· 'ma-hala' itvuktam 'aham' iti* (*Ibid.,* p. 58).

129. Cf. Nilakantha Gurutu, *Śri Śri Parātrimsikā,* Motilal, Delhi, 1985; pp. 91-2. According to Gnoli, *mahāguhyam* would be the creative moment, and *guhyam* the moment of dissolution (Gnoli, *PTv.,* p. 37).

130. A.G. says in the *PTv,* pp. 215-16, 25-8: "As to what happens by resorting to this I-consciousness, ask your personal experience. I have only shown a little bit of the path. One should not rest contented with this much. Who can say with certainty 'this much is all regarding the divine consciousness?' The divine grace has been vouchsafed to me only to this extent. By that (grace), I have been privileged to disclose this much (as means) ... Subtler *tarka* than this ... may occur to other experients either today (in the present) or at some other time (past or future)..." (J. Singh, *PTv,* unpublished translation).

9

Readerly Text, Ideas in Motion, and Kinaesthetic Form: An Indian Approach

Charu Sheel Singh

My notion of kinaesthetic (kinetic + aesthetic) form centres round the figure of *mandala* given below and certain concepts in Buddhism and yoga whose implication in terms of *literariness* I dwell upon in the course of my article. Some of the prominent Western literary theorist's and aesthetes' views are examined, for the belief is that a bi-polar sensibility cannot but combine the two in order to produce synthesis through collective and cumulative imagination which synergises as well as liberates. As my argument proceeds, the Figure on p. 138 will unfold itself, while the body-plexus symbolism will combine and interchange places. This will produce my own categories in the process.

I begin 'with a consideration of my own categories which are reading categories as well. There are six bodily plexuses which are supposed to be the centres of psychic energy in body-organism. Now, the sacral plexus *(Mulādhāra)* and Prostatic plexus *(Swādhisthāna)* combine to form the lyric. The sacral plexus is energy at its most primordial and vibrant

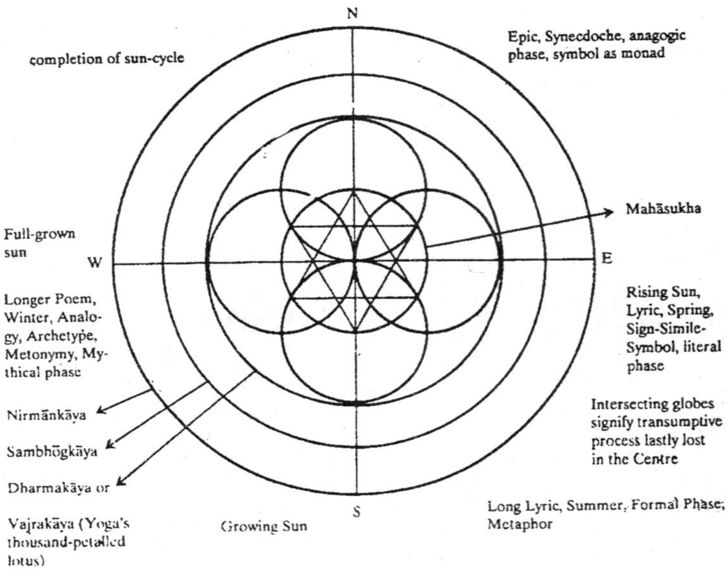

stage, which, when combined with the *ċakrā* above it, acquires the first manifest formation in the form of primary rhythms in primary lines accompanied by anthropomorphic sense of inspiration and imagination. Since the roots grow out of the combined energy of material nature and human nature, harmony with the environment results in a burst of primitive sentiment that, as yet, cannot believe that the outer environment is hiding its own ironies of deviation *(vakrokti)* or believe in the "defrocking of the Shaman" as Mircea Eliade would have called it. It must, however, be made clear that all the *six ċakrās* are one into the other and no exclusive division or compartmentalization is meant when I say that the first two *ċakrās* create the lyric form. The table below will clarify:

Cakrās (body-plexuses)	Poem-Form	Epistemological stand
1. *Mulādhāra* (Sacral Plexus) and *Swādhisthāna* (Prostatic Plexus)	Short lyric	Perception inference-dialec-tic-moral
2. *Swādhisthāna* (Prostatic Plexus) and *Manipura* (Solar Plexus)	Long lyric	Inference-dialectic-moral
3. *Manipura* (Solar Plexus) and *Anāhata* (Cardiac Plexus)	Long poem	Dialectic-moral
4. *Visuddha* (Laryngal Plexus) and *Ajñā* (Cavernous Plexus)	Epic	Moral-dialectic-inference-perception

When the advance is made to the longer lyric, the prostatic and the solar plexuses combine, and instead of mere perception where the subject could not distinguish himself from the object of his perception, he now draws vital inferences which melt the ice of his being and ask him to look inward. Simultaneously, there is a vital increase in volume and intensity of the energy-vibrations; gradually, we advance not only to a larger, growing, and more accommodative and inclusive form, a corresponding journey from ignorance (attachment) to knowledge (disattachment) also takes place. At the level of the longer poem, the inference leads to the birth of the dialectic where the two selves of the one protagonist, question and counter-question respective epistemological stands in order to arrive at a larger truth and effect synthesis. The moral of conflict is implicitly glimpsed at by a self which, as yet, is not visible. It is in the epic stage that the synthesis is effected, disinterest achieved by the protagonist, whose end-result is manifested by the flowering of the thousand-petalled lotus, shown in my first diagram. This I have also called the Diamond Body of Buddha. Read from below *(Mulādhāra)* upwards, my categories designate poetic process through four main formal moulds into which the Truth or Self-malleates itself in its journey upwards to joy divine. Read from outward to inward, from top to bottom, the categories will constitute readerly qualities. This is so because the reader or the audience gets the finished product first; it is not concerned at all with the pains and vagaries the creative artist went through before, the work reached the ultimate stage. After enjoying the work in total in his first encounter, the reader begins to meditate over the constituent parts of which this form was made. And in this process, he unearths the bigger part first, then the smaller, and finally the smallest.

A reader's analytical activity starts from the whole to the part, while the poetic development is from the part to the whole. In terms of the *mandala* circles and the square within it, the reader will enter by the northern gate; then to western, southern and eastern, in order to complete the cycle. The movement of the creative process pursues the course of the sun-cycle, runs in clockwise direction, while the readerly movement follows anti-sun-path and deconstructs all that the sun has traversed in its journey from the east to the north through the south and the west. The sun leaves behind itself a darkness which only analysis can illumine. The creative process absorbs the rays of the sun in all their variety of intensity and depth at various compass-points which vitally correspond to his own body-complex system. This body, however, is a mixture of light and darkness, which interchange and intermix their identities many a time before the final luminous form is achieved. It is the critic's job to unravel such facets of light and darkness that constitute the vitals of the being of creative process. The following *mandala* diagram shows the creative artist's entry into the poetic, form from the eastern gate. It is only when he reaches the northern gate that he gets a vision of the gigantic form, the one Arjuna saw in the form of Krishna in the *Gīta.* The critic, on the

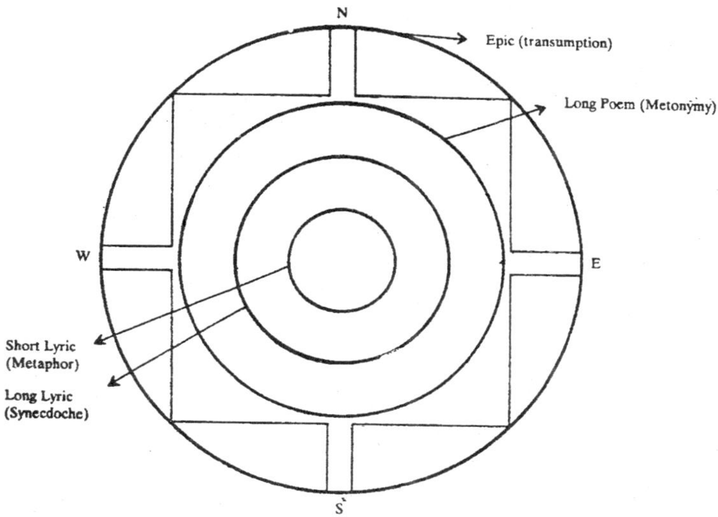

contrary, enters into the art-work from the northern gate, gets a feel of the total form at the outset itself. It is thereafter that he dissects the other parts of it, marches into deeper circles, and unearths the short and the long lyric, and the long poem in the epic itself. The critic's journey is from transumption (of all categories) through metonymy, synecdoche, to metaphor; the poet's is the reverse order—from metaphor through synecdoche, metonymy and transumption. Each figure, however, is in the other (as the critic is in the creative artist and occasionally *vice versa)* though particular figures of speech can only manifest themselves fully at given compass-points, astrological positions, gravitational relationships, and geometrical notations. The *ċakrās* are also the inner zodiac manifesting the respective and relative positions of the planets at a given point of material time and material form.

In an article,[1] Monroe C. Beardsley says that there are two motives behind creation—conscious and the unconscious. He does not answer the question as to why or how the creative process *begins.* My answer to this is that when the creativity, inborn with certain body-organisms, cannot keep the sense of form up to itself, it tries to create an illusion of it. This illusion is poetic form. But since this illusion has come out from within the poet's inmost being, it merely constitutes the circumferential space whose substance is the centre—the argument pursued throughout in this article. This centre in the author, however, is regarded by Geoffrey Hartman, for example, as central to confusion as well: "The author is no longer prophet or interpreter, but the place where this confusion of tongues becomes conscious".[2] Hartman's equation of the author with an incident that reminds of the happenings at the Tower of Babel, celebrates, though in a different way, Roland Barthes's "The Death of the Author" thesis. Murray Krieger, however, disagrees with the view that the original *Book* (my centre) has suffered any altercations with the passage of time. Talking of the successive degradations that the Western man has suffered, Krieger says: "His self-consciousness is a recognition of the successive deprivations Western man has suffered as he has withdrawn from one ontological claim to another in the many centuries that have led from ontology toward fiction. . . the retreat of the eighteenth century rationalistic dogma under the assault of critical philosophy: the retreat from metaphysics to aesthetics, from God's world to the human work, in which the demythologized *is* becomes the *as if.* It is, in short, the retreat from *the* Book to many man-made books."[3]

What is important in Krieger's notion of the poem is that he views it always as the poet's mythograph of the Presence—a notion which is Heideggerian and Derridean. Krieger's stand is that the antinomies of affirmation and denial are always present in the poem's metaphorical thrust, and the best thing that the metaphors achieve is to tell the poet and the reader that beyond the level of communication, serving as a link between the impossible and the possible, metaphors as vehicles or bodies of thought cannot go. "In each of my books I have argued that the metaphor works wholly and miraculously (as a substantive transfer of properties) only while reminding us that, as verbal play, it cannot finally work at all . . .".[4]

Krieger says that all poems have their anti-poems within them and a stage comes when the miracles of the metaphor are broken and splashed on the ground our beings are made of. This is shown in my formulation of things by the contrasting interplay of *gunas,* each into the other; the form is known by the *guna* that ultimately scores over the other two *gunas.* Alhough I accept *in toto* Krieger's assertion, and of so many other contemporary theorists, that the metaphor ultimately serves a reductive function, I, however, do not subscribe to Krieger's view that the metaphorical miracles are "broken up and dragged to earth".[5] I, instead, proceed by a logic of assimilation and integration, where the helplessness of the metaphor is finally not broken but recreated by a faculty in us that enjoys *disinterested play* of wholes and larger wholes *ad infinitum.* The metaphor itself is a whole in a particular mode of its existence within given time-space sequences; simultaneously, it is linked and inbred into other wholes larger than it but not functioning at variance with it. The recreation implies not only a balance of antinomies but a transcendence of them as well. Just as Krieger, a theorist of Presence that he is, says that, "Working from mere phonetic coincidence, the poet forces the word to deny its emptiness and behave in a way that leaps the bounds of ordinary discourse, turning signs into things",[6] I say, and perhaps Krieger would agree with me, that the word cannot but return to its origin which is emptiness. As shown earlier, emptiness is the greatest metaphor for meaning as well as its transcendence, especially in Buddhism. The poet raises miracles of metaphor knowing the facts of death and transience; so, the form that is created is never, final, only "continually final", as Krieger says. The suggestion Krieger gives to perceive the beyond in the temporal is to have one eye from Coleridge and the other from Derrida. This will *re*-construct the *de*-constructed. This is what the concept of Buddha's three bodies implies. The *Nirmānkāya* (Physical Body), the *Sambhogkāya* (Body of Bliss) and the *Dharmakāya*

(Body of Essence) constitute three illusions in Buddhism: the illusion of everyday consciousness, the illusion of the higher levels of inner vision, and the illusion of the essential Being-itself-configurations which do not and cannot constitute it. The work keeps shunting from one position to the other in rounds that become eternal if not attached to a fourth faculty, the centre, which changes the rounds into a spiral and then assimilates them into itself.

The word does not have to die; after re-generation it discovers its eternal lineaments into the Diamond Body of Buddha, the *vajṛakāya,* the Blakean Imagination, whose shadow the word and the world are. Name and form are two denotations temporal form is known by. But in a logic where Buddha *minus* Buddha is Buddha and Buddha *plus* Buddha is Buddha, there is little room either for the loss of meaning or the recovery of it. What is lost and recovered is indeed part of the process. The essence image itself is eternal; it is its reflection in time-space continuum that appears and disappears. Zimmer says of Buddha image: "He denotes pure emptiness and its manifestation in the metaphysical and physical spheres of names and forms, whose Essence is, after all, Emptiness".[7] This is what Bloom discovers in Kabbalah. "Kabbalah too thinks in ways not permitted by Western metaphysics, since its God is at once *Ein-Sof* and *ayin,* total presence and total absence, and all its interiors contain exteriors, while all of its effects determine its causes".[8] It is my view that all theory, either implicitly or explicitly, has to accept this; there are inter-radiations out of creative works that but interpenetrate compartmentalized tokens of our being and compel it to think in terms of micro- and macro-cosmic symbolism—a view I have been assiduously pursuing. There are other than *merely* Western influences on Kabbalah, to which Bloom makes no specific reference, for it is not out of nothing that Kabbalah does not fit into the Western tradition. It openly made use of sources that were available in its ground of growth, unlike the Church Fathers who fanatically refused Pagan and Oriental influences available. I also do not agree with Bloom when he says that "Kabbalah stops the movement of Derrida's 'trace', since it has a *point* of the primordial, where presence and absence co-exist by continuous interplay."[9]

While the latter part of Bloom's statement is acceptable, the former is not. The moment a point in time is postulated (and all points can be postulated only in time) God also becomes part of this continuum which is not what Derrida's "trace" is advocating. It goes at the furthest limits oftime and cries: "It's still time", and therefore, goes on in search of the Inexpressible. Krishna in the *Gīta* goes beyond good and evil; He is the Father, the Mother, the Creator and the Procreator of all contingent beings. He designates Himself as Void and Non-Void, what is and what is not (9.19) and what surpasses both (11.37). The nature of the God-incarnate in the Gīta is often shown to accept the four propositions of Nagarjuna outlined earlier ("is", "is not","both is and is not", and "neither is nor is not"); its own existence, however, is never said to be limited to these four or to any other time-space concept formation. This is what Derrida's "trace" is. This transcendence in contemporary Western thought is first achieved by Nietzsche, then by Kant, and Heidegger thereafter. Bloom rightly remarks that Nietzsche was the first who gave a meaning to human suffering by calling it "the ascetic ideal" in *Genealogy of Morals.* It will be worth-while to recall here that Nietzsche considered Plato's thought as "anti-Hellenic".[10] Nietzsche's own thought was greatly influenced by Hindu and Buddhist thought as was the thought of Schopenhauer, Hartmann and Richard Wagner. In fact, Nietzsche often comes very close to Buddhist concept of emptiness and to the concept of God in the *Gīta,* beyond good and evil, a title Nietzsche was so fascinated by that he gave it to one of his books. Schopenhauer, who himself influenced Nietzsche a great deal, said: "And O! how the mind is here washed clean of all its early ingrafted Jewish superstition! It is the most profitable and most elevating reading which (the original text excepted) is possible in the world. It has been the solace of my life, and will be the solace of my death".[11] Radhakrishnan says that Schopenhauer read

Anquetil Duperron's translation of *Upanishads* he made from a Persian version—Dara Sukoh's *Sarr-é-Akabar*. "Schopenhauer was greatly influenced by Buddhist ideals also. German transcendentalism was affected by Indian thought through Schopenhauer, Hartmann and Nietzsche. Richard Wagner became acquainted with Buddhistic ideas through the writings of Schopenhauer. His *Parsifal* arose out of a French translation of a Buddhist legend. To Mathilde Wesendonk, Wagner wrote in the year 1857: 'you know how I have unconsciously become a Buddhist', and again: 'Yes, child, it is a world view, compared with which every other dogma must appear small and narrow'."[12] The contacts between Nietzsche and Wagner are well known and they influenced each other.

This gives a perspective as to why Nietzsche went beyond opposites and why he gave meaning to human suffering, incorporating Buddhist ideas. Commenting upon Nietzsche's "ascetic ideal", Bloom says that "This change signifies 'a will to nothingness, a revulsion from life', yet still a purposefulness. Life thus uses asceticism in a struggle against death. Nietzsche, magnificently contrapuntal, attains a triumph in antithetical thought by declaring that to be ascetic thus is to be life-affirming. The artist in particular transforms the ascetic ideal by incarnating 'the wish to be different to be elsewhere'."[13]

This is Buddhist doctrine of Emptiness at work, and its further implications will become clear as we proceed along. Kenneth Burke once said that it is only Non-Being which can oppose Being as its dialectical counterpart.[14] He further said that the dialectical process in Plotinus, "beginning with material things, in the end had completely transcended its beginnings. . ."[15] The phenomenon of the transcendence of the latest deposit of karma leaves behind a paradox. This paradox is the clue to meaning in literature. It is immanent and implicit in the creative language used in literature, for its existence lies primarily in the number of outer and inner crusts of meanings that it breeds and multiplies, and finally contrasts them to the essentially empty nature of all metaphors, tropes and figures of speech.

Emptiness is in the meaning as well as out of it, and the body in which it is shrouded, could be the body of myth, metaphor, metonymy, synecdoche, or all of these simultaneously. Emptiness weaves these layers into the symphony of an orchestra, transmits an appearance or illusion of meaning through them, and, at the same time, transcends the periodic and the temporal into the nothingness of itself. A perfect simile could be the coiled snake in the *kundalini* yoga mentioned earlier, who manifests his meaning-power and primordial energy according to the level of creative realization performed prior to its verbalization. The *ċakrās* are psychic centres who are able to see the vitalistic interplay of primal male and female images as per their own perceptive powers peculiar to that stage of enlightenment. The moment the centre is reached, the *ċakrās* are transumpted and assimilated into the all-embracing emptiness where identity and difference meet and are immediately transcended.

Mikel Dufrenne says that beginnings of language are a mystery and "its origin remains hidden in the darkness of prehistory, suggest the idea of a transcendent nature of language" .[16] Dufrenne meticulously advances the thesis that language continuously leads to ontology and metaphysics and shows his agreement with Karl Jaspers's philosophy of the "ciphers". Jaspers I regard as the greatest philosopher of transcendence in the Western tradition. Jaspers was well-versed in Buddhist ideas, and in his book *Philosophie*, III, this is made abundantly clear.[17] In his introductory note to Nāgārjuna's *Vigrah-Vyāvar-tanī*, K. Bhattacharya compares Jaspers with Nāgārjuna, and says that for both of them "silence" was the ultimate in meaning. Jaspers said: "Das Letzte des Denkens wie der communicationist Schweigen".[18] Jaspers further said: "Im Scheitern das Sein zu erfahren".[19] Prof. Bhattacharya compares it with T.R.V. Murti's statement on negation and *Śūnya:* "Negation is thus the despair of thought; but it is at once the opening up of a new avenue—the path of intuition. . . *Śūnyata* is negative only for thought; but in itself it is the non-relational knowledge of the absolute".[20]

In an interesting article[21] Koshiro Tamaki mentioned Jaspers having written on Nāgārjuna and Buddhism. It is for the essentially transcendent character of thought-forms, speech-forms and writing-forms that Dufrenne rejects logical positivists' approach to language. Cassirer also comes in for mixed reaction: "If the Critique of language should be substituted, as Cassirer would like to see, for the Critique of reason, it would only be as a Critique of impure reason".[22] But Dufrenne hastens to add, expecting problems: "But this impurity is necessary: it signifies that man is bound to the world by an original pact, and that, perhaps, even in cases of the purest reflection, man is never able to renounce this pact".[23] Giving an account of Bergson's theory of art T.E. Hulme said: "The two parts of Bergson's general philosophical position which are important in the theory of aesthetic are (1) the conception of reality as a flux of interpenetrated elements unseizable by the intellect (this gives a more precise meaning to the word reality. . .; and (2) his account of the part played in the development of the ordinary characteristics of the mind by its orientation towards action".[24] In fact, the two parts outlined by Hulme are related. The first is a variation upon Buddhist view of reality as dependently-originated, and the second purports to the movement that this interrelatedness of objects generates the action.

Hulme sees a similarity of approach in Schopenhauer and Bergson's view of art. Bergson sees in true art the emancipation of the idea from the fetters of Will. In fact, Bergson's view of art as emancipation comes very close to what I have been trying to arrive at. The human senses and the objects of the outer world of perception become a mould for the artist (as yogi) to enter in and come out at the single command of his conscious desire. Hulme says that the artist who is emancipated from the orientation of his senses is rare, almost an accident produced by Nature. "The artist is the man, then, who on one side of his nature is born detached from the necessities of action. According as this detachment is inherent in one or the other of the senses or is inherent in the consciousness, he is painter, musician, or sculptor".[25] This detachment I have considered in relation to Kant and *Bhagavadgīta* and it forms, in fact, the entire basis of the narrative advancement of the *Gīta* from ignorance to knowledge. Compare T.E. Hulme on Bergson with this verse in *Patanjali's yoga-sūtrās:* "(Concentration not conscious of objects) caused by worldly (means) is the one to which the discarnate attain and to which those (whose bodies) are resolved into primary-matter attain".[26] With reference to my views on the poetic process which invariably acquires the form of a *mandala,* the artist can pierce through the first circle, and pass from the shorter forms to longer ones, only when he shows an advancement in the degree of detachment. To this end my hierarchy of metaphors gradually goes on forming larger and larger wholes, until the complete detachment achieves the highest form and transumption of objects and metaphors takes place. When objects and senses have been transfigured, they are legible to become part of the Buddha-body—the eternal image in time and out of it at once.

There are many verses in Patanjali's *Yoga-sūtrās* which talk of creative process and creative transformation of the yogi. When the artist as yogi perceives objects, those objects do not enter into his psyche and consciousness in the form of hard realities; rather, memory comes to play a vital role here in creative process. "Memory *(Smrti)* is not-adding-surreptitiously *(asampramōsa)* to a once experienced object".[27] The idea, when presented to the senses and the intellect is affected by the object known, shines in the form of two kinds, that of the object known and that of the process of knowing. The truth about perception is that what is perceived of the object is its form and not exactly its inner essence; its form *(ākara)* is reproduced in the thinking-substance *(buddhi-sattva)* which in turn reflects the image cast upon it by the Self. A still more vital thing is that the artist perceives not only time-mutations and the idea of the flux that they carry; he also tries to make creatively viable objects undergo through his own creative process in order to emerge as important form-structure.

"(Concentration becomes) conscious (of its object) by

assuming forms either of deliberation (upon coarse objects) of reflection (upon subtile objects) or of joy or of the sense-of-personality".[28] Deliberation, reflection, joy, and the sense-of-personality are the stages the perceived object is churned through before it acquires manifestable form. In the deliberation, where the other three are subordinated, deliberating activity concentrates upon coarse objects. This corre-sponds to my category—the lyric. When the reflection dominates, deliberation is substracted and a consciousness of bifurcation or mutation or multiplication of the self-grows. In the third stage of the dialectic where the point and the counter-point both are exposed into a certain emptiness of meaning, the joy-feeling is generated, for the dialectic has made the subject forego both of his stands and move to a still higher plane towards the Self which reflects in time but, in fact, is out of it. The sense-of-personality implies a feeling *(Samvid)* where the Self and the personality are one—an integrationist view, corresponding to my epic stage, which integrates the other three categories in the warp and woof of its own being.

In an article, Paul Stern talks of two opinions "apparently quite opposite" on the nature of art: "according to the one, the ultimate function of art is to express convincingly some process or condition of the inner life; according to the other, its function is to create images which, by clarity and harmony of form, fulfill the need for vividly comprehensible appearance, which is rarely satisfied by reality".[29] It is good, however, that Stern does not regard the two as opposite but complementary to each other. The inner life cannot be expressed in and through a vacuous medium; all medium implies images, mental or concrete, for manifestation of feeling and idea. Nietzsche's Dionysian and Apollonian elements, besides being polar opposites, are nevertheless the opposites that are required to carry together the essentiality of any formal being of the universe. Stern tends towards a dynamic whole in his approach and this is appreciable. However, his categories to realize this whole are somewhat general and may well thwart the final attempt at capturing the whole.

The four kinds of concentration that I outlined above have, each of them, an object upon which they rest. I have been holding that each artist can create only that kind of art-work which his already-formulated *body-mandala* permits him to create. For prior to all phenomenal perception, there stands an image of the Self, which, in Patanjali, before the beginning of the creative process, stands in unison with the Self out of time. As Prof. Woods explains: "Organs-of-sense are produced out of the sense-of-personality. Consequently the sense-of-personality is their subtile form".[30] The sense-of-personality itself is the first *mandala* of the lyric, where the subject has emerged out of the elements and is yet not conscious of their separation from him in terms of mode and manner. The distance has not yet emerged. P. A. Michelis says that the English psychologist E. Bullough and the Spanish philosopher Jose Ortega Y. Gasset express two diametrically opposed views on aesthetic distance: "The first thinks that 'the utmost decrease of distance without its disappearance' would provide that 'psychical distance' which is the main characteristic of aesthetic contemplation '. . . . By such 'psychical distance', he maintains, 'the objectification of one's mental states' can be achieved. The second considers that the distance should be the greatest possible; 'to give style', he says, 'is to deform reality, to make unreal'; and he proceeds to explain that in order to derealize we must confront reality not 'as being lived' but as 'contemplated reality'".[31]

What Jose Ortega Y. Gasset means by the derealization of reality is the fact which I mentioned with reference to Patanjali's notion of perception, *viz.*, objects cannot be perceived as they in themselves are; they can only be perceived in the form that their appearance in time creates; moreover, this form has to counter the perceiver's own mental form, his own mental image of his own self, before the form perceived becomes part of the perceiver's memory and multiplies there in its variations in tone, colour, shape, line and contour. There are two basic kinds of concentration in Patanjali—one which is conscious of objects and the other which is not. It is the one which is conscious that has four kinds of formal realizations through four kinds of objects. How distance materializes and how form-mutations form new wholes by creating new psychic centres through a process of hybridization and multiplication is explained by Prof. Haughton-Woods thus: "... (sense-of-personality) together with the (self as) known becomes the idea *(buddhi)*, that is, the feeling which pertains to one self. And because the knower becomes included in this (feeling), one may say that there is a (concentration) conscious of the knower as its object . . . The effect adjusts itself to the cause, not the cause to the effect. Hence this coarse direct-experience becomes associated (by inherence) with coarse (objects) and with subtile (objects), with sense-organs and with the feeling-of-personality, which are four kinds of causes. Furthermore, the other (first three direct experiences, inasmuch) as they have three or two or one cause, assume a triple or double or single form".[32] All forms are effects of causes for there is no effect without a cause. However, perception of apparent forms is not due to the central cause of their manifestation. As the subject marches from the mere sensory, to the inferential, the dialectical and the integrationist moulds of his vision, distance in time grows into distance in space, until, finally, it results into the realization of the space as the body of the subject and time as the manifesting vehicle of that body.

Degrees of distance effect vital variations in form, the deformation of reality, as Y. Gasset calls it. Each psychic centre is a meaning cobweb which has layers often unfathomable. These cobwebs are also the nets of *māyā* or illusion which is what all forms actually are. The vital difference, however, rests in this that some forms liberate in their meaning-dispositionality and point to the region beyond words; others enlume or imprison and suffocate vital nerve-centres of outgoing energy. What all forms singularly try to attain is the centrality of their manifesting cause, what Heidegger would have called, a wish to return to origins. The centre is that vital magnitude in whom are implicit various forms waiting to explode at the single stroke of the Time-machine. Each form exhibits a state of stability; and equilibrium at its own level of manifestation, but, simultaneously, it cannot rest at that level for its centre is part of a more vital centre and its form the solitary child of a more vital form. Patanjali says: "The particularised and the unparticularised (forms) and the resoluble only (into primary matter) and irresoluble-primary-matter are the divisions of the aspects *(guna)*".[33] The four elements, which also figure in my categories and are associated with each of the four poetic modes, are the particular forms of the unparticular elements *(tanmātrās), viz.,* sound, touch, colour, taste and smell. Likewise, there are body-organs of thinking, action, excretion and generation. The central organ has all kinds of things as its intended object. Beyond particularized forms is the Great Substance *(Mahat-tattva)* which is resoluble into the primary matter. Ortega Y. Gasset's notion of deformalising tendency as basis for forms is in terms of what in Patanjali is called the "discarnate". There are two kinds of fluctuations in the central organ of the artist prior to creation. One is the fluctuation which abides in the body. This is called adjusted fluctuation. The other is the fluctuation of the central organ which is itself externalised and hence can never be adjusted to the requirements of the body-organism's vibrations.

As long as the second is not adjusted according to the first, infinite formal realizations occur, journeys from one body to another continuously take place, for this implies an endless karmic fruition of the three *gunas.* Merleau Ponty imagines the human body functioning at different levels, each part accomplishing its own assigned task, but all these tasks are vitally connected with what Patanjali calls "the central organ" and what Merleau-Ponty calls, quoting Lhermitte *(L'Image de notre corps,* p. 238), "an inner eye". Each of us sees himself as it were through an inner eye which from a few yards away is looking at us from the head to the knees. Thus the connecting links between the parts of our body and that between our visual and tactile experience are not forged gradually and cumulatively. . . this translation and this unification are performed once and for all within me: they are my body itself.[34]

> Consider these verses from Patanjali:
> Or (he gains stability) by expulsion and retention of breath (1.34).
> Or (he gains stability when) a sense-activity *(pravrti)* arises con-nected with an object (and) bringing the central organ into a relation of stability (1.35).
> Or an undistressed (and) lumiqous (sense-activity when arisen brings the central-organ into a relation of stability) (1.36).[35]

A thesis I have been meticulously pursuing for the rationale behind the creation of form and the consequent meaning-dispositionality has been with relation to the axial concept of the centre which is there in the body, and the surrounding space which is body itself. What Patanjali's *śūtrās* quoted above establish is that the infinity of space without the comprehension of the corresponding centre is an unmalleable mass of matter, chaos, not yielding to any kind of transformation. In all the three *gunas,* it is only when the central organ is brought into a condition of stability in relation to the object that the kinaesthetic form emerges.

Notes and References

1. "On the creation of Art" in Lee A. Jacobus (ed.), *Aesthetics and the Arts* (New York: McGraw Hill, 1968), p. 53.
2. *Saving the Text* (Baltimor: Johns Hopkins University Press, 1981), p. 140.
3. *Theory of Criticism,* p.189
4. *Ibid.,* p 224.
5. *Ibid.*
6. *Ibid.,* p. 239.
7. H. Zimmer, *Artistic Form and Yoga in the Sacred Images of India,* trans. Gerald Chapple & James B. Lawson (Delhi; Oxford University Press, 1984), p. 88.

8. Bloom, *Kabbalah and Criticism,* p. 53.
9. *Ibid.*
10. See Dr. Oscar Levy (ed.), *Will to Power,* Vol. I (1909), p. 346.
11. Parrega, ii, p. 185; quoted in Wallace, *Schopenhauer,* p. 106.
12. S. Radhakrishnan, *Eastern Religions and Western Thought,* p. 248.
13. *Kabbalah and Criticism,* pp. 51-2.
14. See p. 34 in Kenneth Burke, *A Grammar of Motives* (New York: Prentice Hall, Inc., 1945).
15. *Ibid.*
16. Mikel Dufrenne, *Language and Philosophy,* trans. Henry B. Veatch, Foreword by Paul Henle (Bloomington: Indiana University Press, 1963), p. 16.
17. Berlin, 1932.
18. *Vernunft und Existenz (=Aula-Voordrachten der Rijksuniversiteit te Gromingen,* No.1, 1935).
19. *Philosophie,* III, p. 235.
20. Murti quoted on p. 93 in K. Bhattacharya introduced and E.H. Johnston and Arnold Kunst (eds.), *The Dialectical Method of Nagarjuna Vigrdlwyavartani* (New Delhi: Motilal Banarsidas, 1986).
21. "Jaspers' Auffassung uber den Buddhismus", in *Journal of Indian and Buddhist Studies* (Tokyo), Vol. III, No. 2 (March 1960), pp. 10-20 (768-58); Bhattacharya, *op.cit.,* p. 93.
22. Dufrenne, *Language and Philosophy,* p. 18.
23. *Ibid.*
24. T.E. Hulme, "Bergson's Theory of Art" in Eliseo Vivas and Murray Krieger (eds.), *The Problems of Aesthetics* (New York: Rinehart, 1957), p. 127.
25. *Ibid.,* p. 131.
26. James Haughton-Woods, *The Yoga-System of Patanjali* (New Delhi: Motilal Banarsidas, 1983), I. 19; first published in volume 17 of Harvard Oriental Series, 1914. Prof. Woods clarifies: "The discarnate, that is the gods, attain to the (concentration not conscious of objects which is) caused by worldly (means)...", p. 43, *Ibid.* I shall talk of the role of this withdrawal in relation to the creative process.

27. I. 11, in Woods, *Ibid.,* p. 31.
28. *1.17, lbid.,* p. 40.
29. "On the Problem of Artistic Form", in Susan K. Langer (ed.), *Reflections on Art: A Sourcebook of Writings by Artists, Critics and Philosophers* (New York: Oxford University Press, 1968), p. 71; first published by Johns Hopkins University Press, 1958.
30. Woods, *Yoga-System of Patanjali,* p. 41.
31. "Aesthetic Distance and the Charm of Contemporary Art" in Lee A. Jacobus (ed.), *Aesthetics and the Arts* (New York: McGraw Hill, 1968), p. 32.
32. Woods, *op.cit.,* p. 41.
33. *Ibid.,* II. 19, p. 148.
34. Merleau Ponty, *Phenomenology of Perception,* pp. 149-50.
35. Woods, *Yoga-System of Patanjali,* pp. 72-4.

10

The Trauma of Birth, Abandonment and Homelessness in Three Middle English Romances: New Approaches to Medieval Literary Criticism

Norman Simms

Medieval romance is the stuff of gallant knights and beautiful ladies, heroes questing for the goals of honour, treasure and justice against dastardly foes; its settings are gorgeous in courtly splendour and enamelled landscapes, and it is recited in the elaborate rhetoric of the "colourful" middle style. So what are we to do with a set of popular Middle English narratives that, instead, deal with infants torn from their mothers' breasts or set to die at sea or abandoned in the bowl of a tree, of young boys and girls facing the ordeals of deprivation and loneliness, of enemy knights who behave like cruel ogres and, when defeated, weep like "cradlebairns"? How do we make sense of narrative settings that offer obsessive passages over the stormy seas and, land these children on bleak shorelines, or place them in peasant hovels and pious convents? Where can we categorize popular romances whose rhetoric is mixed and unsteady, verging on the low style of farce and satire and whose very status as complete texts is almost always virtually defused by their fragmentariness, their ripped and torn or gapped presentation? These are questions which unsteady more than our presuppositions about medieval genre; they begin to dismantle fundamental categories of textual criticism and the literary assumptions such theories underlie.

Critics of medieval literature deal with a body of texts that came into being during the manuscript phase of European culture and which generally show all the marks of textuality that link the literature more towards traditional oral expression than towards contemporary print and post-print system of knowledge and feeling.[1] Nevertheless, the medievalist tends today to follow either one or both of two older scholarly highways, one leading, towards positivist registration of linguistic matters, transmission systems, and academic decodings of sources and analogues; the other towards an impressionistic and aesthetic description of reconstituted contemporary readings of the text. Neither approach, while useful and interesting, properly addresses the ontological and epistemological questions which current textual theory opens in the very zones of reading as a deconstructive exercise,[2] especially relevant for manuscript-phase literature.

Naive and Critical Readings

Readings other than the naive and the critical may be termed symptomatic and reflexive.[3] Naive readings assume no prior knowledge of the text other than that which reading, reveals, while critical reading keeps adjusting focus through attention to intellectual, especially literary, contexts. Hence, they occur in a place of problematic reflexivity. But readings that at symptomatic go beyond text and context: they seek to understand not only the text in itself and the contextual reading of it, but to apprehend what lies beyond the author and the surrounding intellectual, spatial, and noetic[4] systems, to discover that which, while implicit in and emerging through the individual and the community's culture, no longer has or has not as yet attained to the grid of words and images already articulated. Thus symptomatic readings seek to informing and constitutive energy of literary creation beyond the text and context: to find, in what belongs to the literature as a presence of continuous duration, which inheres within the historical continuity of discourses: yet in another sense, what lies in the dẹpths of word, image, and generic structure to make the word articulate, the perception imaginable, and the form conceivable. It is also a way of gazing into the *logos* of narrative or dialectic articulation at the centre of articulation as a creative process, where pre-text is transparent to consciousness, and yet invisible to articulation, and there to begin to see archaic, current and emergent meaningful-forms inter-inanimating one another at one with unrealized acts of intentionality. Here, at this metaphysical level of symptomatic reading, the text is experienced as a truth beyond the measurement of language or natural imagery.

The practical reader, however, must catch him or herself short first, reflexively in the act and place of reading, so as to see that act as continuous with a history of naive and critical readings which begin even prior to the writing of the text. The writing in itself is then to be regarded as a specific reading or misreading of the discourses which antedate it. In a manuscript culture, like the European Middle Ages, the necessary time-lapse and often position-change required between one copy of the text and the next makes the history of these readings central to the history of the text's own meaning. The place of our own modern reading, then, cannot be a neutralized area of objective scholarship, but only one more reign of historically-shaped grids of receptivity. An assessment of our place in these zones of current mentality becomes a vital concomitant of such a symptomatic reading of the medieval text.

Just as there can be no recapturing or reconstituting of a naive reading from the past, since the poem or legend textually recorded was never innocently read for the first time, but only re-written as a specific (mis)reading of a more or less consciously perceived continuous discourse, so there can be no unproblematic critical reading, that is, a reading based merely on uncovering contextual codes of obscure and esoteric reference. Nor can we follow the reading of the text symptomatically to the metaphysical core of ontological pre-texts. Instead, we must read otherwise; and to read otherwise[5] means to read the text in terms of the silences and invisibilities in the text, embracing the lapses, gaps, ruptures, contradictions, and other supposed failings of the text. What is deconstructured in this way, however, is not the text *per se* but the naive and critical readings of the text. Holding firmly to the text, one reads away from special pleading and allegorical rationalization, and thus finds the text becoming increasingly dense with incoherences, and inconsistencies. Moreover, the present reading becomes a constant destabilizing of reality in the midst of the competing discourse which begin to constitute the text. To read otherwise, then, is to move towards the epistemological crises of textualization.

The reading moves from text and context to symptoms. A symptomatic reading pretends to make the silence heard and the invisible seen: through a number of strategic tricks, we begin to confront the unspeakable and the unimaginable. But how? The naive reader assimilates the text to a normative oppression of truth, normalized emotions and ideas, and rejects the lacunae in the text as unfortunate accidents, meaningless defects in a history of insignificant transmission. Such reading outside of history sees no problems of text. The critical reader seeks to assimilate the text to a general system of historically knowable, official discourses, and the reading smooths out the rough patches, fills in the gaps, and untangles the overlappings with editorial emendation, reference to documentary statements of normative doctrine, and the ritual citation of sources and analogues. Technical argument justifies and then erases slips of the pen, replaces lost leaves in a folio; and corrects misconstrued and antiquarian editions. Such readings intrude into history and remove the problems from the text. The reading otherwise begins by inscribing the text into the history of reading,[6] of the reading which in each act of copying, performing, or experiencing the text interrupts momentarily the dynamic history of symptomatic discourse, including our own reading as but the latest in these editorial intrusions. Each slip of the pen, loss of a vellum page, or sentimentalization of the text has its place in the reading of the text, is itself a sign of the energies at once always creating and always deconstructing the text.

Symptomatic Readings

The text is then to be read as a zone of symptomatic reading: the text is the focal point of that reading, but as a problematic. The text defines the zone and the problematic. The symptomatic reading begins to bring to the surface of consciousness the silences and invisibilities of our own presence as much as that of all previous readings, including the pre-texts and the actual writing of the text itself. Not an ensemble text, as Clifford Geertz suggests;[7] but a region of competing textualities—that is the problematic area of our reading otherwise. Problematic because it is not a problem to be solved; it is a text defined by its irresolutions and instabilities. A naive reading assumes a single and univocal text, normalized to our own perceptions and understanding. A critical reading hedges in the text by systems of discourse and coordinated reading; nevertheless it discovers textuality, thick with silences and invisibilities; always being created, always being deconstructed. The symptoms draw us in by trickery—false lights, shifting echoes, illusory forms; but otherwise we hold in to our practical selves.

There is then no coherent, consistent original text to be reconstructed either through editorial emendation or to be completed through scholarly apparatus filled with references and citations. Distance in time and space allows us to begin to see that the ruptures, overlayings, and other tears and blockages belong to the mentality of that age, as all mentalities are constituted by the tensions between the seen and heard articulations and the unheard of lapses and contradictions.[8] Our critical reading of the text helps bring to light inadequacies in explanation or motivation for character, failure to coordinate development of plot, imbalances in aesthetic structure: characters speak too long of irrelevant matters and slide or omit reference to the obvious. Structures may be truncated. Lyrics may turn on nonsense words in the refrain. Breakthroughs of the sacred might occur at anticlimactic moments. We might discover the text seething with incompletely assimilated discourses of social, religious, political, and scientific matters. But we should not neo/mis-read the critical text naively. The system of symptomatic reading is a reading towards the text as a centre, of a diachronic and synchronic textuality, the mentality. I offer a simple but not exhaustive outline as a threefold procedure. Each step leads away from what is articulated in word and image towards what is silent and invisible and then towards what is unspeakable and unimaginable. The steps are here separated only make explanation simple, not to indicate primacy of value or historical continuity; throughout a reflexive dialectic between the current reading and the textuality of the written discourse takes place. Only in the broadest terms is the process a movement from naïve through critical to symptomatic reading. The truth is otherwise.

Stages in Mentalities Reading

At first in this mentality reading of medieval literature, the reader describes what is said and seen in the manuscript as the text. This is a rhetorical and performative description, which comes to include, so far as possible, the actual manuscript or manuscripts, provenance, and history of textual transmission from manuscript to contemporary editions. The reader here tends to hold in abeyance personal responses, insofar as they intrude upon the task of supposedly objective "naive" measurement of the text. To a great degree, this is what is normally done as a preliminary to any critical reading by a modern medievalist, and the procedure thus tends to enfold within itself the double naivite of working towards a putative original "innocent" reading and a contemporary "objective" reading requiring only glossarial notes to make the text accessible.

After describing all that has been said and imagined by the text, the second level of mentalities' reading moves towards an assessment of what might have been seen and spoken by the makers of the text. By finding the sources and analogues to ideas, images, speeches, characters, events, and settings, the reader begins to judge what strategies of choice, suppression, and transformation were involved in the articulation of the text being scrutinized. The noetic preconceptions, the social dynamics of the performative moment, and the inner logic of the emotion or adventure being narrated or meditated upon, all these are accounted for by setting what is said and seen against what else might legitimately have been spoken or imagined by the author. The milieu of the text is thus perceived as a region of contextual and inter-textual statement, a region criss-crossed by official and personal discourses of theology, liturgy, philosophy, rhetoric, technologies, social systems, acceptable dreams, and so on. Each statement articulated in the text is taken as a synechdoche and a metonymy of the externally articulated context. The text becomes in this way a sequence of selected representative words or images standing for a total discourse of officially sanctioned language and imagination. More critically the text becomes a problematic presentation of words alluding to other words, ironically displacing and distorting alternatives, and encapsulating traditional experiences of the defining truths of medieval mentality.

But this second stage of reading is not merely critical, insofar as it sets the text along a pattern of contextualized official and personal discourses which encode what is true and false, real and unreal, valid and invalid, normal and abnormal, natural and unnatural, and so on. The second stage of reading is also entering the symptomatic when it begins to locate discontinuities and inconsistencies of the text within a projected zone of problematic silence and invisibility. The reader projects his or her own discomfort into a place of instability where given forms lose their rigidity, their apparent lines, dynamics, and become something formal only in relation to other meaningful patterns dying and being born around it. There are then other grids to be momentarily and playfully constructed between the speakable and the unspeakable, the imaginable and the unimaginable, the knowable and the unknowable. This is, however, more than a trick of saying in metaphor that as music is an alternation of sound and silence, so literature is a way of using language to suggest realms beyond language. This kind of second-stage symptomatic reading begins to discover that the text is motivated into articulation partly by the inadequacy of cultural discourse to express, even in the amplitude of its many competing discourses, the fullness of human experience; it is also to find that the articulation in the text cannot be taken as either naively or critically transparent or equal to the conscious motivations of the contextual tradition, the biographical maker, or the historically original audiences. These conscious articulations of intention—seen and heard in words, images, traditional structures, *topoi* of all kinds—are variously broken, confounded, misplaced, deconstructed by other partly or fully unseen and unheard discourses. Something other seems increasingly to be involved.

The symptomatic reader tries to project these other parts of the text, tries to (mis)read them as part of its sub-textuality. The third stage, going beyond naive rhetoric or performative descriptions and further than critical reconstruction of contexts, attempts to deal with felt absences in the text — those invisibilities and silences known by the traces they leave behind, by the distortions' occasioned by their presence outside the current range of hearing and seeing, by the destabilizations affected on other subsequent readings—scribal errors, faults in transmission, defects in antiquarian editing, naive and critical impositions on modern versions, resistances in our own reflexive ability to come to grip with the text. As a psycho-analyst uses dreams and children's games as projections of inner worlds of unconscious thought or slips of the tongue and hysterical obsessions as haemorrhagings of the suppressed discourse of neurotic imagination, so we begin by seizingon manifest, gaffs, breaks in logic, inadequate response to questions within the text as entree into the unseen and unheard areas of the poem or story we are examining: we start to find projections on the screen of the manuscript of sub-textual discourses only partly remembered by the text. But these apparent or real ruptures do not explain away the text, no more than Freudian screen memories can be dismissed merely as false masks over latently obsessive recollections.[9] There is no end, certainly no allegorical end, to a symptomatic reading: only the practical retreat into the condition of otherwise.

We may make some broad classifications of things which are invisible and silent in the text, but these classifications are neither strict, exclusive, or historically sequential. They are separated and emphasized here for heuristic reasons only: otherwise we could say nothing. Some things are not seen or heard in the text because the author wishes the audience, as though they were a sophisticated coterie, to share the meaning denied to the naive personages or personalities within the romance, tale, or lyric poem. Chaucer, for instance, denies to the pseudo-historical characters in *Troilus and Criseyde* awareness of the Christian universe they inhabit because they are, as characters, able to articulate only a pagan set of social and philosophical discourses. Even further, the unseen author, standing behind the mask of the *ingenue* pedant who edits the putative ancient text in the performative illusion of the poem, shares with the sophisticated reader an understanding of courtly and speculative themes and images only ironically and metonymically present in the actual words of the text. But Chaucer also shares another intimate reading with those who read critically; they read the textuality of his text at the place where the generic and official discourses of his poem are silent to the naive audience at the court who take his text as transparent to their own romantic experience and as an ironic perspective on the lost world of ancient legend. That critically intimate reading which Chaucer articulates in the very performance of the text as text occurs among Chaucer's contemporary readers at the Inns of Court. Their secularizing, sceptical self-conscious textualizing of literature already reads our subsequent presence into the reality of Chaucer's poem.

But other kinds of things are not seen and heard in medieval literature because they belong to the secret, *i.e.*, unofficial, discourses of individuals and groups who lie outside the recording of validating documentation. As Carlo Ginzburg has shown in *The Cheese and the Worms*[10] or Emmanuel Le Roy Ladurie in *Montaillou,*[11] when there are accidental transcriptions of actual peasant or artisan voices, the things that are said and seen seem outrageously unlike that which appears in any of the official state or ecclesiastical discourses we recognize in medieval literature. Sex, age, class, occupation, and geographical isolation can be reason enough for historically silencing a voice or blocking out an image; and yet, to any author living in the Middle Ages, those voices and images would be recognizable, no matter how consciously repugnant or socially inaesthetic. Following Antonio Gramsci, Raymond Williams has argued that any hegemonic ensemble of discourses takes its shape from overt or covert response to counter-hegemonies.[12] Louis Althusser makes a further point that when reading a text we find discrepancies in logic and narrative order we are probably in the presence of gaps:[13] gaps in which the text answers questions not permitted entry into its words, where the questions are either simply not there at all, or where they have been replaced with more acceptable but entirely or partly irrelevant questions; or gaps in which the text asks questions which it does not answer, or which it answers with responses that fail to come to grips with actual problems raised by those questions.[14] It may be that the questions have not yet articulated themselves officially or consciously within the culture but are only latent in the situations which the author begins to read in his or her text as the romance or lyric, or though able to be articulated have as yet nothing but inadequate, traditional responses. The discrepancy between question and response—and here I use this logical figure as a metonym to stand for a wide range of other narrative and lyrical paradigms—can thus indicate an experience felt but not yet granted official status, or an experience inscribed into the traditional discourse but no longer actually felt in the changed circumstances of the real moment. The transference of characters, situations, and emotions from one genre to another may also involve the shift in focus from one formal discourse to another, with the consequence that a sustained and unfamiliar perspective begins to textualize that experience in ways threatening to the normal myths of the culture. Myths here are taken to mean those narrative and, imaginary utterances which any society uses to avoid facing up to the necessarily inadequate formulations of its official articulation of reality. Myths are obsessively retold, always seeming to be recreated anew out of the data of actual experience, but formulated from the topoi of conventional discourse. When shifted generically by literary wit and hence held up to critical scrutiny, myths have to be rationalized, sentimentalized, or allegorized into permissible codings. A symptomatic reading begins to discover, through critical irony, allusions, synechdoche, and other devices of rhetoric, as well as through naive ruptures in the text, the silence and invisibility of the things the normative tradition, the author, and the audience could not allow to be articulated. The zone of reflexivity draws us in, and we grapple with our presence in the world of the text.

The third categorization of things unseen and unspoken actually takes us towards the unimaginable and unspeakable, that is, beyond matters which are 'suppressed either for strategic reasons or for unconscious reflexes in the generation of the text. What we are now dealing with are qualities not simply suppressed or distorted into screen memories. These are things which then had no way of surfacing into articulation as words and images but which are now manifest to us only over vast differences of time and place and through reflexive awareness of our own inadequate mentalities. We feel them uncomfortably, and we search our repertoire of metaphysical tricks to project them out on the screen of the critical text.

There are, to begin with, the historical changes of the long duration. These range at once from transformations in weather to social accommodation to the environment, tracks of a cultural development that occur so slowly that neither individual memories nor even the official awareness of formal groups and institutions can put into words and images; these are realities which therefore seem to be unchanging, to be fundamental, if not absolutely natural and normal, so that barring radical shifts in political relationship, which thus may affect trading routes, or intense foreign invasion or migration, the discourse of the culture fails to register the actual changes involved. This happens either because, as Jack Goody indicates,[15] cultural amnesia always adjusts the words and images of tradition to suit the current realities, or because the encapsulated experiences are asserted as more mystically true than the accidental discrepancies of perceived daily and therefore necessarily profane life.[16] To become more overtly aware of the changes would often mean to discredit the whole system of knowledge and belief which sustains the official structures of power in the society. The more insistent the suppression in myth and ritual, the more neurotic the society. Yet we see, for instance, in the literature of the late Middle Ages in England, a resort to irony and parody, as though the only way to speak and image forth the actual changes in experience were to play off one false discourse against another. There was simply as yet no acceptable alternative literary discourse to express the consequence of several strands of change over the past millennium, changes that were exacerbated by famine, plague and financial crisis during the fourteenth century.

Another kind of change which often occurs at a level of experience unable to express itself in words and images may be seen in the phenomenon of language itself, not in the formal nature of grammar, rhetoric, and logic, but in the shifting verbal commonplaces which a society finds binding together the separate discourses of its diverse modes of existence and which centre themselves on the special topics of their particular methodologies and chosen subjects of enquiry. Just as the crossing of generic lines in literature often involves the danger of interference between categories of discourse held apart by mythical narratives and liturgical constructs, as the realization that one has already passed beyond the confines of a linguistic system may cause awareness of the inadequacies in that traditional mode of thought or discourse. If there is an adequate or comforting alternative model of thought in which to structure one's experiences on the other side, then there can be satirical, playful, parodic gambits in the literature of reflection.

But often in periods of uncomfortable transition, such as were occurring in the late West European Middle Ages, individual authors found themselves caught in the interstices, in the midst of terrible and unspeakable, even unimaginable experiences, paradoxical, contradictory, at once collapsible and often enough infuriatingly reversible. The inner structures of language, like those formal aspects of logic and topoi of official and everyday things, began to become visible, and hence to become incapable of functioning properly, *i.e.,* as unquestioned sacrifices of traditional authority. This started to leave unspoken and unimagined a whole "range of normal and specialized experience. An, overabundance of mere words and a gushing of images, ornate to a degree where their very presence signals a massive lack of content, will be familiar to readers of much of the 15th and early 16th century English and Scottish literature. But a symptomatic reading does not stop by calling such texts verbose; it begins there with the symptoms of things unseen and unheard held under erasure by that flow of verbiage and moves to a place where the original norms, forms and implicit assumptions are viewed otherwise.

A third, but by no means a final, category of things that reside outside the range of language and imagination lies in that set of experiences which begins for all individuals within the womb and carries through to infancy, early childhood, and the traumatic attainment of a self-conscious memory of the self as a distinct ego between seven and twelve years of age. These are the periods of life which begin prior to conscious language and imagination, during the process of learning to use the discourses which sustain and define the world of historical and cultural reality, and which finally give the individual a distinct sense of "self" within those systems of official discourse. These are precisely the zones of scrutiny today supervised by the sciences of psycho-analysis and psycho-history.[17] The traumatic events in these three periods of human development are shaped by the physiological structure of all human beings but they are also subject to shifting specifics of historical patterns of nutrition, vulnerability to disease, culture-based attitudes towards care for the pregnant mother, styles and techniques of birth and care for the parturant infant, child-rearing behaviour, early pedagogical principles, and other medical, social, moral, and political stresses placed upon the growing and emerging personality of the individual.

Psycho-historical Insights

Configurations of parenting, earliest paradigms of sociability, and the actual physical structures of the environment all reinforce, interact with, and call forth the way we dream, articulate ourselves in gesture and language, and recognize our role in traditional and original literary experiences. Since these fundamental experiences take up anywhere from a third to a quarter of normal individual life, we exclude them from our calculations at great peril. Further, as we shall see shortly, these childhood trauma can actually enter into the foreground of popular Middle English literature, even though the little that is said in them in naive word and image is symptomatic of the dimensions of silence and invisibility we have to engage. We must stress that the invisibilities and silences here referred to are not metaphysical realms outside of normal experience that are signalled allegorically in the text; but, rather, they are the effects and fragments of actual discourses disallowed from the surface text for a variety of historical reasons or by the presence by other means of equally real and physical experiences which do not have specific languages of word or image inside the mentality system articulated by the text. Meanings moreover will not be found by seeking to isolate a single voice, partly heard and partly silenced by the historical nature of the text, but by the reader's trick of attending to the multiplicity of voices in the text, the tangle of dynamic discourses, imageries, and other modalities of thought, feeling, and experience which are constantly defining and deconstructing the place in which we recognize the text. Just as Emmanuel Le Roy Ladurie discovers in the mountain villagers of Montaillou a web of conventional topics and pious discourses mixed with half-believed and half-understood Cathar pieties, not to mention all the partly realized, partly recalled materialities of peasant and shepherd life, inklings of Moslem and Jewish discourse, hints and snatches of not yet developed heretical views, all of which constitute the mentality of this fourteenth century community,[18] so Jacques Derrida, Paul Ricoeur, Harold Bloom and other proponents of the deconstructive mode of literary criticism find the text to be an unsettled and unsettling conglomeration of present and absent discourses and imaginations.[19]

Towards Framing a Problem Area

In what follows, my discussion of three popular Middle English metrical romances does not attempt to examine all the facets of critical approach I have outlined above. Instead, my discussion concentrates on a few of the later areas of concern which at once seem central to the texts and which are indices of several discourses silenced and hidden by the very ontological forces which turned these traditional discourses into a set of texts and preserved them for our current reading. What follows also is not a search for the correct naive interpretation or for some critical position which suddenly illuminates a new meaning behind each text. There is no sustained symptomatic interpretation here, only other ways of reading which the text calls forth; and if these other readings destabilize naive and critical interpretations, then we must accept that and carry on in our search for still other projected readings. The movement is from one critical position to a symptomatic other, a movement that does not invalidate —necessarily—those readings moved away from; indeed, the movement should be a binding, entangling journey, drawing as many diverse positions as possible into a reading which is dynamic and not static. Essentially, then, what is deconstructed for abandonment is what Jacques Derrida calls the white myth of metaphysics,[20] the Greco-Christian notion that the univocal voices of metaphysicals and literary critique (they are, at the level we are discussing, the same) equivalent to truth. This is the white myth of Western bookishness, which assumes that by reading away from the naive letter of the text towards some allegorical otherness of sacred or ideological purity, there is a stable reality of the critically true.

We are arguing, to the contrary, for a reading that takes a text, each text, in its physical and historical particularity, as contingently true; a reading process that does not seek to read away from critically, but to read symptomatically inwards to the experience of engagement with the text: a reading which is always otherwise, always moving from point to point, from interpretation to interpretation, and thus finding multiplicity of significance, plurality and contradictoriness of meaning as the very essence of the text as a playful projection of truth. The reader must find himself or herself within that textuality, the current reading neither being an original naive reading or a critically objective gaze outside the text nor the final reading, but merely the latest of all possible symptomatic readings. The discourses of private experience we are concerned with in regard to the three popular Middle English Romances of *King Horn, Havelok the Dane* and *The Lay le Frein* deal with the areas studied under psycho-history and mentalities. Through Freud and those followers who have made particular study of infancy and early childhood, such as Melanie Klein and Erik Erikson, we are today able to envisage some of the trauma which characterize, the formalization of ego-development, the learning of language—in the widest sense of those diverse semiotic systems which conceptualize in word, gesture, image, the individual's place in the world—and the dreamwork mechanisms which underpin all so-called real, ludic, and liminal facets of culture.[21] Naturally, any contemporary generalizations of childhood experience must be modified through careful attention to historical circumstances before we can begin to extrapolate backwards towards understanding of the silenced or partly-silenced discourses making up part of the textuality of the manuscript texts we are concerned with. These hesitations are even more necessary when we come to the matter of prenatal traumata, and the schema drawn up by Lloyd DeMause in his *Foundations of Psycho-history*[22] require nuanced modifications to fit with specifics of thirteenth and fourteenth, century France and England. Nevertheless, once we are alerted to major forces at work in the development of the psyche in the people who created, performed, read, and listened to the romances we are concerned with, not to find any traces of these crucial experiences recorded explicitly in the texts, should signal to us their probable presence in other (absent) ways.

The Romance of Childhood

What the psycho-historians have found is that the normal child of the period we are examining was very much what we would now term a battered baby. Even further, there is increasing evidence of neglect, abandonment, and residual acts of infanticide. Rather than the kind of unawareness of a special phase of childhood in Western Europe which Phillipe Aries suggested a number of years ago,[23] the actual situation that historians are now revealing for the late Middle Ages is one of psychological ambiguity, of cruelty and sentimentality, held in uneasy tension, with the constellation of mother, child, and other near and close members of the household—not all necessarily what we currently define as a family—providing an arena for the often violent projections and introjections of mythic instability. Since each of the popular romances we are dealing with overtly turns on a problematic fantasy opened by the rejection of a child, either for political or personal reasons, we can see more clearly how the suppression of discourses and imaginations takes place. Naturally, merely focussing on this aspect of the romances will not exhaust them of literary significance. One needs very much to consider the interplay of rhetorical, festive, and ludic elements within the articulated textures of the poems, the patterning of ritual passagess the two male and one female protagonists travel through to reach a stage of adult self-awareness, public affirmation of their intrinsic birth-rights to name, prestige, and office, and sexual maturity, and the asserted but not always intrinsic discourses of Christian salvation and sanctification. In other words, we are not asserting, for instance, that the mythic engagement of the foetus in combat with the poisonous placenta[24] explains the *Lay le Frein*, but that the imagery of the ash tree at the heart of the lay cannot begin to work in relation to other intrinsic significations unless that kind of powerful pre-verbal trauma suggested by the psycho-historian is noted. Nor are we suggesting that the contradictions and lapses in the lay are resolved or filled by turning an infared light of psycho-history on the text, so that some hidden or unconscious allegory of the birth process is suddenly revealed. Instead we are suggesting only that the text of literature in certain stages of its developments is to be seen as more extensive place of discursive density, a density opaque with overlayers of screen imagery, and at the same time porous with things that cannot be seen or heard because they are very much unspeakable and unimaginable.

Incomplete Texts of Romance

Let me first give brief sketches of the three Middle English romances we are dealing with.[25] *King Hom* and *Havelok* come from the same manuscript, Land Misc. 108 in the Bodleian Library. Two other manuscripts of *King Hom* also are extant, one dating from about 1225, making it an extremely early popular romance of the Middle English tradition. All versions of these two poems, like that of *Lay le Freine,* which exists in a single manuscript from Auchinleck, are defective either because of missing lines conjectured to be found scattered through the text or with substantial passages gone so that the poems as we have them are at best fragments. It is not my purpose to reconstruct some hypothetical original for each, or to attempt to trace back by peeling away dialectical variations some pure traces of what the composer or translator intended. At best, I shall indicate points of fragmentation or gapping in the text as moments of something other than faulty manuscript transmission or "normal" scribal inattention and error. Since the argument of this paper is that these three poems, perhaps more than more sophisticated "art" compositions, reveal by their very crudeness usually suppressed facets of the late medieval mentality, these points of fragmentation and gapping will be taken as *entrées* to the unconscious levels of that Middle English psyche. Typical critical comments about the kind of entry points may be found in the A.V.C. Schmidt and Nicolas Jacobs edition of *Medieval English Romances* published for Hodder and Stoughton (London) in 1980. Thus in their note to line 2525 of *Havelok,* Schmidt and Jacobs write: "Although there is no break in the MS. here, there is a gap in the, story, part of which the poet seems to have omitted... Skeat here assumed the loss of a passage describing Havelok's return to England; but the journey is implied in the account of the founding of the priory, and the passage as we have it stands, provides an adequate transition: we may not assume that the poet intended otherwise." As we shall show in the appropriate place, this sort of ambiguous transition in the story arises at precisely the point of mythic intensity, and the apparent unsteadiness on the part of scribe or author or editor or what have you. Whoever was responsible for the formation of the text as it comes to us, marks something other than aesthetic (or narrative) confusion.

Another kind of problem shows up in the conclusion to the *Lay le Frein*. If it were just, as sometimes happens, that the last pages of manuscripts get torn away, we could accept the gap from line 341 following as one of those unfortunate accidents of medieval transmission. However, there is another smaller hiatus in the text from Jines 121-133. Donald B. Sands, in his 1966 edition for Holt, Rinehart and Winston (New York), *Middle English Verse Romances,* plugs the gaps by using Henry William Weber's 1810 pseudo-Middle English translation of Marie de France's French version because, as other editors over the years have found, Weber's lines "give us the illusion of possessing *Le Freine* intact". Yet the truth is that we do not have an intact poem: we have a text that is broken at two key points, at least key in the terms of the argument we are making. The shorter gap recounts how the midwife cannot bear to kill the extra twin daughter born to the lady who has made an issue of scorning other women as adulteresses for having two children at once. The young lady-in-waiting agrees to place the baby out, that is, to leave it as a foundling at a convent. As this is a crucial turn in the suppressed anxiety over abandonment and infanticide in the mythic depths of the tale, the textual hiatus seems anything but fortuitous. That being so, the absence of the story's conclusion, once Le Freine marries her young lover at line 340, may very well be more than a tear in the manuscript. Weber's version of Marie's lay indicates that what is missing are the marriage test and recognition scenes and the French poem's incomplete tying up of most loose ends (even in the so-called original the status of the two twin brothers seems curiously unsatisfactory). The readings which follow, then, do not seek to argue away the fragmentariness of the gappiness of the manuscripts, but to take those textual defects as evidence of anxieties in the psyche of the transmitters and patrons of the poems. Such readings are, of course, highly speculative unpackings of myth; and at the same time, while proof is hardly absolute, such readings do yield understandings of the three poems that grant to them more than historical interest as "popularized and simplified translation" down from more courtly or sophisticated romances.

On the Margins of the Inner Sea: Horn and Havelok

King Horn deals with a youthful prince who, at the age of fifteen, is robbed of his true identity and social role and is cast forth into the sea. Then, by dint of adolescent courage and innocent determination, he returns to his proper home and titles. In this way, enacting the stages in an elaborate ritual of process or coming-of-age ordeal, he comes to replace his murdered father. He also avenges his widowed mother, and emerges a potent husband and king. The romantic plot involves several sea-voyages, as well as a number of single-combats on the margins of the land, so that the young hero's coming of age occurs at both ludic and liminal stages of development, stages which we find are defined, as it were, by their relation to the watery world that is imagined as outside of normal space and time.[26] In a similar manner, the so-called Sarazins, who murdered his father, usurp his kingdom from the young prince; and threaten the other peoples and places he journeys to and through, are not as their name might suggest historical Moslem raiders. In fact, while they may more properly be registered as reflexes of the Viking incursions of northwestern Europe, they are, mythically and ritually, the people of the sea-world who enter into and upset the land-kingdoms of Christian folk of whom Horn is the young hopeful leader. *Havelok the Dane* (or as it is entitled in the Laud Manuscript, where along with *King Hom* it is preceded and followed by a number of saints' lives, *Incipit Vita Havelok Quondam Rex Anglie et Denemarchie)* has its hero-child rejected at a much earlier period, and actually focusses on his personal development from the age of two to 12 years. Havelok's romantic and ritual passages towards and into manhood involve a greater transformation in external identity than Horn's, for the young Dane, in his rescue from infanticide, grows up as the surrogate son of a poor fisherman named Grim. As in *King Hom,* Havelok's journey across the sea makes him a mythic figure whose strength lies in association with the margins of the shore, and who can only win his identity-confirming land-titles through a series of dis-guises and combats. Instead of usurping sea-devils, however, the enemies of Havelok and his bride are treacherous and ungrateful father-surrogates, guardians appointed by true fathers over their infant children. Like Horn, too, Havelok must be able to bind together several land-titles so as to achieve the maturity and potency of marriage which crowns his enterprise, the successful ritualized passage from boyhood to manhood.

But whereas *King Horn* plays on the conventions of literary, that is, courtly romance, particularly those topoi of the handsome stranger or fair unknown—the young knight who comes unrecognized to a court and through manifest courage and inherent gentility wins his rightful titles and confirms his privileged right to marry in the royal line—*Havelok the Dane* is a more problematical romance, exploring or at least beginning to sound the themes of class, age, and moral privilege. We can also begin to find the traces of more fundamental discourses of experience in *Havelok,* since it covers a wider distribution of social and occupational types; although paradoxically it is in *Horn* that the starkest mythical patterns can be noted. At lines 1910-13 of *Havelok,* as the hero battles his way towards his proper titles, he is confronted by sixty attackers. Havelok lays on them stoutly, cracking arms, knees, shanks and thighs. Then:

> He maden here backes also bloute
> Als here wombes and made hem rout
> Als he weren cradelbarnes—-
> So dos the child that moder tharnes.

There are other sorts of epic-type similes from time to time in the battles that take place in this popular romance, but none so apt to the themes of this essay—and to the immediate context; just prior to the attack by the sixty, Havelok rouses his two brothers to action, reminding us of his collective upward curve of regaining family honour and responsibilities. Now these four lines are rendered by A.C. Gibbs as:

> They made their backs as soft as
> their bellies, and made them bawl
> like babies in their cradles — just
> like a child who lost its mother.

The revenge of Havelok, then, is to turn his enemies into cry-babies, since the beginning of his misfortunes lies in the trauma of near infanticide, loss of his mother, and abandonment. The simile goes further in inflicting upon the enemy a worse state of humiliation than merely weeping infants. The foe are beaten to a pulp, with their backs as soft as their bellies, not so much "cradelbarnes" as fatal forms, virtually aborting themselves, and thus as much themselves destroyers of their mothers as victims of her violent ejection of them from her hostile (poisonous) womb into the world. In inflicting this punishment on his enemies, Havelok also projects outwards his own sense of loss of having been violently pushed or punched from his mother's womb "Whil he was litel...ful naked" (1.7). When his father dies, as we have seen, Havelok is subject to torments and indignities, and is forced to watch his two younger sisters being murdered and cut to pieces, and then, in an inverse parody of his refuge in the once nurturant womb, he is cast into the sea. As we have shown, this leads to his rebirth in England and the narrative process of his gradual return to true titles and privileges. This process, as we mentioned above in relation to a similar pattern experienced by King Horn, involves obsessive, ritualized, and mythical movements back and forth across the sea in order to effect the restorations required by the romantic plot of return and recognition.

The Tree as Placenta: Le Frein and Le Codre

Yet the third of the romances in Middle English metrical forms we are considering, *Lay le Frein* appears to be far more elemental and more mythic than either of the two other popular romances discussed above. Though a translation from the French, or possibly a recreation of Marie de France's *lai* of the same name, the English version deepens and darkens the verbal ambiguities in the title character's iconic role. For it seems that the incomplete coordination of the stark fable of the twin sisters and the sentimental vignette of the power of love to transform an unjust situation embraces a range of psychologically deep projections of pre-natal and infantile crisis. In the romance, a noble mother, having denounced her husband's closest friend's wife for having an illegitimate lover as the cause of her twin sons' birth, finds herself soon afterwards the parent of twin daughters. Unable to accept the social consequences of revealing the double birth, though, she abandons one of the infants, who upon being found in the hollow bowl of an ash tree outside a convent, is named Le Frein after the French name of the tree. But the young girl, upon attaining the age of sexual maturity, not only is told of her foundling status and given the marks of her unrecognized high titles—a golden ring and an embroidered blanket. She also enters into an affair with a young knight and eventually runs off with him to live in his castle as his mistress. Only by showing selfless love to, the young man on the eve of his wedding to her unrecognized sister similarly named after a tree, 'the princess Le Codre, does Le Frein regain her proper identity as daughter to the rejecting mother and so become available to marry her young lover.

The discontinuity between the mythic pattern of twin sons and twin daughters which is revealed by the role of Sir Guron and the unnamed husband found for Le Codre, as well as the ambiguity in the function of the two women who attend the mother at the birth of her twin daughters, the midwife who refuses to perform infanticide and the foster-child who substitutes abandonment,—these glaring inconsistencies surely alert us to the presence of suppressed aspects of the psychic fantasy celebrated in the lay. The play on the arboreal names of the twin daughters is furthered in the Middle English by the vague pun on the title and the language of the original but more so by the emphatic association of the English name of the tree and the protagonist and the feeling of *shame* attendant upon her birth. The logic of the *Lay le Frein* coherence lies, then, not in assimilation and metaphoric suitability but in juxtaposition and partial similarities. Just as the Christian allusions in *Havelok* seem forced and inadequate to the problematic opened by the mythic drama of the romance, so the stated and implied signification of the heroine's name in *Le Frein* indicated experiences held under erasure by these spoken and imagined aspects of the texts. It is not that either the allusions to Judas or the sounding of the proverb that "Better than Ash is Hazle I ween" are all wrong or that they entirely mislead the reader to irrelevance. But these intrusive discourses at once reveal and hide other interpretations in the poems. These are interpretations which psycho-historical insight alerts us to discover.

At the centre of *Lay le Frein* we find the death and rebirth of an abandoned twin daughter. Left in the bowl of the hollow ash by the mother's maid-servant, "Why ther y-nortured had y-be" (122), the tree which "fair and high/well-branched, of great worth," at once possibly identified as tomb and new womb, or on the one hand poisonous placenta, unyielding breast, rejecting mother, and on the other, nurturant placenta, succulent breast, the loving mother. The infant girl is found by a porter at the entrance to the convent, the home of sacred yet sterile nuns, who are loving and caring but milkless brides of Christ and imitation mothers of the infact Jesus. The old man then takes the foundling, first, home to his daughter, "For sche was melche and couthe theran." The delay and further deflection of the child's birth away from the tree to the convent involves this structurally awkward but insignificant interlude with the porter and his daughter. The passage contains apparently realistic details of nurturance, *i.e.*, a warm and caring mothering that exists neither in the proper home of the twin nor in the convent itself since the women there (nuns) have no milk. On how the baby is fed thereafter, once she has been taken into the nunnery and announced by the abbess as "mi kinswoman", the text is silent. Associated with the christening of the child under the name Le Frein goes repeated discussion of the meaning of that name in relation to the ash tree, and yet, as we have said, the actual details of mothering are suppressed. We are merely told that the young child "thrived from yer to yer". The female child is obviously taken care of for the twin reasons of the abbess's maternal instincts—the baby had become her own kinswoman, her foster-child—and of Christian love, "For Marie love," in imitation of the Queen of Heaven. Thus the ash tree outside at the gate of the nunnery mediates between the mother's palace (placenta), which is cold and poisonous to the rejected daughter, and the convent as a conventionalized, *i.e.*, artificial, substitute womb. In that sense, the tree is at once a parody of nurturance and yet a real site of mothering, but in a partly suppressed and deflected image of motherhood. The ash tree is, in the mythic fantasy-language of the poem, the body of the mother, real and parodied, particularly a placenta which nurtures the other twin, Le Codre, and poisons the rejected sister, named after the tree.

When Le Frein reaches the age of 12, we are told that she is renowned for her beauty but also that she "couthe ought of manhed". She is sexually mature and innocent. At the age of puberty, then, when young medieval girls are ready to begin their ritual passage into wife-hood; Le Frein asks about her origins, and is told as much of her identity as the abbess knows. She is given the golden ring and the cloth she was wrapped in as an infant. But the next step towards her official sexual maturity must be from the outside, the intrusion of Sir Guron. He falls in love with her, disguises himself as a lay-brother, and then talks her into running off with him as his mistress, not his wife. It seems to the good abbess that Le Frein's departure is a form of death; "She made morning in hir thought". This second time, instead of the girl being rejected by her mother, she abandons her foster-mother. She seeks emotional maturity in a sexual alliance with the knight, but though she behaves very much as a lady in his castle and is beloved and respected by others there, she is not really married to Sir Guron. She is as yet unrecognised in her true identity. Hence, the knight fairly easily gives into the pressures of his barons to marry properly and breed a rightful heir and to forsake his *lemman,* the beautiful stranger, Le Frein. Yet here the Middle English manuscript ends, truncated—as though the scribe were traumatized by something unspeakable, unimaginable and unthinkable. Following the story as given by Marie de France and rendered in pseudo-medieval verse by Henry William Weber, we can gain an acceptable version of the French conclusion.

The negotiations for a bride bring Sir Guron into an alliance with the parents of the other twin daughter, Le Codre, named after, for no apparent reason in the text, the hazle tree. The sounding of the proverb by the wedding guests that hazle is better than ash merely seems to augment ironic blindness of Guron and the others who fail to see the family resemblance between Le Frein and Le Codre. It is only when Le Frein, in a fit of self-effacing love for her erstwhile paramour, brings her *mantel* to lay on the bridal bed that a connection is made. Her mother recognizes the cloth, asks where she got it, and, hearing the naive account of her abandonment with it and the golden ring, faints. Swooning and sighing, the mother, as it were, suffers the ordeal of her labour again, so that she painfully admits her errors in abandoning the child and pretending she was never born. At that, the lady and the knight her husband embrace Le Frein as their daughter. The marriage to Le Codre is annulled, and Le Frein is wed to Sir Guron. Le Codre's own subsequent marriage to another unnamed knight is quickly stated but not dwelt on, even though the final lines of the French poem define the lay as about not just but both female twins:

> Thus ends the lay of tho maidens bright,
> Le Frein and Le Codre y-hight. (407-408)

As we have shown, there seems to be more to this poem than the comic motifs of loss and recovery, separation and coming together, and the rise of the fair unknown lady to the titles and status she deserves by birth. The problematic of twinning, the trauma of abandonment, and the suppressed mysteries of nurturance in relation to scared virginity are all part of a mythic dimension neither the Middle English nor the Middle French lays seem able to articulate. The gaps which fragment the Middle English at least focus our attention on the unspeakable qualities of tale as myth, while Marie de France's more controlled artistry seems to smooth away the unresolved tensions.

Our purpose has been to return attention to these unresolved tensions and, where possible, to suggest some of the kinds of unspeakable, unimaginable and unthinkable aspects there are in the mentality of the period which gave rise to these poems. This is by no means to explain away what the romances present to us as inexplicable but to make us aware that psycho-history can be a tool in the cabinet of contemporary readers of Middle English Poetry, part of our necessary *bricolage.*

Notes and References

1. It would now be impossible to list all the books relevant to this argument, but an almost random listing will orientate the reader towards the mentalities approach adopted in this essay: Maurice Clanchy, *From Memory to Written Record: England 1066-1307* (London, 1977); Alexandru Dutu, *Modele, Imagini, Privelisti: Incuriuni in Cultura Europena Modema,* (Cluj-Napoca, 1979); Lucien Febvre and Henri-Jean Martin, *The Coming of the Book: The Impact of Printing, 1450-1800,* trans. by David Gerard, ed. by Geoffrey Nowell-Smith and David Wotton (London, 1976); Wilbur Samuel Howell, *Logic and Rhetoric in England, 1500-1700* (Prince-ton, 1956); Richard A. Lanham; *The Motives of Eloquence: Literary Rhetoric in the Renaissance* (New Haven and New York, 1976); Walter J. Ong. *Ramus, Method, and the Decay of Dialogue: From the Art of Discourse to the Art of Reason* (Cambridge, Mass., 1958); and Brain Stock, *The Implications of Literacy: Written Language and Models of Imerpretation in the Eleventh and Twelfth Centuries.* (Princeton, 1983).
2. Because "deconstruction" is now something of a buzz-word, I should give my own working definition and admit to a more than critical reception of Foucault and Derrida. By deconstruction, I mean the ability to read a text as a manifestation of a complex historical and psychological process, as discussed in this essay and my forthcoming *The Humming Tree;* " text in this light becomes dynamic rather than fixed, and deconstruction means dismantling the illusions of such rigidity and closure particularly evident in romantic close-reading exercises and normative historical (positivistic) interpretations. The text thus becomes a *locus* of dynamic

energies, of forms emerging and collapsing, of idiosyncratic personal trauma and long-shared cultural experiences.

3. Again these are words which, while they have specific origins in certain Marxist critics, have gone through many seachanges, and now must be understood, at least in this essay, as defined in the paragraphs which follow. See my *Humming Tree* (forthcoming).
4. By "noetic" is meant a knowledge system on the analogy with a "poetic", a system of organizing literary texts (including prosody, rhetorical schemes, and cultural expectations): hence, a "noetic" includes the laws or rules of logic, proof and evidence, the schemes of presenting information as "facts" and "history", and the expectations of academics and other officers of the learned professions.
5. To read "other" means to swerve away from positivist and romantic notions of interpretation, to hold in abeyance the "normative" expectations that poetry will be based on metaphoric similarities that narratives will be coherent and novelistic, and so forth. The otherness is a mark of scepticism, critical interrogation, cynical deconstruction, etc.
6. In addition to the books mentioned in note 1, see also the following as guides to the ideological presuppositions of this essay: Mikhail M. Bakhtin, *The Dialogic Imagination: Four Essays*, ed. by Michael Holquist, trans. by Caryl Emerson and Michael Holquist (Austin and London, 1981); Lennard J. Davis, "A Social History of Fact and Fiction: Authorial Disavowal in the Early English Novel", in Edward W. Said, *Literature and Society;* Ravindra K. Jain, ed. *Text and Context: The Social Anthropology of Tradition* (Philadelphia, 1977), especially Juan M. Ossio, "Myth and History: The Seventeenth-Century Chronicle of Guaman, Literature Studies Poma de Ayal" (pp. 51-93) and Jack Goody, "Literacy and Classification: On Turning the Tables" (pp. 205-25); David Margolies, *Novel and Society in Elizabe-than England* (Totara, NJ, 1985); D.F. McKenzie, *Culture, Literacy & Print"in Early New Zealand: The Treaty of Waitangi* (Wellington, 1985); Fred C. Robinson, "Print Culture and the Birth of the Text", *Sewanee Review*, 89:3 (Summer 1981), 423-30; Jonathan D. Spence, *The Memory Palace of Matteo Rici.* (New York, 1984); Peter Stallybrass and Allon White, *The Politics and Poetics of Transgression* (Ithaca, NY, 1986); George Steiner, *On Difficulty*

and Other Essays (Oxford, 1978); and Tzvetan Todorov, *The Poetics of Prose,* trans. by Richard-Howard (Oxford, 1977).

7. Clifford Geertz, *The Interpretation of Cultures: Selected Essays* (New York, 1973) and *Local Knowledge: Further Essays in Interpretive Anthropology* (New York, 1983).
8. For example, these terms are explained in Meir Sternberg, *The Poetics of Biblical Narrative: Ideological Literature and the Drama of Reading* (Bloomington, IN, 1985); see also my discussion of this and related books in *The Humming Tree.*
9. Sigmund Freud, "Screen Memories (1899)", in *Collected Papers,* ed. James Stracky, Vol. V (New York: Basic Books, 1959), pp. 47-69.
10. Carlo Ginzburg, *The Cheese and the Worms,* trans. John and'Anne Tedeschi (Baltimore, 1978).
11. *Montaillou:* The *Promised Land of Error,* tran Barbara Bray (New York, 1978).
12. On Gramsci's theory of hegemonies and- counter-hegemonies, see *Selections from his Political Writings,* trans. John Mathews (New York, c. 1977); but especially the interpretations of Raymond'Williams in *Marxism and Literature* (Oxford, 1977).
13. Louis Althusser, with Etienne Balibar, *Reading "Capital",* trans. by Ben Brewster, rev. abridged ed. (London. 1970; orig. French, 1965).
14. See Sternberg's discussion of the "gappiness" in biblical narrative, note 8 above.
15. Jack Goody (ed.), *Literacy in Traditional Societies* (Cambridge, 1977) and see his own. *The Domestication of the Savage Mind-* *(Cambridge,* 1977) and more recently *The Logic of Writing and the Organization of Society* (Cambridge, 1986).
16. While these terms derive from the History of Religions, with authorities such as Mircea Eliade and Jonathon Z. Smith, they are used here in a more psychologi-cally dynamic sense based on the interaction of poetics and noetics, forming and unforming world views, etc.
17. See Lloyd de Mause, *Foundations of Psychohistory* (New York, 1982). See also Lloyd de Mause (ed.), *The History of Childhood* (London, 1976), esp. de Mause, "The Evolution of Childhood", pp. 1-74, and Mary Martin McLaughlin, "Survivors and

Surrogates: Children and Parents from the Ninth to the Thirteenth Centuries", pp. 101-82; and Shulamith Shahar, "Infants, Infant Care, and Attitudes toward Infancy in the Medieval Lives of Saints", *Journal of Psychohistory,* 10:3 (1983), 281-309.

18. See note 11 above.

19. See note 2 previous page.

20. Jacques Derrida, "White Mythology: Metaphor in the Text of Philosophy", in his *Margins of Philosophy,* trans. with additional notes by Alan Bass (Chicago, 1982), pp. 207-71.

21. Vitlor Turner, *FrtJmRitual to Theatre: The Human Seriousness of Play* (New York: Performing Arts Journal Publications, 1982), see "Liminal to Liminoid" *in Play, Flow, Ritual: An Essay in Comparative Symbology,* pp. 20-60.

22. See esp., p. 237.

23. Phillipe Aries, *Centuries of Childhood: A Social History of Family Life* (New York, 1962), but see de Mause, "The Evolution of Childbood", esp. pp. 20-60.

24. On the poisonous placenta, see for example, Uoyd de Mause, "The Foetal. Origins of History", in *Foundations of Psychohistory,* pp. 244-332.

25. The texts used here are based on the following editions: Donald B. Sands (ed.), *Middle English Verse Romances* (New York, 1969); Thomas C. Rumble (cd.), *The Breton Lays in Middle English* (Detroit, 1965); A.C. Gibbs (ed.), *Middle English Romances* (London, 1966); Al.C. Schmidt and Nicholas Jacobs (eds.), *Medieval English Romances,* Part I (London, 1980).

26. On the myth of the sea, its margins, and passages over it, see Alain Cabantous, "Espace Maritime et Mentalites religieuses en France are XVII-e et XVII-e siecles", *Mentalities/Mentalites,* 1:1 (1982).

11

Raja Rao's *The Serpent and the Rope:* An Indian Novel

Ragini Ramachandra

It is perhaps trite to say so late in the day that The *Serpent and the Rope* in the very grandeur of its conception and epic proportions is the most exciting experience in contemporary Indian fiction. With many firsts to its credit, the novel marks an important breakthrough—its distinction largely determined by its metaphysical concerns and preoccupations. By refusing to make socio-political, historical, psychological and even moral issues his main consideration, Raja Rao has not merely avoided the familiar terrain trodden by many of his contemporaries, but also at the same time hinted at the glorious possibilities open before an intelligent human mind on the one hand and the present-day fiction writer on the other. The very title that takes. us back to Sankara's metaphor of Appearance and Reality, *Satya* and *Mithya:* the epigraph from Sri Atmananda Guru and the motif of Sakyamuni leaving behind his wife and babe in Kapilavastu to reach a point of no return are richly suggestive of the nature of Raja Rao's undertaking. Raja Rao is not interested, say, in the manner of a Narayan in capturing and recording with fidelity all the microscopic details that surround ordinary life or the incongruities in human nature nor like Khushwant Singh, Bhabani Bhattacharya or Manohar Malgonkar in offering a historical perspective of India. In fact, so opposed is Raja Rao to India's historicity that he makes Ramaswamy say in the course of the novel, "to integrate India into history—is like marrying Madeleine". (p. 337)

The novel might very well be an answer to Churchill's facile remark made somewhere: "India is a geographical term. It is no more a united nation than the Equator." Page after page of the *Serpent and the* Rope-exemplifies, that for its author India is "an idea, a metaphysic" which he carried wherever he went, and not a spot on the map, a country like France or England: Nevertheless Raja Rao is more conversant with its topography than many who profess to know her contours from Kashmir to Kanyakumari. Yet it is good to remind ourselves that had Raja Rao been interested in discovering only the geographical entity of his country, he might have ended up producing another saga of "heat and dust" creating not even a mild ripple in the process! Thanks to Raja Rao's efforts at rescuing the novel form from photographic realism, the scope of the novel itself has been enlarged to include history, philosophy, myth, legend, poetry and religion in a manner one had not hitherto come across in Indian creative writing. All this rich, diverse material could not have more convincingly proved "Why the novel matters".

A great conqueror in history like Alexander might have felt sad at the end of his career that he had no more worlds to conquer, but a writer who lives in the country of the mind and the spirit with ever new and uncharted territories to explore might resemble a Goethe on his deathbed asking for. . . light. . .! Coming back to Raja Rao, it is this light, this *Jñanam* that is India, that he is interested in exploring. His supreme distinction lies in having realized its value and imparting it to his characters and readers alike. Support can be drawn from the novel itself where Rama observes in one of his, dialogues With Madeleine towards the end:

Can you understand that all

> things merge, all thoughts and
> perceptions, in knowledge.
> It is in knowledge that you know a thing,
> not in seeing or hearing. (p. 336).

Here is a novel which simply cannot be evaluated by the conventional Western yardstick of 'plot', 'character', 'situation', for despite all its rich layers yielding a multi-dimensional experience, what 'plot' in the strict sense of the term can we find? In this respect it looks as though Raja Rao is conforming to a well-known rule of Sanskrit literary criticism which considers the plot merely as an "outer vesture" which serves its purpose best when it thrusts itself least on the attention of the readers. In fact, in a perfect drama, says Hiriyanna, we should not become conscious of the plot at all. Accordingly, Sanskrit rhetoricians look upon any obtrusion of the plot as a sort of materialism in poetry. Though this canon was formulated basically in relation to drama, it could by extension be applied to other forms of literature as well, for the term *kāvya* was all inclusive in ancient times. The sheer immensity of the novel, the wide and breathtaking range of its experience, its enormous learning permit us to place Raja Rao in the mainstream of Indian tradition, for one might recall how ancient Indian critical system also most emphatically outlined the need for *Vyutpatti* – *learn*ing or erudition as one of the most essential requirements of a good poet. The entire novel is an enactment of Raja Rao's conviction that life is a pilgrimage – though he does not know what it is and to where. In his desire to understand this great mystery, he resorts to an arche-typal pattern in conceiving of Rama's life as a kind of journey, not an 'absurd' one at that but as a voyage of self-discovery. It is the "sad and uneven chronicle" of a "holy vagabond" whose quest starts quite early in life. Born a brahmin, that is devoted to truth and all that, Rama not merely gives us an exalted definition of a brahmin as "he who knows Brahman" but also traces at once his lineage to the great sages of the past, whom he feels in his bones – his legendry and upanishadic ancestors, Yajnavalkya and

Madhava and Sankara and others who left hearths and riverside fields, and wandered to mountains distant and hermitages 'to see God face to face'. An unusual opening for a novel one would feel, which at once lifts the reader out of himself and his mundane times with all that talk of sages who were filled with a thirst for God, with a *devakama* and dying, yet knew did not die. This opening paragraph with its poetic evocation of the past and preoccupation with Man's higher functions implied in his quest to "see God face to face" immediately sets the tone for the novel and also prepares the reader for the various twists and turns he is subsequently called upon to make in following the hero's quest, for understandably the pilgrim's path must be strewn with so many hurdles. Rama was not merely born a brahmin, but *was* a good brahmin, we are told; knew Grammar and the *Brahma Sutras,* read the upanishads at the age of four, was given the holy thread at seven—because his mother was dead and he had to perform her funeral ceremonies, year after year—his father having married again. The loss of his mother and his profound sorrow over it presented with great feeling acquires a metaphysical status, particularly in his poignant outbrust: "I was born an orphan, and have remained one". That and the subsequent query, "am I always going to be an orphan?" might be in the nature of a comment on man's orphaned existence on earth in general.

It is this predicament which induces Ramaswamy to meditate on several other deaths in the family, of Grandfather Kittanna and Aunt Lakshamma, his step-mother and his own father not to speak of the horse Sundar driving him in turn to speculate. . . "if they've died, I ask you, where indeed did they go?" (p. 8) . . . "Where is Sundar now? Where?" (p. 9) Being a true heir to the Vedantic tradition he cannot believe in the finality of death and so comforts himself with the thought that "one does not die". In fact, so strong and vital is this Vedic tradition which runs in his veins that on another occasion he quotes with power and authority the *Rig Veda* which says, "Never at any time am I subject to Death". And that is not all. His scriptural knowledge encourages him to go even beyond and assert:

> The only real illusion mrityu,
> *moral* is Death. Man must seek
> forever the death of death (p. 389).

Anyhow his father's death takes him to Benares, a 'surrealist' city whereone never knows "where reality starts and where illusion ends". (p. 13) One of the first things that he is quick enough to realize is that in Benares "death is as illusory as the mist in the morning". (p. 13)

It is Raja Rao's splendid evocation of Benares, the 'eternal' city, that reveals an aspect of the immemorial India on the one hand and brahmanism in its decadence on the other. It is a city of contradictions, we come to learn:

> There the dead do not die nor
> the living live. (p. 24)

Going down the steps of Harishchandra Ghat he can relive and recreate how Tulasidas wrote his *Ramayana* "just there, next to the Rewa Palace", and how Kabir had been hit on the head by Saint Ramanand and farther down the Buddha himself had walked down the river and washed his alms-bowl, gone up the steps and set the wheel of Law turning, etc., etc. And against this background sits "each Sadhu, a Shiva", lost in such magnanimity as though to affirm the undying roots of this great Indian past and hint at its unbroken continuity for ages to come. It is here as well that one gets to know the resonance and the majesty of Sanskrit language particularly through those beautiful hymns of Shankara, thus establishing a kinship with another great link from the past. So rooted is Ramaswami in his Sanskritic tradition that standing on the banks of Mother Ganga he is moved to say, "you cannot have so much Sanskrit in your being and not feel". Devi Sureshwari Bhagavathi Gange... The truth of Rama's observation that "he who possesses Sanskrit can possess himself' is borne out in his extraordinarily mature and restrained behaviour with Madeleine even when his marriage with her is breaking down. Interestingly one of the things that Rama and Savithri have in common is they both know Sanskrit and can entertain each other with *Uttara Rama Charita* or *Raghuvamsha.*

So Rama traverses through the whole of the Gangetic plain with the recognition that it "is one song of saintly sorrow as though Truth began where sorrow was accepted, and India began where Truth was acknowledged". (p. 37) The Ganga that "knew our secret" and "held our patrimony" for Rama "is ever so knowing", "so wise"; in fact "if wisdom became water the Ganges would be that water, flowing down to the seven seas". Contrast this with Madeleine's picture of Benares that conforms to the average Western man's notion of the holy city:

> Of Benares all I know is the
> bits of floating human flesh and
> the pyres of dead, and that the
> Ganges water when chemically
> examined shows no bacteria. (p. 42)

And this from one who confesses to being a "pagan"! Rama who is more truly a pagan has heard such things but has not seen them himself, he observes, for his preoccupations being different, his mind telescopes back to the times when "on these very banks the Upanishadic Sages, perhaps four, five or six thousand years ago, had discussed the roots of human understanding. And Yajnyavalkya had said to Maithreyi, 'For whose sake, verily, does a husband love his wife. Not for the sake of his wife, but verily for the sake of the self in her'." (pp. 25-6) If the past can transmit so much wisdom, the present can do no less. Talking of the prostitutes of Benares, Rama can reflect on the futility of it all and say, "when you see so many limbs go purring and bursting on the ghats by the Ganges, how can limos have any meaning?" (p.14)

Even so natural a phenomenon as the mingling of the Brahmaputra with the Ganga, reminds Rama of an ancient truth. He finds self-unconsciously murmuring to himself:

> Duality is anti-Indian; the non-
> dual affirms the truth. (p. 43)

It is somewhere in the mountain stillness of Hardwar he feels a new knowledge, an *absence,* and so looks up to the mountains for an answer. The Himalaya which was like Lord Shiva himself made "the peasant and the Brahmin feel big, not with any earthly ambition, but with the bigness, the stature of the impersonal, the stature of one who knows the nature of his deepest sleep". (p. 44) This is the way Raja Rao with his predilection for a transcending metaphysics makes use of time-honoured associations and invests even physical topography with a spiritual dimension. Yet it is interesting to note how he juxtaposes the spiritual and the temporal in offering side by side the description of the timeless Ganga and that of the silk shops and the bangle shops of Benares which makes us realize that here is a novelist who tries to recover for us the ancient Indian ideal of combining the *iha* with the *para.*

If the whole Section on Benares is an eloquent testimony to the vitality of a living tradition that has made the present meaningful and enriching, that dealing with Saroja's marriage is a splendid reiteration of the novelist's faith in traditional values that have sustained Indian society through the ages. It is refreshing to note that even in a novel with a strong penchant for the transcendental, adequate attention is paid to the preservation of family bonds that have been the chief integrating force in Indian society. In fact, such sanctity is attached to them by Rama himself that his sense of belonging to his family seems to extend even beyond death:

> "Living in the intimacy of my own family....
> gave a feeling of complex oneness, from which
> one could never get out save by death, and even
> after that one could get into it again in the
> next life, and so on till the wheel of existence
> were ended". (p. 280)

Rama who lives so far away can still be of help to his family imply by writing to them and going to them every two or three years so that the children feel protected and know there is one whom they have to obey! Rama comes all the way from France to India to attend his sister's wedding, for he, her elder brother, was also the head of the family following his father's death and it was but proper that he came home to give away his sister in marriage. Even as he lands at the Bombay airport he finds himself uttering the *Gayathri mantra,* something that had become a part of his life for twenty years. Standing on Indian soil he longs to see the India of his "inner being", the India of "Brahma and Prajapathi; of Varuna, Mithra and Aryaman; of India, of Krishna, Shiva and Parvathi; of Rama, Harischandra and Yajnyavalkya; (p. 248), for this India was a "continuity" that he felt not in time but in space standing like a cloud over a plain whose waters have perennially "fertilized our minds and hearts". (p. 248) Not being hemmed in by time, they are ever present, we gather.

It is perhaps in this sense that India is "outside history", says Ramaswamy, and it is this India that he cherishes in his heart and his creator celebrates in the novel. The wedding itself is a masterpiece of enactment, a marvellous recreation of the pomp and splendour of an Indian marriage. Women in rustling silks, flashing their gold belts and diamond nose rings; playing, screeching children; piping music, the smell of rose and attar, jasmine and coconut and betelnut complete the picture. The rituals like the *Saptapadi* are performed in a way which suggests, the essential India has not changed nor for that matter when the *tali* is tied round the bride's neck and she looks "a Lakshmi". This concept of auspiciousness is quite pervasive in the novel, as though Raja Rao is continuing Mammata's tradition which believed: "Poetry is a cessation of the inauspicious". The wedding is important not merely in its fidelity to external details, but also from the point of view of what it does and means to a girl in a Hindu household. Saroja's reluctance to marry Subramanya Sastri is made quite explicit in the novel. Driven to frustration and despair over it she compares herself to a cloth thrown to the *dhobi* on Saturday mornings. She even wishes she were a European woman, for then she could have enjoyed more freedom. But the same girl turns completely different once the marriage hour draws close—goes to her brother and says:

> Brother, bless me. I need only
> your tender hands, your firm
> protective hands over my head. (p. 273)

Later she even assures him:

> Brother I shall but bring a
> fair name to the household
> Do not worry. (p. 273)

What deep maturity had come into her young face, what responsibility sat on her young shoulders now, Rama marvels.

Various are the ways in which these imperishable values are brought home to us. Raja Rao cannot merely capture our folk wisdom but convey it too in peasant idiom, in the very tone of its voice when he makes Little Mother say, "To learn English is easy, but to say Rama, Krishna, it takes a hundred lives". Hence, it is that the story of Sri Rama which highlights the importance of religion in the lives of ordinary people falls into its place in the novel. This is how Raja Rao wins attention and respect to even humble people who are after all the more trusted guardians of a spiritual culture than the educated, for history has shown how the deepest and the most abiding values have come down to us through them. Different are the ways Ramaswamy's Indianness manifests itself. Such is the catholicity of his outlook shaped largely, no doubt, by his religion that he can look upon Mother Rhone as "sister to Ganga", the Mediterranean as an "Indian sea", a "Brahmanic ocean"—"green as a silken sari" (p. 246) with a "human richness that no ocean can give" (p. 60); Paris not a city, but "an area in oneself, a concorde in one's being" and "feel" England in his "bones and breath". Indeed, such is his involvement with Cambridge he can with rare feeling and insight describe King's Chapel as "not made by workmen but by the prayer of pilgrims"; colleges built "not by the donations of noblemen and kings" but by the "leap of light within" (p. 170). Generosity cannot go farther when he even accepts Madeleine in the belief that all "difference is self-created". (p. 22) He kneels down too before her gods in the affirmation, "to wed a woman is to wed her god". Indeed for a man who could create his Benares anywhere he lived, the gods are "neither Hindu nor Greek; being creations of your own mind they behaved as you made them—if Shiva was what I wanted, Shiva himself would come to the Durance". (p. 56)

Superstition too has its part in one's life, Raja Rao seems to believe, for when the news of Rama's father's illness reaches him and he has to go home, he almost feels that if she came "father could not die, he would not die. How, when the first daughter-in-law came home, could the father die? (p. 58) Interestingly this father had 'disliked' Rama's marriage, chiefly because, Rama thinks, his wife "could not sing at an *Arathi*". (p. 19) So deep is his Indian sensibility that he involuntarily mutters to himself:

> Auspicious, so auspicious—with *kumkum*,
> coconut and *choli*-piece, bangles on the
> arm, the necklace of black beads is life. (p. 58)

But the absence of it is implicitly Madeleine. Savithri symbolizes to Rama all that Madeleine does not. This Cambridge undergraduate who smokes like a chimney and dances to a barbarian jazz, yet wears a broad *kumkum* on her face has a deep knowledge of Bhartrihari and the Mira tradition, sings *Murare* to Rama and says "I've known my Lord for a thousand lives, from *Janam* to *Janam* have I known my *Krishna...*" (p. 214). In fact so thin is the veneer of her Western Civilization that it can be removed with a "*babul* thorn", says Rama confidently. Her very name with all its rich, complex associations gathered from the Vedic times to the present—when Aurobindo immortalizes her as a Symbol of Knowledge—could be a deliberate choice not without significance. The coronation of the Queen in the end is the coronation of the feminine principle which Savithri represents—an aspect of the Absolute. On seeing her even Madeleine acknowledges: "It's three thousaneer of her Western Civilization that it can be removed with a "babul thorn", says Rama confidently. Her very name with all its rich, complex associations gathered from the Vedic times to the present—when Aurobindo immortalizes her as a Symbol of Knowledge could be a deliberate choice not without significance. The coronation of the Queen in the end is the coronation of the feminine principle which Savitri represents—an aspect of the Absolute. On seeing her even Madeleine acknowledges: It's three thousand years of civilization that produces a thing like her." (p. 144). It is natural that the toe-rings (Little Mother's parting gift to Rama), used symbolically by the novelist, I should be the precise size for her. For Madeleine they would have been too big. (p. 215).

After this ritual marriage, it does not really matter whom Savithri marries. Even stump Pratap would do. She would obey him as the plane obeys the radar, it is her *dharma*. To disobey it is to give "pain to the infinite sky". (p. 369) Paradoxically all marriages in the novel prove to be failures—whether of Rama and Madeleine, Georges and Catherine, Oncle Charles and Tante Zoubie, Subramanya Sastri and Saroja or Pratap and Savithri, for all marriages have been imperfect, not having realized the truth:

> You can marry when you are one.
> That is, you can marry when
> there is no one to marry
> another. The real marriage is
> like 00, not like 010. When
> the ego is dead is marriage true. (p. 276)

But how one can transcend one's ego-centric predicament becomes Rama's obsession after the breakdown of his marriage with Madeleine. He realiies in the extremity of his crisis that a Guru is what be needs and longs to go to Travancore, for he has nowhere else to go now, "no home, no temple, no city, no climate, no age". (p. 407). His passionate longing not for God, a rounded object but a Guru who can vouchsafe to him the vision of Truth, the gift that Yagnyavalkya made to Maithreyi; "the gift Govinda made to Sri Sankara" (p. 408) so long ago, is not a simple expression of the traditional faith in the indispensability of a Guru, but an artist's way of making an ancient ideal an everpresent reality. Rama's speculation, "There must be a way out, Lord a way out of this circle of life" (p. 236) which echoes the deepest aspiration of the soul in the Indian context, is also a fitting finale to a novel which concerned itself with knowing what this pilgrimage was all about.

Raja Rao has made available to us all this wisdom largely through the fictional mode, largely because as Prof. C.D. Narasimhaiah has pointed out there are occasions when all that philosophy and metaphysics fail to get integrated into the texture of the novel and stand out as unassimilated pieces of abstruse philosophy. Barring this limitation, one might say that here is a novel which has made India real not only to the European but to the Indian as well. Of its author one might say here is a writer who has redeemed our prestige by reclaiming a valuable and sizable portion of the past. If the canons of Sanskrit literary criticism which were laid down chiefly in relation to poetry and drama were to be extended to the novel form as well rather a late-comer in Indian literature), one might posit that here is a novel which meets the requirements of some of the major ancient Sanskrit rhetoricians with their insistence on *rasa, guna, dhvani, vakrōkti, auchitya* and *Shantha.* The profundity of the theme and the way it is worked out by the novelist sets the entire critical process in operation beginning from *hṛdayasamvada* to *tanmayibhavana* to *rasanubhava* ensuring not merely supreme satisfaction for the reader but also his enlightenment. To the extent the novel helps the reader in the understanding of *satya* and *mithya* (illusion and reality, the Serpent and the Rope), if fulfils one of the chief obligations of a good *kāvya,* namely, a *prayōjana* and a *purushartha.*

12

Towards a Viable Aesthetics for Indian Literature in English

R.S. Pathak

Ever since its inception, Indian Writing in English has grown steadily in bulk, variety and maturity. As Mulkraj Anand points out, it has come to stay as part of world literature. For quite some time, Indian Writing in English was considered as a degenerated offshoot of English literature. "I am tempted to say, in fact", wrote Gokak, "that Indo-Anglian literature is a hothouse plant rather than one that has sprung from the soil and sprouted and burgeoned in the open air".[1] It would be, however, incorrect to call Indian literature in English "a hothouse plant". It is a genuine specimen of literature produced by Indians and, like literatures written in Indian languages, is a legitimate expression of the joys and sorrows, problems and plights, yearnings and aspirations of Indian people. It is "but one of the voices in which India speaks".[2] Indian literature in English has been described, on account of its medium, as 'a Janus-faced literature" born of "a cross-fertilization of two faithful cultures", *i.e.*, Indian and European.[3] The contact with the Western mind stirred the soul of India and, ultimately, ushered in the Renaissance of the nineteenth century, which is, said to be "the greatest gift of the English" to India.[4] An intellectual climate, pregnant with unforeseen possibilities, transformed the general outlook of the educated Indians. Macaulay's untiring efforts to create a class of persons who would be "Indian in blood and colour but English in taste, in opinion, in morals and intellect",[5] resulted in the "diminant minority"[6] of Indian society which can be credited with the inception of Indian literature in English.

Indian literature in English is now more than a century and a half old. The first known volume of poems written in English by an Indian was Henry Derozio's *Poems*, which was brought out in 1827. The first novel in English by an Indian, Bankim Chandra Chatterjee's *Rajmohan's Wife,* was published in 1864. Since then Indian writers have made considerable contribution in the fields of poetry and fiction. Initially, however, Indian literature was not taken seriously. It was dubbed by Gordon Bottomly as "Matthew Arnold in a *saree*". Some others described it as "Shakuntala in skirts", implying that this literature was an incompatible union of diverse elements taken from Indian and Western sources. Even certain Indians were not very optimistic about the future of this literature. Uma Parameshwaran, for example, would "set A.D. 2000 as the dirge date for Indo-English literature". As compared to India's classical and vernacular literatures, she adds, Indian literature in English appears "immature and insignificant" and its future seems to be "bleak, offering little but the prospect of extinction".[7] Time has already proved such prophecies wrong. Indian literature in English, notwithstanding all its limitations, has taken impressive strides especially in the spheres of fiction and poetry and has emerged as an acceptable body of writings of acknowledged worth. It has been flourishing even after Independence more successfully than it did before. The fact that it has been studied and subjected to serious appraisal in and outside the country is a proof that it has merits other than those of novelty and exoticism.

The considerable amount of literature written in English by Indian authors has created enormous problems of its evaluation. In the Preface to the Second Edition of his work, *Indian Writing in English,* K.R. Srinivasa Iyengar has pointed out that literary criticism is a "tricky and subjective" business which "calls for the total knowledge, integrity and humility".[8] The critical response to Indian literature in English has to perform all the more onerous task. On the whole, Indian critics have not done justice to this literature, and Indian literature in English has been negotiating an uneasy passage between the Indian's diffidence and the Englishman's indifference. What Gokak said about the earlier Indian Professor of English is also applicable to most Indian critics in English: "He moved like a 'ship of desert', quenching his thirst with the holy waters that he had stored within himself from native springs during his stay at Oxford, Cambridge or London. . . . He measured all literary expression by the English yardstick and found no literary excellence outside English masterpieces".[9] It is highly improper to treat Indian literature in English as a minor tributary of English literature. Some critics have tried to evaluate Indian literature written in English on the basis of Western norms. What is still worse is some others' tendency to emulate the Western world in its diatribe against Indian thought and sensibility and their expression in literature. Most critics are caught in a strange predicament. In a review Shyam Ratna Gupta drew our attention to "an ambivalent trend, a kind of schizophrenic trait or alienation of literary criticism in India".[10] This view may look somewhat exaggerated, but it is based on an acknowledged fact. Indian English literary criticism, as M.K. Naik suggests, has a "woefully stunted look" and although Indian literature is more than a century and a half old, 'it is a sad fact that its total contribution in the field of literary criticism still continues to be extremely meagre".[11] The chief reason for this unsatisfactory state of affairs has been the derivative and imitative nature of Indian criticism. It has been sedulously aping standard practices of Western critical schools and their precepts. This Anglo-mania has been the bane of all our thinking. Other Indian literatures also had to suffer on account of this unfortunate tendency, which made their objective evaluation in accordance with Indian norms practically impossible.[12] And, as Naik aptly maintains, "The peril involved in judging our literature exclusively by Western norm, cannot. . . be over-emphasized" because "our aesthetic cannot be divorced from our roots".[13] An attempt has been made in the present paper to consider the issue in detail and suggest a viable aesthetic for a proper evaluation of Indian literature in English.

II

Forgetting that Indian literature in English is deeply rooted in a native tradition, most of the critics sought its resources and insights in English literary tradition. They failed to recognize the fact that Indian literature is neither a part nor an extension of English literature. In general, attempts to examine Indian literature in English on the basis of the norms and patterns of models belonging to a different soil and governed by a different ethos have miserably failed. An analysis of the remarks on certain well-known Indian masterpieces will make it clear how futile and lopsided such appraisals can at times be. Raja Rao's novel, the *Serpent and the Rope,* is a remarkable achievement in Indian literature in English. In his critique of the novel, David McCutchion asked: "Is this a novel at all?. . . All the central concerns of the Western novel are absent —social relations, psychological motivation, characterization, judgement, a passion for the concrete".[14] The *Time's* reviewer also felt uneasy on account of "the Eastern profundities that sprinkle the book like sacred coconut in the curry" and, quoting from the novel, wittily added: "Sentences are nothing but words, So are novels."[15] These remarks coming from Western critics are not so surprising as the following comment from an Indian reviewer, who regarded the novel as "a cleverly contrived sham"— "all slightly sickening" and littered with "pseudo-Lawrencian metaphysical attitudinisations, based on bogus mysticism".[16] An extensive damage has already been done by opinions like the ones given above. The *Serpent and the Rope* is nothing less than Raja Rao's "spiritual autobiography."[17] As the novelist himself told an interviewer, "Everything one writes is autobiographical. But it is a metaphysical novel."[18] The epigraph given in the beginning of the novel clearly indicates the nature of its theme and its Vedantic orientation.[19] There are at least half a dozen, references to Yājñavalkya in the novel and quite a few to Sankarāchārya and his philosophy. At each step the novel bears resemblances to *Purānas* and *Upaniṣads,* and the language itself is reminiscent of Sanskrit constructions. It is hardly fair to evaluate it on the basis of Western models of the novel.

Another work which has suffered at the hands of critics is *All About H. Hallerr.* Despite its thematic complexity and technical darings, it makes a delightful reading. It was nevertheless dismissed by Meenakshi Mukherjee as "merely a spoof—a tract against imposter ascetics which has sometimes been regarded with undue seriousness".[20] It may be noticed that when Desani's book appeared in 1948, it was greeted with rare enthusiasm by distinguished critics like T.S. Eliot. "In all my experience", Eliot commented, "I have not met with anything like it. It is amazing that anyone should be able to sustain a piece of work in this style and tempo of such length."[21] In his introduction to the novel, Anthony Burgess described it as "a wonderfully heartening book".[22] Although the narrative manner of *H. Hatterr* seems to be Western and its technique uses surrealistic devices, its organizational principle bears unmistakable affinities with that of the *Panchatantra*—especially its reiteration of certain themes and motifs and employment of the chain-story throughout. Desani has called the novel a "gesture", by which he means "a means of self-expression", adding that "Melodramatic *gestures* against public security are a common form of self-expression in the East".[23] The novel, says Desani, resulted from provocation from all kinds of solemnity,[24] yet it had serious intentions. The novelist would like us to believe that Hatterr does "include in his feelings the attraction for the Unknown, the Mysterious and the desire to submit to the authority of an Overlord. ... He has a direct realisation of God. He has a religious experience by the Ganges, in spite of what he himself says about it".[25] These facts should be taken into account before passing any judgement on Desani's novel. He called it a "sacred" work and, anticipating criticisms of the novel, remarked: "If a professional book-reviewer or an aspiring critic cannot see this, he or she is deficient."[26] An evaluation of such a work in accordance with Western models is not likely to take us very far.

The treatment accorded to Indian poets in English has been still worse. The Indian poets who were steeped in indigenous traditions, either poetic or philosophical, never received a fair deal at the hands of those critics who judged their work on the basis of Western yard-sticks adopted by them. A few examples will suffice. Sri Aurobindo's poetry has been denigrated for what the editors of the first notable anthology of Indian English poetry called the "greasy, weak-spined and purple adjectived 'spiritual' poetry" and its "rubbery sentiments".[27] Aurobindo's poetry is mystical in nature, and his *Savitri* is a deeply philosophical epic in Hindu tradition. Some Indian poet-critics seem to have denounced his work to justify their own practice. Nissim Ezekiel, for example, remarks that "anyone who thinks highly of Sri Aurobindo as a poet has no feeling for the English language".[28] Adil Jussawalla found *Savitri* "one vast onion of a poem... unwinding like an interminable *sari*"[29] – *Draupadi ki chir*. Keki N. Daruwalla "read only one poem each by Toru Dutt and Sri Aurobindo" and had "no intention of reading any more".[30] Nevertheless he has the audacity to condemn Sri Aurobindo's poetry. He says: "No other Indian poet was half as bad, none so nebulous or verbose, or who so thoroughly confused the inflated with the sublime".[31] Such verdicts speak of a colossal incompetence to respond to poetry like Aurobindo's on the part of these critics. They remind us of the complaint of the *Times Literary Supplement* about his want of music. Sri Aurobindo is one of the greatest poets ever produced by this country. He writes on elevated themes in an elevated style. In the very first chapter of *The Life Divine* he writes: "All problems of existence are essentially problems of harmony", and only a poet like him could unravel it. To use the poet's words about himself, he "explores the ceaseless miracle of himself". He sees poetry as a rhythmic voyage of self-discovery. It is another name for that creative energy which makes one aware of one's immense possibilities. Only a responsive person with a trained sensibility can really enjoy and evaluate Sri Aurobindo's poetry.

Daruwalla is not alone in denouncing Toru Dutt's "infantile manner".[32] In the short period that she lived, she produced only two volumes of poems, which failed to receive adequate critical attention. As C.D. Narasimhaiah points out, "The critic's ineptitude or ignorance of her work or his prejudic against the work of a mere girl and a colonial to boot may have operated in Toru Dutt not getting praise".[33] Her poetry is generally treated as the creation of a sick young woman who, under the influence of Shelley, Keats and Walter Scott, tried to portray beauty and sweetness in tantalizing colours.[34] Besides French literature, she had read sanskrit literature with great interest, and a sensitive and perceptive reader of her poetry will find proofs of her familiarity with the *Ramāyana*, the *Mahābhārata*, the *Visn.purān.a*, the *Śrimadbhāgvatpurāṇa* and *Abhijnānaśākuntalam* besides the echoes of English literature of the Romantic Revival.

Sarojini Naidu was also said to have been "extensively and formatively influenced by English Romantic poets".[35] The sadness and melancholy in her poetry is believed to contain distinct echoes of the poetry of Coleridge, Shelley, Tennyson and Swinburne.[36] It is also maintained that "Her love lyrics may well pass for the outpourings of a more passionate Elizabeth Barrett Browning".[37] Some modern poet-critics have been unduly critical of her poetry. Nissim Ezekiel, for example, takes her to task for knowing nothing of the literary revolution taking place in English poetry in 1920s.[38] To P. Lal, her poetry is "clumsy, incongruous and sentimental" and represents the last phase of "Indo-Anglian romanticism" which ended with her, "leaving fire-flies to dance through the neem".[39] Sarojini Naidu's poetry has thus been denigrated for being too close to English Romantic poetry and also for not keeping pace with the contemporary trends in British poetry.

Much of the poetry written by Indian poets in English, including that of Rabindranath Tagore, has been downgraded chiefly on account of its romantic sentimentality and stylized expressions of effusive emotions couched in a decorative language. The charges levelled against most Indian poets in English are made without taking into consideration the traditional patterns of Indian life and outlook and their expression in their poetry. The conventions of Indian poetry in English have their roots in the cultural ethos of the country and its people. Indians are typically sentimental (in the good sense) people. Their literature, right from the earliest times, abounds in unrestrained expressions of sentiments. On the whole, it has laid tremendous emphasis on ornamentation. According to Indian poeticians, beauty and embellishments are synonymous. "Beauty is Embellishment", maintained Vamana, for example.[40] Kuntaka defined Poetry as "embellished word and meaning *Sālaṅkṛta śabdārtha* and stated that "the embellishment and the embellished. . . together constitute poetry".[41] According to *the Agnipurāṇa,* "Poetry devoid of figures of sense is like a widow".[42] A later rhetorician Jayadeva categorically maintains: "One who asserts that there can be poetry without figures of speech is capable of saying that there can be fire without 'heat."[43] Lastly, the variety and colourfulness, decorativeness and lushness of Indian literature in English is, in fact, an expression of the variety and colourfulness of the physical and cultural landscape of the country.

It will therefore be unfair to evaluate Indian poetry in English on the basis of Western models. A native aesthetics is the most imperative need of the day. The critics who keep on aping Western modes can be called *(apropos* Ezekiel) "seducers of experience". It may be noted that some practising Indian poets themselves are not unaware of the problem. O.P. Bhatnagar, who has thought deeply on this issue, has something very significant to say on this issue. "Indian poetry in English has to be Indian," he maintains; it can subsist only by drawing "its sustenance from its surroundings".[44] He pleads for a "new aesthetics", maintaining that "the native aesthetics is very much the need of the hour".[45] Bhatnagar urges Indian writers to cast off the British slavery and naturalize the English language to suit Indian needs, ethos and sensibility. According to him, "set and stereotyped" modes and patterns will not serve any real purpose. He is in favour of granting perfect freedom to the poet. He says: "...if English is to be kept a continuing medium of expression in India, it must be bent to Indian aesthetics and image-making, however quaint it may be, than hoist a victory flag on a lost ship".[46] Bhatnagar's pronouncements clearly affirm the need of a native aesthetics and also the right of Indian writers to make use of the language and imagery rooted in Indian ethos.

III

There have been some critics who tried to carve out a passage for themselves, in spite of various problems. Writings like those of C. Narayan Menon, S.C. Sengupta, Nalini Kant Gupta, CD. Narasimhaiah, V.K. Gokak,K.R. Srinivasa Iyengar, Sisir Ghosh, V.Y. Kantak, S. Nagarajan, G.S. Amur and Krishna Rayan have shown that it is possible for Indian critics to think originally on critical matters. Commenting upon the existing state of affairs, Gokak wrote: "It is not only possible, but inevitable that there should grow up, in course of time, an Indian school of criticism, as applied to English literature. . .".[47] This is however, yet to take place. Even in the assessment of Indian literature in English, we have not become self-reliant as yet. Tom between conflicting demands of Indian poetics and Western critical theory, Indian scholars continue to have an ambivalent attitude. With a few honourable exceptions, no Indian critic has ever been fully aware of his critical heritage. It has rightly been said that "In a sense, the history of twentieth century Indian critical theory is nothing but a chain of fresh beginnings. Almost every critic seems to have played the role of a pioneer, the needle of whose compass points towards an unrelated critical tradition, distant in time. . . or in culture-space. . ." .[48] What is still worse is their reluctance to forge links with their own tradition.

The modern Indian, Patankar argues, has completely lost his roots in the ancient tradition and has adopted since "an elitist pseudo-culture which has permanently condemned him to second rateness". Modern Indian critics, he adds, cannot derive any benefit out of Indian poetics, which, for the most part, is "like an ancient piece of architecture, meant to be looked at and not to be lived in". Patankar further remarks: "The Sanskrit theory cannot be fruitfully used for judging modern works because it would be very arbitrary to use it when it is not demanded by the content of modern works and then we find that the modern conceptual framework is adequate and does not need to be changed. The second reason for not re-introducing the Sanskritist theory is that there is no provision in it for certain evaluative principles which are demanded by modern literary works."[49] There is no substance in Patankar's theory. Even after Sanskrit ceased to be extensively used, its literary norms continued to guide the practice of drama and poetry. Like ancient Indian philosophy, Indian aesthetic thought continues to have vitality and validity.

Recent studies on comparative poetics[50] have proved beyond any pale of doubt that in certain significant respects Indian approach is far superior to the Western tradition.[51] Few people will endorse today the view of Wilson who remarked that "Indian criticism ... has always been in its infancy. It never learned to connect causes and effects. . . It never became either poetical or philosophical. Technicalities were the only objects within its comprehension."[52] Indian aestheticians were really aware of some of the crucial problems pertaining to poetry and poetic language, and their postulates are, by and large, amazingly modern. Although Indian scholars did not use the terminology of modern criticism, linguistics and stylistics, their approach in many respects is more striking than that of most Western critics. "It cannot be maintained", remarks De, "that these theorists have said the last word on the subject, or said it [always] clearly or consistently; but they have certainly dealt with some of the fundamental aspects very ably."[53] Certain issues contained in the form of germs were to be taken up for fuller treatment by Western critics and philosophers in modern times.

It is undoubtedly true that the later Indian poetics gets bogged down to purely rhetorical preoccupations. It presents grave obstacles to communication, for its treatises are written in terse and difficult style. The texts bristle with linguistic technicalities and are at places obscure. Their wealth of details, mystical dross, quaint terminology and abstruse discussions would create insuperable barriers to readers who are not well-versed in Sanskrit and have not been properly initiated to this type of study. A careful study of Indian poetics, however, after weeding out inessential details, scholastic niceties, worn-out assertions and unnecessary technicalities enmeshed in a dense, opaque diction, will reveal profound foundations of Indian views on various aspects of literary activity. Taken as a whole, Indian poetics is more profound than a system of rhetoric and in its highest reach soars into aesthetics and linguistic philosophy. The discipline of poetics, as it developed in India, is full of logical, philosophical, linguistic, epistemological and metaphysical problems, and a systematic use of the insights provided by it is most likely to unfold more effective ways of analysing Indian literatures including Indian literature in English. In fact, as Edwin Gerow suggests, "Certain contemporary literary and cultural modes of expression, notably the novel and the Indian film, can better be understood in their aesthetic impact by reference to the well-developed, indigenous classical traditions of aesthetic criticism; they can be better understood, that is, than often are when treated primarily as derivative responses to, and in the context of, recent Western literary and cultural modes."[54]

No system of aesthetic inquiry is foolproof and valid for all ages and in all places. Most of the seminal conclusions of Indian poetics were arrived at before the end of eleventh century, when some of the modern literary forms were not even born. However, most of the charges levelled against Indian poetics are, in general, baseless. One of the greatest limitations of it, according to De, is "its almost total disinterest in the poetic personality by which a work of art attains its particular shape and individual character".[55] Self-expression has not been included by Mammata (*Kāvyaprakāsa* 1.2) in his list of the purposes for which poetry is composed. In the same breath, however, De admits that scattered evidences go to prove that Indian thinkers were not unaware of the problem of individualized expression, "but they either regarded it to be outside their scope or did not attack it in its entirety". Indian tradition, it is true, does not attach so much importance to the individual *(vyaṣti)* as to the whole community *(samaṣti).* Nevertheless scholars like Bhāmaha Tauta, Kuntaka and Abhinava Gupta were fully cognizant of the individualistic aspect of poetic creation. Good poetry can be created, said Bhamaha, only by rare persons endowed with intuition and imagination.[56] Anandavardhana maintained that there is no end to poetic individuations.[57] It was Kuntaka who underscored the important part played by the individual power of the poet. To him, poetic function itself is poetry.[58] He maintains that the entire poetic creation is essentially an act of imagination on the part of the poet and that it finds a befitting means of self-expression in an oblique mode.[59] Kuntaka's classification of Styles *(ritis)* is also based on the temperamental differences of poets themselves.[60] This proves that Indian theoreticians were conversant with the significance of "poetic function" *(kavi karma),* which De explained as "the organic expressive activity of poetic intuition".[61]

It is also said that Indian poetics lacks in textual criticism.[62] It is to the credit of Indian literary theoreticians that they did not develop theories of literature that would apply only to certain forms of literature. Theirs is a truly general theory free of external considerations. Their works contain theoretical formulations based on their experience and familiarity with their predecessors' and contemporaries' creative works; they did not aim at giving detailed textual criticism. Kuntaka's work nevertheless contains perceptive textual analyses of some major works. Moreover, there has been an excellent tradition of commentaries *(tikās)* and commentators like Mallinatha who gave the ablest specimens of textual criticism besides explaining grammatical peculiarities of the text. As theorists of literature, Indian aestheticians remain far superior to their Western counterpart. A careful perusal of Indian poetics, as C.D. Narasimhaiah points out, will prove to anyone "not merely the great advances made by Indian aesthetics in relation to Aristotle but its amazing modernity and unparalleled adequacy in the midst of the chaos of modern critical theories".[63] Only Coleridge, amongst English critics, has made consistent efforts to come out with theoretical pronouncements, but even he does not fare well when compared to Abhinavagupta.[64] It may be instructive to remember in this context what Conrad Aiken has to say of Western criticism (which our critics have blindly followed): "What literature of criticism we have in English—and it is *slight,* for the Anglo-Saxon is not by nature a good critic—is littered with *sham jewels* of sort, which have a pleasant gleam, but *give little light.* And this *deplorable vagueness,* this almost total *lack of any system or scale of values ...*". [65]

The Sanskrit critic, says Naik, is not interested in the social and political conditions affecting a creative work and are "generally too reverential and permit critical evaluation and encourage independence of thinking".[66] Although Indian poetic theories do not conform to the narrow grooves of modern critical approaches, the comprehensiveness of their grasp can hardly be doubted. Even lexicographers like Amarasinha were not oblivious of the contemporary social ethos. They did not pay an excessive attention to socio-political conditions simply because doing so was beyond their immediate concern. As for Indian aestheticians' being "too reverential", it should be enough to point out that even the *kavikulaguru* (poets' poet) Kālidāsa is not spared for his excesses and shortcomings. The Indian tradition did respect ancients *(prācināh)* but it also permitted to criticize, if necessary, even one's own teacher *(doṣāḥ vācī guror api).*

Indian aestheticians' works are characterized by a remarkable analytical rigour. Some scholars, however, are not prepared to allow them the right to linguistic orientation and scientific rigour. According to De, for example, these works are no better than textbooks and manuals: "Sanskrit poetics purportedly engaged in solving the poetic riddle delighted, rather, in the pleasure of abstracted thought and formal calculation. Its method is suitable for the study of botany or zoology, but affords hardly any assistance for the understanding of aesthetic facts or principles. While it has an intuitive realization of the true nature of poetry, it allowed its intellectual prepossession to confine itself to the formulation of pedagogic expedients or normative abstractions. It is like studying the index of a book than the book itself."[67] Such remarks originate from an incomprehension of the basic aims and methods of Indian poetics. They tend to deny the "verbal and formal" character of these treatises.[68] It is worth remembering at this point that even some West or theoreticians were highly impressed by Indian scholars' incisive perception and analytical wisdom. Coleridge, for example, named India as one of the four countries where, he thought, the analysis of the mind had reached its zenith while experimental research was still in its infancy in the West.[69] Two years of study of Sanskrit classics, Buddhistic texts, Patanjali's metaphysics left T.S. Eliot "in a state of enlightened mystification" and led him to conclude that "the Indian philosophers . . . make most of the great European philosophers look like schoolboys".[70] It is really unfortunate that Indian approach to literature has been denigrated on the grounds on which it has been commended in the Western world.

Despite certain limitations of Indian poetics, its positive qualities should not go unacknowledged. Indians were probably the first to assert the autonomous status of art. As Raneiro Gnoli remarks, "The conception of art as an activity and an independent spiritual experience, freed of practical interest which the intuition of Kant perceived for the West, was already in Tenth Century India an object of study and controversy."[71] Even a more significant contribution of Indian aestheticians is their detailed treatment of aesthetic emotions. Their analysis is more plausible and has a definite advantage over their delineation by Western critics.

In this connection Susanne Langer has the following observation to make: "The Hindu critics understand very much better than their Western colleagues the various aspects of emotion in the theatre which our writers banefully confuse; the feelings experienced by the actor, those experienced by the spectators, those presented as under-gone by the characters in the play and finally the feeling that studies in the play—the vital feeling of the piece."[72] Moreover, Indian poetics has emphasized the role of a responsive reader in the proper appreciation of literature in a better way than it has been done in the traditional Western criticism. The great Indian aesthetician Ānandavardhana forcefully maintained that the animating principle of poetry resides in the meaning that can capture the heart of connoisseurs.[73] The process of enjoyment of poetry has been described by him as comprising three processes: The connoisseur's mind first becomes attuned to the emotional situation portrayed *(hṛdaya-saṁvāda);* it is then absorbed in its portrayal *(tanmayībhavana);* and, finally, his absorption results in the aesthetic enjoyment *(rasānubhava).*[74] The concept of *sahṛdaya,* as developed by Abhinava Gupta, "contains the most satisfactory theory of literary appeal."[75] In all these respects Indian poetics has a definite edge over Western criticism.

IV

The greatest need of the hour is to re-examine the native aesthetic tradition and salvage whatcan be useful from Indian poetics. This is what scholars like Hiriyanna, C.D. Narasimhaiah, G.S. Amur, K. Krishnamoorthy and some others have tried to do. However, certain other critics of Indian literature in English, who are otherwise amongst the best, have brushed aside the proposal to revive Indian poetics. This would be, according to them, nothing but "fake patriotism"[76] and "chauvinism".[77] They are of the view that our critic has no option but to be "conversant with the Western standards of criticism and aesthetic doctrines and use his knowledge of them to fertilize his own tradition".[78] There is no harm in familiarizing oneself with Western critical tradition, but accepting it in a wholesale way and rejecting our own critical heritage lock, stock and barrel would be disastrous. Some of our leading scholars like Sri Aurobindo and A.K. Coomaraswamy synthesised the ancient Indian poetics with the Western critical theories and produced excellent results. As Nehru points out, the Indian Renaissance's impact on India was "twofold: she looked to the West and, at the same time, she looked at herself and her own past".[79] An acquaintance with the Western critical tradition should help our critics re-discover their own aesthetic tradition and consolidate their response rather than carry them off their feet.

Any attempt to evolve an aesthetic for modern Indian literatures including Indian literature in English should thus be grounded on ancient tradition of literary appreciation. Indian theories and concepts such as *rasa* (aesthetic emotion), *dhvani* (suggestion), *vakrokti* (oblique expression), *auçitya* (propriety), *sādhāraṇikaraṇia* (universalisation) are definitely relevant even to the modern context. The key concepts, theories and terms from Indian poetics can be redefined to suit modern critical needs, eschewing their scholastic superfluities and hair-splitting divisions and sub-divisions. Bharata had mentioned only four figures, but by the time Appaya Dīkṣita wrote his *Kuvalayānanda* their number had risen to one hundred and twenty-five. The modern critic does not have to bother about twenty-five varieties of simile and ninety-six types of metaphors and ten thousand four hundred and four kinds of suggestion. In case there are certain gaps or loopholes in our tradition, we can depend upon Western critical theories and terms. The practice of a principled eclecticism in this respect will produce ideal results.

It may be noted that the necessity of a judicious synthesis of the Indian and European traditions has already been recognized by V.K. Gokak and others. But this synthesis is "yet to be realised in all its particulars".[80] Sri Aurobindo and Tagore thought in terms of a "universal literature" (Goethe had done the same). Literature, according to them, is an expression of the Universal Man. Its main purpose is, to use

Keats' terms, to take care of "eternal verities" and unfold "the vale of soul-making". This universality of reference may be profitably placed at the centre while studying literature. This approach will enable us to acquire a changed non-insular, humanistic critical perspective which will be, with its deep roots in Indian tradition of poetics, *bhāṣyas, purāṇas, Upaniṣads* and Tantric and Buddhistic dialectics, of considerable help. Despite all claims of modernity, Indian literature in English is deeply rooted in our own traditions. No other critical tool can be really helpful in our study and appreciation of what Sri Aurobindo calls "the expression of spiritual truth and experience of all kinds" in it.[81] Our critics also have to forge a new critical idiom and be in a position to understand and explicate various kinds of symbols, images and archetypes which the Indo-English writers draw from Indian sources. Any real contribution in this sphere can be made by them only when they develop an "inwardness" to the language and get "over its alien culture."[82] The key to solutions to most of their problems lies in their remembering what the *Gīta* (III.35) says: *sva dharme nidhanam śreyaḥ paradharmo bhayāvahaḥ*".

Notes and References

1. V.K Gokak, *English in India* (Bombay, 1964), p. 164.
2. K.R. Srinivasa Iyengar, *Indian Writing in English* (New Delhi, 1985), p. 3.
3. K.R. Srinivasa lyengar, "Indian Writing in English", in *Contemporary Indian Literature* (New Delhi, 1959), p. 35.
4. Sir Jadunath Sarkar, *India Through the Ages* (Calcutta, 1944), p. 52. This Renaissance, says Sri Aurobindo, was "the attempt of a reawakened national spirit to find new impulse of self-expression which shall give the spiritual force for a great reshaping and rebuilding": The *Renaissance in India* (Pondicherry, 1972), p. 397.
5. *The Miscellaneous Works of Thomas Babington Macaulay*, ed. Lady Trevelyan (London, 1907), XIX, pp. 192-93.
6. Nirad C. Chaudhuri, *The Continent of Circe* (Bombay, 1966),

p. 355.

7. *A Study of Representative Indo-English Novelists* (New Delhi, 1976), pp. 1-6.
8. *Indian Writing in English,* p. xi.
9. Gokak, *op. cit.,* p. 3.
10. *Indian and Foreign Review* (July 1, 1975), p. 24, quoted in Iyengar, *Indian Writing in English,* p. 774.
11. M.K. Naik, *Studies in Indian English Literature* (New Delhi, 1987), p. 158.
12. A.K. Warder comments: "The scholars who tried to supply information on Indian Literature applied whatever critical ideas they had picked up from their environment accordingly taking Western models as the only possible standard of good literature". *Indian Kavya Literature* I (Delhi, 1972), p. vii.
13. Naik, *Studies in Indian English Literature,* p. 165.
14. *Indian Writing in English* (Calcutta, 1969), p. 72.
15. *Times* (February 22, 1963), p. 54.
16. M.S. Prabhakar, "India in Dispute", *Encounter* (January, 1965), p. 95.
17. B.M. Razdan and 80 m P. Ranchan, "The Serpent and the Rope" 3, The *Illustrated Weekly of India* (April 10, 1966), p. 45.
18. Annie Brierre, "An Interview with Raja Rao", The *Illustrated Weekly of India* (March 10, 1963), p. 26.
19. The epigraph reads as follows: *rajvāṁ sarpo bhrāntikālina eva bhrānter nāśe naiva sarpo'pi tadvat.* Sri Sankaracharya, *Vivekacudamani* verse 197. (The rope is supposed to be the snake only so long as the mistake lasts and there is no more snake when the illusion has vanished.)
20. *Twice Born Fiction* (New Delhi, 1971), p. 110.
21. Peter Russell and Khushwant Singh (eds.), G. *V. Desani: A Consideration of All About H. Hatterr and Hall* (London, Amsterdam, 1952), Inner cover.
22. *All About H. Hatterr* (New Delhi, 1972), p. 11.
23. *Ibid.,* p. 12.
24. Desani remarked: "*Hatterr* ... was written when I was boisterous. All kinds of solemnity used to provoke me—from religion to

Shakespeare—and this is the chief reason for writing *Hatterr*". S.V. Vasudev, Interview with G.V. Desani, in P. Lal (ed.), *The Second Writers Workshop Literary Reader* (Calcutta, 1973), p. 25.

25. G.V. Desani, "Difficulties of Communicating an Oriental to a Western Audience", in C.D. Narasimhaiah (ed.), *Awakened Conscience* (New Delhi, 1978), p. 403.

26. *Ibid.*

27. P. Lal and K. Raghavendra Rao (eds.), *Modern Indo-Anglian Poetry: An Anthology* (New Delhi, 1959), pp. iii-v.

28. Nissim Ezekiel, "Replies to the Questionnaire", in P. Lal and Raghavendra Rao (eds.), *Modern Indo-Anglian Poetry: An Anthology and a Credo,* 2nd rev. ed. (Calcutta, 1971), p. 169.

29. Quoted in William Walsh, *Readings in Commonwealth Literature* (OUP, 1973), p. 76.

30. Lal & Rao (eds.), *op. cit.* (1971), p. 94.

31. *Two Decades of Indian Poetry, 1960-1980* (New Delhi, 1981), p. xv.

32. *Ibid.,* p. xiv.

33. *The Swan and the Eagle* (Simla, 1969), p. 25.

34. See Iyengar, *Indian Writing in English,* p. 59.

35. T.G. Prasad, "Sensuous Gloss: An Aspect of the Poetry of Sarojini Naidu", in H.M. Prasad (ed.), *Indian Poetry in English* (New Delhi, 1985), p. 90.

36. Amarnath Jha, *Sarojini Naidu: A Personal Homage* (Allahabad, 1949), p. 75.

37. P.E. Dustoor, *Sarojini Naidu* (Mysore, 1961), p. 12.

38. Nissim Ezekiel, Review of *The Feather of Dawn,* The *Sunday Standard* (February 11, 1962).

39. *Modern Indian Poetry in English* (Calcutta, 1969), p. xii.

40. *Saundaryatn alaṅkāraḥ; tadatiśayahetavastvalaṅkārāḥ. Kāvyālaṅkārasūtravṛtti* I.i.2; III.i.2.

41. *Alaṅkṛtir alaṅkāryam apoddhṛtya vivecyate/ tadupāyatayā tatrvaṁ sālaṅkārasya kāvyatā/Vakrokttivītta* 1.6.

42. *Agnipurāṇa* 344/2.

43. *Candrāloka* 1.8.

44. O.P. Bhatnagar, "New Dimensions in Indo-English Poetry",

Commonwealth Quarterly (1980), p. 11.

45. G.P. Baghmar, "Horizon of Reflection" (Interview with O.P. Bhatnagar), collected in G.P. Baghmar (ed.), The *Vision and the Voice* III (Nagpur, 1987).
46. O.P. Bhatnagar, "Future Directions: The Indian Poetry in English", in O.P. Bhatnagar (ed.), *Studies in Indian Poetry in English* (Jaipur, n.d.), p. 68.
47. Gokak, *op. cit.*, p. 144.
48. S.K. Desai and G.N. Devy, (eds.) *Critical Thaught* (New Delhi, 1987), p. viii.
49. R.B. Patankar, "Communication and Literature", *New Quest* 36 (1982), pp. 363-68; "The Three Alternatives", *The Literary Criterion* 19/1 (1984), pp. 51-3.
50. See, for example, C.D. Narasimhaiah (ed.), *Literary Criticism: European and Indian Tradition* (Mysore, 1965); G.B. Mohan, The *Response to Poetry* (New Delhi, 1968); Krishna Rayan, *Suggestion and Statement in Poetry* (London, 1972), *Text and Sub-Text* (New Delhi, 1987), Shrikrishna Mishra, *Coleridge and Abhinav Gupta* (Darbhanga, 1979); R.S. Pathak, *Oblique Poetry in Indian and Western Poetics* (New Delhi, 1988), *Vakrokti and Stylistic Concepts* (New Delhi, 1988), *Poetic and Non-Poetic Discourse* (New Delhi, 1988); M.S. Kushwaha (ed.), *Indian Poetics and Western Thought* (Lucknow, 1988).
51. See Thomas Munro, *Oriental Aesthetics* (Cleveland, 1965), pp. 74-5; Philip Rawson, "An Exalted Theory of Ornament: A Study in Indian Aesthetics", in H. Osborne (ed.), *Aesthetics in the Modern World* (London, 1968), pp. 222-23.
52. H.H. Wilson, *The Theatre of the Hindus* (Calcutta, 1955), p. 6.
53. S.K. De, *Sanskrit Poetics as a Study of Aesthetic* (Bombay, 1963), p. 51.
54. "The Persistence of Classical Aesthetic Categories in Contemporary Indian Literature", in Edward C. Dimock *et al.* (eds.), *The Literatures of India* (Chicago, 1979), p. 212.
55. De, *Sanskrit Poetics as a Study of Aesthetic,* p. 72.
56. *Kāvyaṁ tu jāyate jātu kaśyacit pratibhāvateḥ/Kāvyālaṅkāra* 1.5.
57. *Dhvanyāloka* I. 5-6.
58. *kaveḥ karma kāvyam. Vakroktijīvita,* ed. S.K De (Calcutta, 1961), p. 3.

59. *Rasasvabhāvālaṅkārāṇāṁ sarveṣāṁ kavikauśalameva jīvitam.Ibid.,* p. 146.
60. *Kavisvabhāvabhedani bandhanātvena kāvyaprasthānabhedāḥ sāmañjasatāṁ gāhate. Ibid.,* p. 46.
61. De, *Sanskrit Poetics as a Study of Aesthetic,* p. 30.
62. Some of these charges have been mentioned by M.K. Naik in his *Studies in Indian English Literature,* pp. 158-74.
63. Narasimhaiah (ed.), *Literary Criticism: European and Indian Traditions,* p. 6. cf. Bhayani: "Numerous views of R. Jacobson, J. Culler, R. Sholes, M. Riffaterre, of Russian formalists and of the sponsors of stylistics, structuralism, semiotics and hermeneutics can be looked upon as almost restatements of what was said very early by Bhamaha, Vamana, Anandavardhana, Kuntaka, Abhinava Gupta, Jagannatha and others". "Is There a Climate of Criticism in Our Literature?", *Indian Literature* (1983), p. 87.
64. Shrikrishna Mishra concludes: "... not only Coleridge but all other critics of the world shall have to yield the palm to the great critic... Abhinava Gupta", *Coleridge and Abhinavagupta,* p. 555.
65. *Collected Criticism* (OUP, 1968), p. 55. Emphasis supplied.
66. *Studies in Indian English Literature,* p. 170.
67. *Sanskrit Poetics as a Study of Aesthetic,* pp. 78-79.
68. *Ibid.,* pp. 73-4. For a detailed discussion, see RS. Pathak, *Vakrokti and Stylistic Concepts* (New Delhi, 1988).
69. S.T. Coleridge, *Biographia Literaria,* ed. George Watson (London, 1975), I, p. 89.
70. *After Strange Gods* (London, 1934), pp. 40-1.
71. *The Aesthetic Experience According to Abhinavagupta* (Rome, 1956), p. xxxii.
72. *Feeling and Form* (New York, 1953), p. 323.
73. *yo'rhaḥ sahṛdayaślāghyaḥ kāvyātmeti vyavasthitaḥ Dhvanyāloka* 1.2.
74. *Ibid.,* pp. 11, 15, 24.
75. V. Raghavan, *Bhoja's Śrigāraprakāśa* (Madras, 1963), p. 467.
76. V.A. Shahane, "Critical Approaches Towards Indo-English Writing", in A.K. Srivastava *(ed.), Alien Voice* (Lucknow, 1981), pp. 16-8.

77. C. Paul Verghese, *Essays on Indian Writing in English* (New Delhi, 1975), p. 115.
78. *Ibid.*
79. Jawaharlal Nehru, *The Discovery of India* (Bombay, 1961), pp. 330-31.
80. Gokak, *op. cit.,* p. 158.
81. *Letters of Sri Aurobindo* III (Pondicherry: Sri Aurobindo Ashram), p. 248.
82. S. Nagarajan, "The Literary Criticism of Sri Aurobindo", in C.D. Narasimhaiah (ed.), *Indian Literature of the Last Fifty Years, 1917-1967* (Mysor , 1970), p. 312.

Index

A

A General Hermeneutic of Hṛd-Guha and Guha, 103-06
a posteriori, 46
a priori, 46
Āgmic, 104
Ātmān, 108, 109
Abhijnāna Sakuntalam, 48
Abhinava Gupta's and Kashmir's concept of Guha, 112-17
Achilles, 71
ad infinitum, 143
Africa, 6
Agnipurana, 207
Aham Brahamasmi, 86
ahorātravada, 115
Aiken, Conard, 212
Ajna, 139
ajnānatimira, 116
akanksa, 87
akasa, 104, 105, 107, 108, 109
Alankara, 46
Alexander, 189
All about H. Hallerr, 204
Althusser, Louis, 166
Amarsinha, 212
America, 62
American criticism, 8
American literature, 52, 53
Amero-British, 6
Amur, 208, 214
anahata, 139
Anand, Mulk Raj, 48, 56, 200
Anandvardhan, 49, 211, 214
anavamala, 114
"ancient India, The", 23
Anglican pundits, 42
Anglo-American, 22
Anglo-Indian Literature, 53, 54, 57
Anglo-Indian race, 53
Anglophone World, 43
Anglo-Saxon, 45, 46, 47, 212
antar-vyoman, 104, 118
anti formalism, 12
anti-feminism, 12
anti-text, 33
anugraha, 105

Anuttata, 119
apadana, 94
apercus, 28
apoha, 49
Apollonian elements, 150
aprikatva, 114
Arabic, 18
Arathi, 197
Ardha-Norishwara, 47
Aristotelian modes, 46
Aristotle-Kant-Croce, 20
Arjuna, 140
Arnold, Matthew, 22, 41, 201
Aryaman, 195
asana, 108
Ash, 181
ASRC, 2
Astrologer's Day, The, 88, 90-97
Asudhadhvam, 113
ati raharyam, 120
Auchinleck, 174
Aucitya, 46, 199, 215
Auden W.H., 62
Aurobindo, Sri, vii, 20, 21, 197, 198, 205, 206, 215, 215
Australia, 6, 42
Australian English, 56
Australian, 17
"authorities", 38
avant garde, 21, 23
avaranadevtas, 112
avidya, 109
ayin, 114

B

Bacchux, 59
bahya timirabhāvana, 114
Barthes, Roland, 23, 142
Beardsley, Monroe C., 141
"Beauty is Embellishment", 207
Beethoven, 41
Benares, 192, 193, 194, 197
Bergen-Belsen, 41
Bergson, 148, 149
"bhāvalāvanya yojana," 47
bhaga, 112
Bhagavadgita, 148
Bhagavata, 50
Bhairava, 104, 118
Bhakti period, 67
Bhamana, 211
Bhandar, Bharati, 77
Bharair, 49
Bharata, 46, 50
Bharata-Anandavardhana-Abhinavagupta, 20
Bhashya, viii, 216
Bhatnagar, O.P., 207, 208
Bhattacharya, Bhabani, 189
Bhattacharya, K., 147
Bhattanayaka, 47
bhava, 87
bhavapūrvapatni, 72
Bhopal Arts Centre, 3
Bhowani Junction, 54
Bible, 18
black commonwealth, 24

Blakean Imagination, 144
Bloom, Harold, 144, 146, 171
body-mandala, 151
Bombay Library Review, The, 3
Bombay University, 7
Bombay, 2, 195
Bottomly, Gordon, 201
Bradley, 49
Brahama, 195, 211
Brahma Sutras, 191
Brahman *(brahmapura),* 108, 109
Brahmputra, 193
bricolage, 184
Bridge, 60
British literary ethos, 46
British Raj, 53
British, 7, 24, 45, 47
Browning, Elizabeth Barrett, 206
Bṛh Up, 108, 109
Buddha body, 149
Buddha, 140, 144
buddhi, 108, 109, 110, 152
buddhi-sattva, 149
Buddhism, vii, ix, 107, 136, 148
Buddhist art, 46
Buddhist doctrine of emptiness, 146
Buddhist ideas, 146
Bullough, E., 151
Burke, Kenneth, 146

C

Caha nahi... 67
Cakes and Ale, 54
cakra, 104, 106
Calcutta, 2, 39
Caleridge, S.T., 45, 206, 212, 213
Camatkara, 49
Cambridge, 196, 197, 202
Canada, 6, 42
Canadian (Anglophite) literature, 17
Canetti, Elias, 35
Carana Kamala, 66
Caribbean English, 56
Cassirer, 148
Cathar, 171
Catherine, 198
Caturvedi, Makhanlal, 67
Cave in the Temple..., The, 111
Cavern and the Mystery..., The, 119
cave-buddhi, 109
Chaitany, Krishna, 21
chaos, 107
Chapel, 196
Chatterjee, Bakim Chandra, 201
Chaucer, Geoffrey, 165
Chaudhuri, 56
Cheese and the worms, The 166
Chidra, 104
Christ, 181
Christianity, 17
Churchill, 189
Cicero, 45
CIEFL, 2
Cinta, 74, 75
Circe, 59
Classic Sanskrit literature, 46

Commarswamy, Ananda, 20, 215
Commonwealth Literature, 17, 24, 25, 52, 53
Commonwealth Literature: Problems of Response, 41
Commonwealth Review, 3
Commonwealth, 2, 6, 10, 24, 42, 57
Comus, 59
'Content', 10
'Context', 10
Cosmic Cavern...The, 112-114
Crisis? No crisis?, 14-25
Critical Thought, 19, 20, 87
Critique of Impure Reason, 148
Critique of Indian criticism..., 26-44
Croce, 21, 45, 46, 47
Crystal, David, 65

D

Dachau, 141
dahara vidya, 108, 109
dahara, 104, 107
Dar, B.K., 35
Darkness of the Covern, The, 114-17
Darruwalla, Kiki, 56, 206
"Das Letzte des..." 147, 148
Das, Kamala, 56
Davy, Derek, 65
De, S.K., 209, 210, 212
"Death of Author, The", 142
Deconstruction, ix, 7
Delhi University, 7, 43
Delhi, 2, 39
Derozio, Henry, 201
Derrida, Jacques, 23, 143, 144, 171
Desai, Anita, 38, 56, 204, 205
Desai, S.K., 20
'desi', 6
Determinati's ost negatio, 50
devakama, 191
"devatama", 51
Devy, G.N., xi, xiii, 5, 14
Dharmakaya, 143
Dhatus, 90, 91, 92
dhobi, 196
Dhvani, 46, 48, 49, 199, 215
Dhvanyaloka, 3
Diamond body, 140, 144
Dickens, Charles, 62
Dikshita, Appaya, 215
discoursal function, 91
dohe, 55
Draupadi ki chir, 205
Dufrenne, Mikel, 147
Duperron, Anquetil, 146
Durga, 107
Dutt, Toru, 205, 206
Dwivedi, A.N., 35, 38
Dylan, Thomas, 74

E

Ehattānārayana, 115, 116
Ein-Sof, 144
Ekarthibhava, 86, 87, 88

Ekavākyata, 86
Eliot, T.S., 6, 41, 48, 62, 67, 68, 74, 204, 213
Eliot's theory of tradition, 48
Empson, William, 62
Emptiness, 144, 147
England, 22, 42, 62, 189
English literature teaching... 22
"englobment" of the literary act, 32, 33
enthuse, 71
Epic, 139, 141
"epistemic choices," 62
Epstein, E.L., 65
etad guhyam maha... 119
Etymologies..., 106-12
Eurocentric critical theories, 43
European tradition, ix
Existentialists, 49
Ezekiel, Nissim, 2, 20, 42, 206, 207

F

Far Flung Pavilions, 54
Five Gates...., The, 110
Fminist and Foucaulists... 41
Formalist Criticism, ix
Foster, 54
France, 189, 195
French, 49
Freud, Sigmund, 23
Future Poetry, The, 21

G

Gagentic, 193
gahana, 107
gahvara, 104-09
Ganadara, 50
Ganga, 192, 193, 196
Ganges, 204
garbhāgṛha, 112
Gayatri mantra, 195
Geertz, Clifford, 161
gehvara, 107
Genealogy of Morals, 145
George, 198
Gesset, Joese Ortega y., 151, 152, 153
Ghos, Sisir, 208
Gibbs, A.C., 178
Gita, 140, 145, 149
Gitanjali, vii, 47, 48
Gnoli, 213
Goethe, 41, 189
Gokak, V.K., 20, 200, 202, 208, 215
Goldmann, Lucien, 33
Gopis, 68
Govinda, 199
"grammar of narrative", 85, 86
Greek, 22, 45, 107, 197
Greek-Latin theories, 45
Greimas, 85
Grim, 177
gudhartha, 107
guha, 103, 104, 105, 106, 107-12
guhāmāyā, 112
guha-buddhi, 110
guhahita, 107
guhaka, 107

guhanihita, 108
guhavaktra, 107
guhera, 107
guhervara, 107
guhyakali, 107
guhyakodhipati, 107
guhyam, 107
guhyapati, 107
guhyesvari, 107
Gujarati, 22
Guna-dosa, 46
Gupta, Abhinava, xi, 22, 23, 50, 103, 112, 113, 114, 115, 116, 117, 118, 119, 120, 121, 211, 212, 214
Gupta, G.S. Balarama, xi, xiii, 52
Gupta, Shyam Ratna, 202
Guron, Sir, 180, 182, 183
Guru, Atmananda, 188

H

Halliday, 65, 75
Haradatta, 50
Harishchandra Ghat, 192
Harishchandra, 195
Harishchandra, 195
Hartman, Geoffrey, 142, 146
Hasan, 75
Havebok the Dane, 177, 178, 180, 181
Haveloke, 174
Havelok, 177, 178, 179, 180, 181
Hayakawa, 63
Hazle, 181
Heidegger, ix, 145
Himalaya, 51, 72, 75, 78
Himgiri, 74
Hindu societies, 17
Hindu tradition, 4
Hinduism, 17
Hindustani, 6
Hiriyana, M., 20, 21, 190, 214
histoire de metalites, 32
Hodder, 175
Hoermann
Holt, 175
Holy Grail, 68
Homer, 62
Hopkins, G.M. 60
Horace, 45
Horn, 177
hṛdayākasa, 118
hṛdayabhūmi, 118
hṛdaya-Ilihitacittah, 118
hṛdaya-sainvada, 214
hṛd-granthi, 108
hṛd-guha, 104, 105, 107, 108
hṛdya-padma, 118
Hulme, 148, 149
Hyderabad Central University, 2
Hyderabad, 2

I

Iliad, 71
Incipit Vita Havelok, 177
Incomplete Texts of Romance, 174-76
Indian aesthetics, 7
"Indian but alienated", 2

Indian criticism... 209
Indian English Criticism, 14-25
Indian English language, 11
Indian English literary criticism, 202
Indian English Literature, xi, 19, 20, 21, 24
Indian ethos, 47
Indian Literary Review, The, 3
Indian Literature in English Translation, 53
Indian literature in English, 16, 17, 18, 20, 42, 43, 201, 203
Indian literature, viii
"Indian Renaissance", 23
Indian species of feminist criticism, 10
Indian Writing in English, 201
Indian Writing in English, 26, 37, 53, 200
Indianisation, xi
Indianised language, 15-25
Indianization of English Studies, 52-58
Indianness, xi, 4
Indo-Anglian literature, 45, 48, 50, 200
"Indo-Anglian romanticism," 206
Indo-Anglian, 47
Indo-English literature, 55, 56, 57, 201
Interiorized Pilgrimmage, The, 110
'International' tradition, 9
Ira, 82
Ireland, 42
Iyengar, K.K. Srinivasa, 202, 208

J

Jacobs, Nicolas, 175
Jagannatha, 47
Jamaica, 6
Jasper, Karl, 147, 148
Jaya mangala, 47
Jayadeva, 207
Jesus, 181
Jewel in the crown, 54
Jewish discourse, 171
JIWE, 27
Jnaneswari, 55
Johnson-Caleridge-Arnold, 20
Journal of Indian Writing English, 26
Jusswalla, Adil, 7, 205

K

Kāmāyani, 55, 65, 69, 70, 71, 74-82
Kabbalah, 144
Kabir, 55, 192
kala-tattva, 116
Kalidasa granthita vastuna, 48
Kalidasa, 46, 48, 50, 51, 52, 212
Kama Sutra, 47
Kama, 70, 82
Kannada, 55
Kant, ix, 23, 145, 213
Kantak, V.Y., 208

Kanthapura, 49
Kanyakumari, 189
Kapilavastu, 188
Kapoor, Kapil, xi, xiii, 85
Kapoor, Ranga, xi, xiv, 85
karmendriya, 116
Karttikeya, 107
karuna rasa, 50
Kashmir, 189
Kasmir Saivism, xi, 104, 105, 112, 119
Kaulini, 119
Ka-up., 109
Kavya Bharati, 3
Kavya, 87, 88, 190
Keats, John, 206
Kelkar, Ashok, 20, 21
Kenopanisad, 51
Kha-cakra, 104
kha-madhya, 104
King Horn, 174, 176-79
King Horn, 178
King, Bruce, 2
Kipling, Rudyard, 54
kiratarjuniyam, 49
Kittana, 191
kraunch, 48
Krieger, Murray, 142, 143
Krishna, x, 68, 140, 145, 195, 196
Krishnamoorthy, 214, 215
Kriya-sakti, 116
kryptos, 107
Ksemaraja, 115, 116, 117, 118
Kubera, 107
Kula, 118, 119
kulanayika, 119
Kumarsambhavam, 72
Kuntaka, 207, 211
kuvalayananda, 215
Kuvempu, 55
Kva Suryaprabho, 72

L

L'Image de notre corps, 153
Lacan, 23
lai, 179
Lakhsmi, 195
Lakshmana, 191
Lal, P., 2, 206
Land misc, 174
Langer, Susanne, 214
Latin, 22, 46
Lay le Frein, 174, 175, 176, 179, 180, 181
laya, 105
Le codre, 179-84
Le Frein, 176, 179-84
Leavis, F.R., 6, 22, 41
lemman, 182
Leninist ideology, 48
Leto, 71
Levi-Strauss, 85
Lhermitte, 153
Life Divine, The, 205
Literary criticism in India..., 1-3
Literary methodology, 45-51
Literary theory, 19-20
literatures-vachanas, 55

Long lyric, 139, 141
Long poem, 139, 141

M

māyā, 105, 108, 112, 113, 114, 115, 152
māyā-bilam, 112
māyā-devi, 112
Macaulay, 209
Macaulaysque, 47
Madeleine, 189, 193, 197, 198
Madhava, 191
Madhvi Lata, 48
madhya, 104
Mahāguhā, 116, 117, 118, 120
Mahabharata, 47, 48, 50
Mahapatra, Jayanta, 2
Mahaprasthānam, 55
Mahat-tattva, 153
Mahavakya, 86, 87, 97
Mahavakya: The Indian Theory of Literary Discourage, 85, 99
"Mahavakya", 87
Mahesvarananda, 115
Maithreyi, 199
mala, 113, 114
Malgonkar, Manohar, 189
Malgudi Days, 90
Mammata, 195, 210
Manas, 110
Mandala, xi, 106, 137, 140, 149, 151
Manipura, 139
mantra, 21
mantras aham, 105
Manu, 80
Marathi, 21, 22, 55
Mardhekar, B.S., 20, 21, 42
Marie, 181, 182, 183
Markandeya, Kamala, 56
Marx, 23
Marxist, 48
māyā-bilam, 112
maya-devi, 112
Maya, 105, 108, 112, 113, 114, 115
maya-sakti, 113
McCutchion, David 203
Medieval English Romances, 175
Medieval India, 22
Medieval romance, 157-58
Meghadutam, 72
Melodramatic *gestures*, 204
Memory (Smriti), 149
Menon, C. Narayan, 208
Michelis, P.A., 151
Middle Ages in England, 168
Middle English Literature, 170
Middle English matrical forms, 179
Middle English metrical romances, 171
Middle English Poetry, 184
Middle English romances, 174, 175
Middle English tradition, 174
Middle English Verse Romances, 175
Middle French, 183
Middle-Indo-Aryan, 17

Milton, John, 59, 71
Mimansa, 86
Mithra, 195
"Modern Europe, The," 23
Modern Indian English Poetry, 2
Modern-Indo-Aryan languages, 17
Moha, 113
Montaillou, 171
Moslem, 171, 177
Moving Frontiers of English Studies in India, 52
Mukherjee, Meenakshi, 204
Muladhara, 137, 139, 140
Murare, 197
Murti, T.R.U., 147
Muse, 71
Myers, L.H., 54
Mysore University

N

Nagarjun, 147, 148
Nagrajan, S., 208
Naidu, Sarojini, 206
Naik, M.K., 35, 202, 203, 212
Naive and Critical Readings, 158-61
Nalavikagni mitram, 50
Nara, 120
Narasimahia, C.D. 5, 41, 42, 52, 53, 199, 206, 208, 212, 214
Narayan, R.K., 56, 88, 90, 92, 94, 188
Narie de France, 175, 176, 179
navamalika, 48
Nayak, Guru, 90, 92, 93, 94, 97
Nehru, Jawaharlal, 215
Neo-classcism, 45
neo-Marxist criticism, 10
New Criticism, 28, 29, 30, 40
New Zealand, 42, 43
Nietzsche, 145, 146
Nietzsche's Dionysian, 150
nimesa, 115
Nirmānkāya, 143
Non-Being, 146
North America, 43
novel-poetics, 22
Nowottny, 60
nutana, 23

O

Objective interpretation, 10
Orissans, 2
Ortiz, Javier Vgaz, xi, xiii, 100
Oxford, 202

P

Pada, 86
pada-siddhi, 93
Panchtantra, 204
Paninean grammar, 87, 88
Panini, xi
para maya, 113
Paradise Lost, 71
Parameshwara, 201
paranisa, 115
parme vyoman, 109, 110

Parsifal, 146
Parthsarthy, R., 2
Parvati, 195
Parvati-Samkara, 72
Patanakar, R.B., 20, 21
Patanjali, 149, 153, 154
Patanjali's Yog-sutras, 149
Pathak, R.S., xi, xiii
Patnakar, 209
Perry, John Oliver, xi, xiii, 1
Persian, 6, 18
"Perspectives," 31, 34, 35, 36
Phenomenology of hṛd-guha 103, 104
Philosophie III, 147
Phonetic Form of the Utterance, 89
Platonic, 46
Plotinus, 146
Poems, 201
Ponty, Morleau, 153
Prajapati, 195
"prakhyatam iti vrittam", 49
prakriti, 92, 113
Pralaya pravaha, 76
prana, 110
Prasad, Jayshankar, 55, 65, 70
Prasad, Ratnasankar, 74, 77, 78, 80
Pratap, 198
pratipadika, 88, 90, 91, 92
pratyaya, 91, 92, 93
Pravarti, 154
Prayojana, 199
pre-darwinists, 40
"Preface", 73, 74, 75
Primary function of criticism, The, 15
Primary texts, viii, ix, x
Primitivism, 12
Propp, 85
prounciamentos, 41
prthvi andas, 114
psycho-cosmic "states", 101-03
Psycho-historical Insights, 170-171
Psycho-history, 43
pūmna-ahambhava, 105
pumdarika, 104
Puranas, viii, x, 204, 216
puranic abode in the Himalayas, 51
Purusa, 76, 113
purushartha, 199
Purva Mimansa, 86

R

Radhakrishnan, S., 145
Raghus, 72
Raghuvansam, 46, 72, 193
Rahman, A., 35
Rajmohan's wife, 201
Rama, 87, 93, 189, 190, 191, 195, 196, 197, 198
Ramanand, 192
Ramanujan, A.K., 55
Ramaswamy, 189, 191, 192, 195
Ramayana Darshanam, 55

Ramayana, 48, 50, 86, 87, 206
Ramchandra, 81
Ramchandra, Ragini, xiv, 188
Ramcharitmanas, 60
Rao Raja, vii, x, 42, 49, 56, 188, 189, 190, 191, 192, 193, 194, 195, 196, 197, 198, 199, 203
Rao, Narayan, 9
rasa theory, 20
rasa, 46, 48, 50, 51, 101, 199, 215
rasa-dhvani, 21, 46, 48, 50
rasanubhava, 214
Ravana, 93
Rayan, Krishna, 20, 208
Readerly Text, Ideas in Motion and Kinaesthetic Form..., 137-156
religious literature, 102
"religious" text, 101
Renaissance, 200, 215
Rewa Palace, 192
Rhone, 196
Richards, I.A., 59
Ricoeur, Paul, 171
Rimmon-Kenan, 85
Rinehart and Winston, 175
Riti, 46
Romantic and post-Romantic theories, 29
Romantic Revival, 206
Romanticism, 70
Roy, Emmanuelle, 166, 171
Rushdie, Salman, 42, 56
Ṛg Veda, 107

S

Sādhāranikarania, 215
saṁkoca-vikara, 105
"Sacred texts," viii
Saffikara, 109
Sahaleara, 48
Sahitya Akademi, 3
sahityadarpana, 87
Sakyamuni, 189
Salankrta Sabdartha, 207
Sambhogkaya, 143
Sambhu, 115
Samkhya Yoga, 97
samnidhi, 87, 97
Samvid, 150
saṃhara, 105
Saṃkara, 103, 109, 188
Sanatana, 23
Sands, Donald B., 175
Sankaracharya, 204
Sanskrit Grammar, 97, 98
Sanskrit literary criticism, viii
Sanskrit poetics, ix, 22
Sanskrit, 18-19, 40
Sanskrit-Persian-Arabics, 18, 19
Santa rasa, 50
Saroj, 198
Sarozins, 177
Sastri, P.S., xi, xiii, 45
Satpadi, 195
Satya, 188
Savirtri, vii, 47, 48, 49, 205
Savitri, 197
Schmidt, A. V.C., 175

Schopenhauer, 145, 146, 148
Scotland, 42
Scott, Paul, 54
Scott, Walter, 206
Scrutiny Contingent, 42
Secondary text, ix, x
Self, 149, 150, 151
"sementic field", 72, ·73
Sengupta, S.C., 208
Serpent and the Rope, vii, 188, 199, 203
Shakepeare, William, 19, 52, 62
Shakuntala, 201
Sham jewels, 212
Shankara, 192
Shantha, 194
Sharma, R.S., xi, xiii, 58
Shelley, P.B., 67, 206
Shiva, 51, 72, 107, 117, 118, 119, 120, 192, 195, 197
Short lyric, 139, 141
siddhi, 88
Simms, Norman, ix, xiii, 26
Singh, Charu Sheel, 137
Singh, Khushwant, 189
Sivaratri, 117
skandha, 107
Speaking of Siva, The, 55
Spinoza, 50
Sraddha, 70, 71
Sraddha, 82
Sri Sankara, 199
Sri, Sri, 55
Srimadbhagavatpurana, 206
Srivastva, R.K., 35, 38
sṛsti, 105
Stages in Mentalities Reading, 162-170
Steel, Flora Annie, 54
Steiner, George, 41
Stern, Paul, 150
Sthitata, 108
sthithi, 105
sthula māyā, 113
Stoughton, 175
Structuralism, ix
Study of Poetry: A Linguistic Model..., 58, 84
sūksma, 112
Subtext, 10
Suddhadhvan, 113
Suddha-vidya, 113, 114, 116, 120
Suddluasudhadhvan, 113
Sudras, 67
Sukoh, Dara, 146
suksma-māyā, 113
Summa, 121
Sumonadhikarana, 110
Sunya, 118, 147
Sunyata, 147
Sureshwari, 192
susira, 107
susumna, 104, 118
Swadshisthana, 137, 139
Swinburne, 206
Syam, 68
Symptomatic readings, 160, 161, 162

T

Tagore, Rabindranath, vii, 55, 207, 215
Tai up, 109
Taj Mahal, 48
Tamaki Kosiro, 148
tamas, 105, 116
Tamilnadu, 50
Tanmatras, 116, 153
tanmayibhavana, 214
Tantric literature, 104
Tantric Saivism, 103
Tat tvamasi, 86
Taylor, Meadows, 54
Telgu, 55
Tennyson, Alfred Lord, 52, 206
Terms for the Central Domain, 117-119
'text', 40
the Margins of the Inner Sea..., 176
The primary function of criticism, 15
Theory of Guha (1), 104, 105-06
Theory of Guha (2), 105, 106
Third World, 10, 42
Three illusion of Buddhism, 144
Times Literary Supplement, 205
Times, 203
Timira, 116
timirodapi, 116
topoi, 164
toridhana, 105
Towards a Viable Aesthetics..., 200-216
Towards Framing a Problem Area, 171-174
Towards the Development of a Hermeneutical Model...., 100-136
Tradition of "broken images", 48
Transcendental Subjectivity, 105
Trauma of Birth Abdonment..., The, 157-87
Tree of Plecenta, The, 179-84
Tukaram, 21
Tulsidas, 100, 192

U

Ūadhav jāhu..., 68
Udho, 68
Uma Haimavati balu sobhmāna, 51
Unimesa, 115
United Kingdom, 1, 2, 8
United States, 2, 8
Universal Man, 215
Unmesanimesa, 105
Upanisadic Doctrine of the Cavity, 108
Upanishads, viii, ix, 47, 108, 146, 204
Urdu, 18
Utpaladeva, 117
Uttara Rama Charita, 193

V

Vāg arthav iva sampriktau, 46
Vāgarthaprapratipattaye, 72